The Theory of Wages in Classical Economics

The Theory of Wages in Classical Economics

A Study of Adam Smith, David Ricardo and Their Contemporaries

Antonella Stirati
Lecturer in Economics
University of Siena

Translated by Joan Hall

Edward Elgar

Originally published in Italian as *Salario e mercato del lavoro nell' economia politica classica* by Rosenberg & Sellier, Torino, 1991, and © Rosenberg & Sellier, 1991
English edition © Antonella Stirati 1994

Published by
Edward Elgar Publishing Limited
Gower House
Croft Road
Aldershot
Hants GU11 3HR
England

Edward Elgar Publishing Company
Old Post Road
Brookfield
Vermont 05036
USA

British Library Cataloguing in Publication Data
Stirati, Antonella
Theory of Wages in Classical Economics:
Study of Adam Smith, David Ricardo and
Their Contemporaries
I. Title
331.2

Library of Congress Cataloguing in Publication Data
Stirati, Antonella.
Theory of Wages in Classical Economics : a study of Adam Smith, David Ricardo and Their Contemporaries / Antonella Stirati.
    p. cm.
Includes bibliographical references.
    1. Wages 2. Classical school of economics. 3. Economics
-History. I. Title
HD4909.S75 1994
331.2 101—dc20   93–42452
                                                          CIP

ISBN   1 85278 710 4

Printed and bound in Great Britain by
Hartnolls Limited, Bodmin, Cornwall

Contents

Acknowledgments

This book is based on my doctoral thesis completed at the University 'La Sapienza' in Rome.

The thesis was supervised by Prof. P. Garegnani, to whom I am greatly indebted for the attention with which he followed my research and, more generally, for his contribution to the revival of the classical approach. It was this perspective that stimulated my interest in the themes dealt with in this volume. Prof. A. Ginzburg, as referee, attentively read and discussed the thesis with me, and provided many precise observations and very useful suggestions for improving the study.

I also wish to thank other advisors and colleagues who read all or parts of the book at various stages of its evolution: F. Bettio, G. Caravale, A. Picchio, A. Roncaglia, A. Rosselli and F. Vianello. Their comments have been very helpful to me in clarifying my ideas and improving the exposition. Particular thanks are due to S. Cesaratto who patiently read the various drafts of the manuscript and provided precious advice and criticism. Of course I accept full responsibility for the arguments.

Lastly, I would like to thank my colleagues in the doctoral programme in Rome for creating a climate of discussion and collaboration that favoured the successful completion of the work, and the Lisli and Lelio Basso Foundation which, by awarding me a 'Fausto Vicarelli' grant, enabled me to extend and develop my thesis research and to realize the present volume. Financial contribution from the Italian Ministry of University and Scientific and Technological Research is also gratefully aknowledged.

Joan Hall has skillfully translated the text, often improving it in the process.

Introduction

The question of how wages are determined has been given little attention in recent debates on the theory of value and distribution in the works of the classical economists, except in connection with Ricardo's wage theory. And while that subject has been widely debated, I believe the discussion has been limited by an inadequate understanding of the ideas of Ricardo's predecessors, including Smith.[1]

The relatively scant attention devoted to this question may seem surprising in view of the recent revival of interest, not only historical but also theoretical, in the interpretation of classical economics. This revival, stimulated by Sraffa's work,[2] has led to a lively debate in which the main issue is whether the theoretical approach of the classical economists was different from and alternative to the later marginalist view. According to some scholars, the earlier writers tended to consider real wages as a magnitude determined independently of the price system by a combination of social and economic forces, and this has been seen as an important distinctive feature of their economic theory (Garegnani, 1990, p. 118; also Blaug, 1987, pp. 435–6).

The possibility that the classical economists might offer indications for alternative analyses of wages and the labour market is of particular interest today, because in this area the reigning theory seems to have serious difficulties in explaining observed phenomena.

1. The latest, and as far as I know the only monograph devoted specifically to the study of the theory of wages of the classical economists, including the authors treated here, is that of Wernel, 1939. In that work the evolution of the classical theory of wages is interpreted in a manner very different from that proposed in this book, as an evolution of various formulations of an 'iron law of wages'. More recently some studies have proposed an interpretation of the classical theory of wages, with particular reference to the contributions of Smith and Ricardo, which has some elements in common with the view that emerges from the present research: Garegnani, 1984, pp. 294–6 and 1990, pp. 118–22; Picchio del Mercato, 1981.
2. I refer here to Sraffa, 1951 and 1960. In the latter study Sraffa declares that he intends to adopt the 'submerged and forgotten' point of view of the 'classical economists from Adam Smith to Ricardo' (p. v).

A succession of hypotheses and models has been proposed to explain the existence of widespread and persistent unemployment, but each of these seems inadequate in the light of subsequent critical appraisal. The current theory posits an inverse relation between the wage rate and the demand for labour – a notion which is hardly compatible with the existence of persistent unemployment. The labour market is also characterized by widespread and persistent disparities between the wages and occupations of groups of workers (of different race or gender, for example). In the literature these disparities are often attributed to discrimination, and are hard to reconcile with the usual view of how competition works.[3] In this context an analysis of the point of view of the classical economists, and a critical reflection upon it, may provide a stimulus and a contribution to the interpretation of contemporary reality.

In this study I have sought to explore in depth the whole complex of ideas held by these economists regarding the factors that determine the natural wage, those that make it a centre of gravitation for actual wages at any given moment, and those that cause it to vary over time. My aim, therefore, is not only to outline the position and the contribution of each individual author, but also to reconstruct a general perspective on the problem of wage determination – a perspective which, despite their different views about other aspects of economic theory, was shared by them and indeed was widely accepted in the historical period under examination.

The analysis is conducted from the viewpoint of the history of economic analysis. Thus, I am concerned with the structure of the theory – the causal links between economic magnitudes – more than with economic policy implications and their relation to historical events.[4]

---

3. For a reflection on the way both aspects constitute a serious problem for contemporary theory, see Solow, 1980.
4. As we shall see there is not always a correspondence between opinions on economic policy and underlying economic theory. In some cases different conclusions with regard to economic policy derive from similar theoretical views, while in others similar conclusions are drawn from different analyses. An example of the first case can be seen in the contrast between Turgot and Necker concerning the liberalization of the corn trade, and of the second case, in the similar positions of Malthus and Ricardo regarding the necessity of abolishing the Poor Laws (see below, Chapter 3, p. 79; and Chapter 4, pp. 116–7).

Definition of 'classical'

The debate over the interpretation of classical economic thought begins with its very definition, and with the limits of the historical period in which it prevailed. As this subject is too wide and too open to be dealt with exhaustively here,[5] I shall merely give a broad outline of its terms and indicate my own frame of reference.

The term 'classical economists' was, of course, coined by Marx, who saw the classical period as extending from Petty to Ricardo in England and from Boisguillebert to Sismondi in France.[6] By about 1830, according to Marx, Ricardo's influence was already waning in England and his teaching was being superseded by 'vulgar' elements in economic thought.[7] On the other hand economists like Jevons and Cannan, and later most historians of thought, have laid more stress on the break created by the 'marginal revolution' around 1870. They have accentuated the elements of continuity between economists like Senior and J.S. Mill and the preceding classical tradition, which in their view began with Smith's *Wealth of Nations*.

While these two periodizations (from around the mid-seventeenth century to 1820, or from 1770 to 1870) have been the major contenders, others have been proposed which extend the range of the controversy. Among these, perhaps the best known is that of Keynes, who described as 'classical' all the economists before himself, from Ricardo to Pigou. He was certainly influenced by Marshall, who saw a continuity between his own theory and the classical one. But Keynes also wished to emphasize that his criticism of Say's law represented a break with the whole preceding economic tradition, whose unifying element lay in the acceptance of that economic law.[8]

The different periodizations, and the different opinions regarding

5. For a review of the different positions and definitions see Blaug, 1987.
6. However, as Groenewegen notes (1987, p. 21, n.), Marx held that the classical school was not limited to the economists of these two countries; he includes, for example, Italians such as Galiani, Genovesi, Beccaria and Verri.
7. This reconstruction by Marx is shared by contemporary economists such as Dobb (1973, pp. 96–102) and Meek (1967, pp. 66–73). Schumpeter, though he gives completely different judgements of Ricardo's contribution, also maintains that his teaching was already in decline in the years immediately after his death, and that his influence died out after about 1830 (1954, pp. 476–8). An analysis similar to that of Schumpeter is proposed by O'Brien, 1975, pp. 43–4. On the meaning attributed by Marx to the term 'vulgar' economics see Garegnani, 1984, pp. 303–4, and Groenewegen, 1987, pp. 21–5.
8. For a critical examination of Keynes's definition of the 'classical economists' see Meek, 1967, pp. 53–66, and Garegnani, 1978, pp. 24–8.

the existence of a continuity between Smith and Ricardo (whom Marx saw as the main exponents of English classical political economy),[9] are naturally underpinned by different interpretations of the history of economic thought and different views about what elements characterize and distinguish classical economic theory.

The analysis conducted in this book adopts and supports the periodization indicated by Marx. The strong elements of continuity and affinity between the authors studied with regard to the perspective and the object of this analysis – the theory of wages – make it reasonable to speak of a vision peculiar to that period and those authors. The vision changed just after Ricardo's death, as the wage fund theory became accepted.

I have tried to give a fairly complete picture of the English side of classical economics, which was most influential in the history and development of economic thought. I have also included a partial view of the French side, with special attention to Turgot and Necker. These two economists may be considered representative of ideas that were incorporated in the work of Smith, and through it influenced the subsequent development of economic thought.[10]

Problems encountered by traditional interpretations

In addition to the considerations mentioned above, this study is motivated by the fact that the usual interpretation of the classical theory of wages has encountered (and still encounters) difficulties that cannot but raise doubts as to its adequacy. Thus it should be possible, and certainly useful, to reconsider the matter from new points of view.

Recently Samuelson has boldly asserted that there is a substantial similarity in approach between classical and contemporary economists (Samuelson, 1978, p. 1415). But in fact nearly all scholars dealing with the theory of distribution in classical economic thought show a certain uneasiness or surprise at the differences between the

9.   Schumpeter, as is well known, saw Ricardo's theory as a 'detour' from a tradition which otherwise united Smith with the later developments of economic theory.

10. For example McNulty mentions Turgot, together with Petty, Child, Locke and Steuart, as one of those who had the greatest influence on Smith's theory of wages (1980, pp. 49–51). All these authors are examined in the present research which bears out McNulty's view. On the relations between Turgot and Smith see also Groenewegen, 1969. Bharadwaj has recently emphasized the influence of Necker on Smith's theory of wages (1987, p. 544), see below, Chapter 3, p. 31, n. 5)

classical economists' way of thinking and that of modern economists. In particular, the classical theory lacked the symmetry of the explanation of income distribution that prevails today, whereby the remuneration of labour, capital and land are all determined by a single principle – the interaction of supply and demand curves – and reflect the marginal contribution of each factor to production.

Thus, Schumpeter seems disconcerted by the fact that in Smith (as in other classical economists) wages, profit and rent are determined by different principles, and that profit and rent are seen as 'residual' incomes even though it is recognized that capital and land, as well as labour, 'contribute to production'.[11] To Knight the classical theory of wages seemed so far from the reasoning of contemporary economists that it 'sheds no light whatever on the economic principles of distribution, and is an amazing tissue of inconsistency and irrelevance' – a point of view clearly shared by Cannan (Knight, 1956, p. 75; Cannan, 1893, pp. 379–83).

This perplexity with regard to the classical theory of distribution is aggravated by the difficulty of explaining certain elements of that theory on the basis of its traditional interpretation.

In the traditional view, the classical theory of wages rests on two pillars: the theory of the wages fund and the theory of population. Wage rates in any given period are said to depend on the relationship between a predetermined 'fund' designated for wages and the size of the fully employed working population. Wages are then driven towards subsistence level by population changes in response to the difference between the current wage and subsistence.[12]

At the same time, however, scholars have regarded Smith's theory of wages as a 'compendium' of numerous and diverse theories which are contradictory and in fact mutually incompatible (Blaug, 1985, p. 44; Hollander, 1973, pp. 185–6; Schumpeter, 1954, pp. 268–9; Knight, 1956, pp. 80, 83). In particular, the role that Smith assigns to the bargaining power of capitalists has been seen as inconsistent with

11. Schumpeter, 1954, pp. 268, 557–61, 566–7; see also Cannan, 1893, pp. 200–2, 382 and Hollander, 1987, p. 73 (cf. below, Chapter 3, p. 32, n. 7)
12. Such a view can be found, among others, in Cannan, 1893, pp. 231, 237, 242–3; Schumpeter, 1954, pp. 266, 665–8; Blaug, 1985, pp. 44–5, 90; St Clair, 1965, p. 100; Skinner, 1979, pp 164–6; Blith, 1987, p. 836. Some scholars have also maintained that the classical economists at times simply asserted that wages are set at the level of subsistence, without any real theory to explain why this happens (Cannan, 1893, pp. 232–34; Knight, 1956, pp. 80–81).

the theory of the wages fund (which was nonetheless attributed to him) or with the role of competition in determining wages (Blaug, 1985, p. 44; Knight, 1956, pp. 81–3). The role of 'common humanity', which according to Smith limits the fall of wages, has been said to conflict not only with all the wage theories attributed to him, but even with common sense (Cannan, 1893, p. 235; Blaug, 1985, pp. 45–6).

In the case of Ricardo the most obvious problem is to reconcile his conclusion that introducing machines may cause unemployment with the traditional interpretation of his theory of wages. This conclusion has been explained in terms of a peculiar attitude whereby Ricardo, abandoning the approach adopted in the rest of his analysis, supposedly refers here only to the very short-term consequences of the introduction of machines, ignoring the corrective effects that wage reductions would have on unemployment over a longer period (Wicksell, 1934, I, p. 137; Schumpeter, 1954, p. 683; Blaug, 1985, p. 133). But unfortunately, as Blaug notes with some perplexity, Ricardo speaks of unemployment created by machines as a phenomenon that may last for 'a considerable interval' of time (1985, p. 133). In fact Ricardo's position was not so unusual. Schumpeter states that from the end of the eighteenth century the introduction of machines was more and more often indicated by economists as a cause of unemployment (1954, p. 273).

Lastly, the traditional interpretation has also had difficulty in explaining the view – held by Smith, Ricardo and other classical and preclassical economists – that direct taxes on wages, or indirect taxes on goods consumed by labourers, would always be followed by an immediate adjustment of wages such as to leave the workers' real disposable income unaltered. Clearly such a rapid adjustment could not be attributed to variations in the population.[13]

In the light of the analysis developed in this book, these difficulties in interpreting the classical theory of distribution reflect a profound change in perspective – a change that has made it hard for contemporary economists to understand what Sraffa called the 'submerged and forgotten' point of view of the classical tradition.

---

13. St Clair, 1965, pp. 126–32; Shoup, 1960, p. 73; Hollander, 1979, pp. 393–5; Hollander, 1987, pp. 158–60 (see also below, Chapter 3, p. 82, and Chapter 5, pp. 139-41).

Sraffa's contribution to the reconstruction of that point of view, and the rejection of the terms in which the classical theory of wages has traditionally been interpreted, open the way to an analysis whereby that theory proves both internally consistent and fundamentally different from the modern theory of distribution. This interpretation makes it possible to overcome the problems outlined above.

A central thesis of this book is that the wage fund theory, held by economists like McCulloch, Senior and J.S. Mill, is absent from the works of the classical economists. In other words, they did not posit the inverse relation between wages and level of employment which characterizes both the wage fund theory and the later marginalist theory. Once this fact is recognized, we can see that in their view persistent unemployment or underemployment were not only possible but 'normal'. The distributive variables can thus be considered determinate, at their normal level, even in the presence of unemployment. This view is accompanied by another important characteristic of the classical approach – the central role of social norms and conventions, both in determining the natural wage and in ensuring that the actual or 'market' wage gravitates around it.

Contents of the book

The first chapter of this book aims to clarify the meanings of the main concepts used in the following discussion, as they should be understood in the context of classical theory. In this connection, I shall have occasion to bring out certain differences between classical and contemporary theory, thus to some extent anticipating the conclusions of later chapters. In Chapter 2, I examine some ideas about factors contributing to the determination of wages, as they emerge (though not systematically) in English economic writings between the end of the seventeenth and the middle of the eighteenth century. In this literature, though the subject is still treated in a fragmentary way, one can already see some elements which resurface in later works, including Smith's *Wealth of Nations*.

Chapter 3 is the central part of the study. Here, through examination of the works of several authors (Steuart, Turgot, Necker and Smith), it has been possible to reconstruct a fairly precise picture of the forces they saw as determining the natural rate of wages and the way that rate changes over time – a picture which I believe can be taken as characteristic of classical political economy.

In the interpretation proposed here no role is assigned to mechanisms of population change in the gravitation of wages towards their natural rate. The role of population theory in the classical analysis of the labour market, from Cantillon to Malthus and Ricardo, is specifically examined in Chapter 4. Particular attention is given to the role of population theory in explaining how the availability of labour tends to adjust to the demands of accumulation. Differences between the authors are also noted, especially certain aspects of Malthus's theory that distinguish it from the preceding tradition and from Ricardo's position.

Chapter 5 deals with Ricardo's theory of wages, bringing out the inconsistencies and ambiguities that have made its interpretation extremely controversial. A better understanding of the tradition preceding Ricardo can throw significant light on that controversy. I shall indicate some strong elements of continuity between the wage theories of Ricardo and Smith, and suggest that the ambiguities in Ricardo's formulation arose because, in order to support his conclusion about the effects of decreasing returns in agriculture on the rate of profit, he introduced into his wage theory some elements of rigidity that do not fit well into the overall view derived from Smith.

The last chapter draws the threads together into a synthetic view, combining the main elements of the analytical scheme developed in the preceding chapters. The classical economists' approach to the analysis of the labour market is then compared with the other two main explanations of wages in the history of economic thought, the wage fund theory and the marginalist theory. This comparison further clarifies the analytical foundations of the classical view.

1. Labour Supply and Demand, Unemployment, Natural Wage: Some Definitions

INTRODUCTION

Terms such as labour supply and demand, or unemployment, may assume different meanings in different theoretical contexts, and in the works of the classical and preclassical economists they do not have the same connotations as in contemporary economic analysis.

The distinctive features of the classical analysis of the labour market and of income distribution, and hence also the meanings assigned to the terms listed above, will be discussed in the following chapters. At this stage, however, it may be useful to anticipate some of the conclusions of the analysis, in order to highlight the changes in meaning of the most commonly used terms – changes which, if ignored, might lead to misunderstanding.

Problems of interpretation can arise not only because the classical economists used some terms similar to contemporary ones with different meanings, but also because some of their expressions are by now relatively unfamiliar and their original sense is not always clear. This is the case, for example, with the term 'natural wage' used by Smith and Ricardo. As the determination of the natural wage within the classical theory is the main object of this study, let us begin by defining this concept.

THE NATURAL WAGE

The classical economists generally used the term 'natural wage' to indicate an amount of money. But the object of the theory of wages is to determine the 'natural' level of real wages, to which a certain

1

money wage must correspond once the prices of goods consumed by the workers are determined.

The focus of classical wage theory is the determination of a single rate of remuneration of labour, the natural wage. This calls for an explanation, as observation immediately reveals the existence in the labour market of different pay rates for different occupations. By the term 'natural wage' the classical economists explicitly mean the wages paid to 'common labourers' – i.e. adult male workers without particular qualifications or skills, who are considered to represent the majority of wage earners.[1] This, however, does not mean that the classical economists ignored the existence of pay differentials. Their focus on the wages of common labour is an abstraction, analytically justified by their view that pay differentials tend to be very stable over time. This means that changes in the wage rate for unskilled labour are accompanied, as we would say today, by a shift in the whole wage structure with the ratios among the wages of different categories remaining unchanged.[2]

The adjective 'natural' was introduced by Smith and adopted by later economists. Contemporary interpreters have sometimes attributed some peculiar connotations to this word. The classical economists, it has been maintained, saw 'natural' values as 'just' values reflecting an intrinsic harmony of the natural and social order. It has also been maintained that this view would introduce an unscientific attitude into classical economic theory, making it impossible to distinguish between normative and analytical elements

---

1. These are the workers at the bottom of the pay scale, except for child and female labour, who, according to the descriptions and references found in the texts of the authors under discussion, receive still lower wages.
2. In this connection, Smith writes: 'Though pecuniary wages and profits are very different in the different employments of labour and stock; yet a certain proportion seems commonly to take place between both the pecuniary wages in all the different employments of labour, and the pecuniary profits in all the different employments of stock. This proportion [...] depends partly upon the nature of the different employments, partly upon the different laws and policy of the society in which they are carried on. But though in many respects dependent upon the laws and policy, this proportion seems to be little affected by the riches or poverty of that society, by its advancing, stationary or declining condition; but to remain the same or very nearly the same in all those different states' (Smith, 1776, book I, chap. vii, par. 36; from now on: I.vii.36); 'Such revolutions in the publick welfare, though they affect the general rates both of wages and profit, must in the end affect them equally in all different employments. The proportion between them, therefore, must remain the same, and cannot well be altered, at least for any considerable time, by any such revolutions' (ibid., I.x.c.53); see also Ricardo,1821, I, pp. 20–1.

(Zamagni, 1987, pp. 99–100).

The use of the term 'natural' to designate economic magnitudes such as prices and wages probably reflects the intellectual influence of natural law philosophy on the development of classical political economy. However, as Taylor has suggested, even though to some extent the classical economists were influenced by a philosophy that led them to look for a harmonic order underlying observed phenomena, 'the doctrine of economic harmonies [...] was not necessarily a hindrance in the early stages of the search for regularities or laws'.[3] As he notes, in the natural sciences some important discoveries were made under that very influence. The fact that certain philosophical premises may be considered outdated does not necessarily rule out the scientific validity of studies carried out by their adherents.

Moreover, the philosophical influence of natural law does not necessarily imply that for the classical economists natural values reflect a just and harmonious 'natural order'. What economic analysis mainly had in common with the philosophy of natural law was the idea that material or social phenomena rest on an underlying order which can be discovered through reasoning and experience, and that to understand this order means to identify the 'laws' that govern material or social phenomena.

The idea of a divine origin of such laws, and the consequent perspective whereby they lead to the best of all possible worlds – while present in part of the philosophical tradition of natural law – does not appear to have a role in the economic theory of the classical authors, particularly in Smith and his successors. O'Brien has argued that '[t]he classical economists from Smith onwards recognized fundamental flaws in the harmony of the unregulated natural order. Ultimately they believed that harmony could be achieved only through the creation of a legal and non-legal framework within which man had to operate' (1975, p. 24).[4]

---

3. Taylor, 1929, p. 17. In this connection see also Schumpeter: 'There is no point in throwing out the analytic baby with the philosophic bath water. And this is precisely what is being done by those who dispose of the economics of the scholastic doctors or their laical successors merely by pointing to its associations with a system of moral and legal imperatives – of natural laws in the analytic sense because of its association with a system of natural laws in the normative sense' (1954, p. 111).
4. On the absence in Ricardo of the idea of harmony in the economic system, see also Taylor, 1929, p. 17.

As we shall see, these features of the classical theory are particularly evident with regard to income distribution. In this area there is an explicit recognition of the existence of conflicting interests, and hence a non-harmonic conception of relations between social classes. Even the Physiocrats, who from a philosophical and political point of view had a harmonic vision of class relationships, developed an economic analysis which ultimately (against their own intentions) revealed the existence of potentially conflicting interests among different social groups with regard to income distribution (Vaggi, 1987, pp. 177–82). By contrast, in the second half of the nineteenth century, when the classical approach was virtually abandoned, a harmonic conception of economic mechanisms appears to have grown stronger, not weaker (Taylor, 1929, pp. 30–31).

The sense of the adjective 'natural', then, is not different from that of 'normal' – that is to say, a magnitude that results from the full and free operation of the forces which the theory considers decisive for explaining the phenomena under study.

The natural values (prices, wages) of the classical economists are comparable to those Marshall defined as 'long period normal' (1920, pp. 314–15).[5] Like the latter, they are determined without taking account of the possible influences of temporary and accidental events that may at any moment disturb the operation of the systematic and persistent forces governing the movements of the economic system,[6] or of changes in what the theory takes as the data determining the natural magnitudes themselves.[7] Changes in these data cause what Marshall (1982, p. 315) calls 'very gradual or *secular* movements' of normal magnitudes.

The object of the following chapters will be precisely to identify what the classical economists considered to be the data and the economic forces that determine the natural wage at a certain time and place, and to show how changes in these data can influence the

5. The adjective 'natural' has continued to be used in this sense in economic theory after the classical period: think for example of Wicksell's natural rate of interest, and the natural unemployment rate in modern macroeconomics.

6. 'Natural simply means that disturbances other than such as may have been included in the data are assumed to be absent, or that we intend to investigate a process or state as it would be if left to itself' (Schumpeter, 1954, p. 112, n. 5).

7. '[The] doctrine of Adam Smith and other economists [is] that the normal or "natural" value of a commodity is that which economic forces would bring about if the general conditions of life were stationary enough to enable them all to work out their full effect' (Marshall, 1920, p. 289).

'secular' movements, to use Marshall's word, of the natural wage.

For the sake of simplicity, in what follows I shall use the terms 'natural' and 'normal' wage interchangeably, even when referring to authors who used different terms or periphrases with the same meaning.[8]

THE DEMAND FOR LABOUR

The influence of contemporary economic theory may lead to the belief that when they spoke of the demand for labour the classical authors were referring (though in an imperfect and approximate way) to a functional relationship which, as in today's dominant marginalist theory, links the demand for labour with the real wage rate.[9]

However, by the 'demand for labour' the classical authors meant a single quantity (the number of working hours or workers required by capitalist entrepreneurs),[10] rather than a function or 'demand curve' representing the different equilibrium levels of employment corresponding to different levels of the real wage, as is the case in contemporary economic theory.[11] This question will be taken up again in the following chapters, and it will be re-examined in the concluding pages. Here, in support of the above argument, I shall only call attention to the analogy between the 'demand' for labour and the 'effectual demand' for a commodity.

The definition of the latter is provided in Smith's discussion of the natural and market prices of goods:

The actual price at which any commodity is commonly sold is called its market

8. Cantillon speaks for example of customary wages, Turgot speaks of the 'natural proportion' between the prices of goods consumed by workers and the 'price of wages', i.e. money wages.
9. For example this function is attributed to Smith in Blaug, 1985, p. 44.
10. There seem to be some differences, probably reflecting historical conditions, in the type of demand for labour considered by the economists of the period. When Ricardo speaks of labour demand or employment he generally refers to wage earners employed by capitalist entrepreneurs. Smith usually also includes servants hired at a wage to provide personal services to the rich. Steuart, Cantillon and Necker (and often Smith) include artisans selling their products and services in the market.
11. This follows the absence, in classical political economy, of the direct and indirect substitution between factors with changes in distribution, which is the foundation of the demand curves for labour in modern economic theory (see below, Chapter 6, pp. 188-95).

price. It may either be above or below, or exactly the same with its natural price. The market price of every particular commodity is regulated by the proportion between the quantity which is actually brought to market, and the demand of those who are willing to pay the natural price of the commodity [...]. Such people may be called the effectual demanders, and their demand the effectual demand. (Smith, 1776, I.vii.7–8)

The concept of 'effectual demand' defined by Smith[12] in these lines is that of a determinate quantity, and the 'proportion' between supply and demand is the ratio between two quantities: the number of hats (bushels of grain, yards of cloth) on sale, and the number of these items which consumers wish to buy under normal conditions, i.e. when the price is the natural price. This relationship obviously cannot determine the market price, but as Smith says, it regulates it – in other words it determines the direction of change in market price with respect to the natural price.[13]

---

12. The term 'effectual demand', with the same meaning as in Smith, had already been used by James Steuart (1766a, I, p. 117).

13. Garegnani, 1983, pp. 77–9. The interpretation of Smith's 'effectual demand' as a given quantity of goods, and of the 'proportion' between the quantity actually available and the effectual demand as a ratio between two quantities, is also accepted by historians of thought with a different approach. See for example Hollander, 1987, pp. 66–7, where the author recognizes that Smith speaks of the demand for a consumer good as a single quantity. This conflicts with the interpretation suggested by Benetti (1979, pp. 85–98), whereby the 'effectual demand' would be a sum equal to the natural price of the good times the quantity bought at that price. That sum (no more and no less) would always be spent for that good. The market price of the latter would prove equal to the ratio between that sum and the quantity of the good actually available; thus for each commodity we would have:
$$Pm = PnQn/Qm$$
where Pm is the market price, Pn the natural price, Qn the quantity demanded at the natural price, and Qm the quantity actually available. In this interpretation the market price is perfectly determined once the actually available quantity of the good is known, and it is a market clearing price because when there is an excess supply it continues to fall until all the goods are bought. This interpretation, however, is clearly contradicted by the texts of the classical economists. Smith, in discussing the fluctuations of market prices, explains that in the case of an excess supply of a commodity over the normal quantity: '[t]he market price will sink more or less below the natural price [...] according as it happens to be more or less important to them [the sellers] to get immediately rid of the commodity. The same excess in the importation of perishable, will occasion a much greater competition than in that of durable commodities' (Smith, 1776, I.vii.10). This clearly implies that not all the goods must necessarily be sold, at least immediately, and that the market price is not thought to be determined as in the above equation, since other circumstances (in this case the perishability of the goods) contribute to its determination. Similarly, in the case of a scarcity of the commodity compared to the normal quantity various circumstances are indicated by Smith as important in determining the deviation of the market price from the natural price: apart from the size of the deficiency of the good, the latter will depend on the 'wealth and wanton luxury' of the purchasers, and on how important it is to them to acquire the

By extension we may say that the demand for labour, like the demand for a commodity, is a determinate quantity. The term 'demand for labour' is thus synonymous with 'level of employment', with the qualification that this is employment in the capitalist or market sector of the economy. More precisely still, since in principle the quantity of labour demanded might exceed the existing supply, it can be defined more generally as employment plus vacancies.

Thus when the classical economists speak of the relation between the demand for labour and the population, they refer to the ratio between the number of employed workers and the population, the variations of which are seen as an indicator of labour market conditions.

In contrast with the above picture, the classical economists' theory of wages has been most commonly interpreted in terms of the wages fund theory. On the basis of this interpretation, in the context of the classical analysis the term 'demand for labour' would indicate not the employment level, as I have suggested, but a predetermined 'fund' for the payment of wages. The classical theory would thus imply an inverse relation between the real wage rate and the level of employment, similar to that introduced later, on different theoretical grounds, by the marginalist theory.

But in the texts of the authors studied here there is nothing to suggest the existence of an inverse relation between wages and employment. On the contrary, as we shall see (Chapter 6, pp. 182-4) there are elements in the analysis that contradict the possibility of such a relation.

good (ibid., para. 9). As an example of the role of this last factor Smith cites the 'exorbitant price of necessaries' at times of siege or famine (Ibid.). This last example leads one at once to doubt that he considered the overall sum spent for a certain commodity to be given for all cases. Rather, in further contrast with the formula given above for determination of market prices, it must be recognized that according to Smith a scarcity of necessaries might induce individuals to give up other items of consumption in order to obtain a certain quantity of goods of first necessity, thus increasing the sum spent for the goods in question. Hence the 'effectual demand' cannot be interpreted as a predetermined sum spent in all cases for the purchase of a certain commodity. Smith's treatment can be considered representative also of Ricardo's point of view. In his chapter on natural and market prices Ricardo explicitly refers to Smith: '[i]n the seventh chapter of the Wealth of Nations, all that concerns this question is most ably treated' (Ricardo, 1821, I, p. 91). Also in contrast with the above interpretation is what Ricardo writes in *Protection to Agriculture*, 1822, IV, p. 220 (quoted below, Chapter 6, p. 192).

THE SUPPLY OF LABOUR

In current economic language the supply of labour (or labour force, in statistical surveys) is the number of workers (or hours of work) offered at the current wage. Statistically, that number comprises employed people plus those who are out of employment but actively seeking work. Current economic theory regards the labour supply as a variable which, for a given population, depends on the wage level according to a specific quantitative relation (function), which in general is held to be increasing. Hence, for a given population, the number of persons prepared to work (or the number of hours workers are prepared to do) is expected to increase, with an increase in real wages, at least within a certain interval of the values that wages may take.

For the classical economists, on the other hand, the labour supply is identified with the population belonging to those social classes which can get the income they need to live only by selling their labour. It is obvious, and the classical economists certainly knew it, that there is always a part of that population which is not able to work – for example very young children, invalids, the elderly. But this does not mean the population cannot be used as an approximate measure of the size of the labour supply, if the section of the population which is unable to work remains sufficiently stable over time, or if the factors which would cause changes in the size of that section can legitimately be assumed constant. In those circumstances, the population able to work varies proportionally with the total population. However, the question of the existence of a sector of the population which cannot work, for what might be called demographic reasons, enters the picture when the classical authors discuss the effects of wage variations on the growth of the population, and of that growth on wages. Population growth is seen as the result mainly of an increase in birth rate and a reduction of infant mortality. Thus before its effects show up on the labour market as an increase in supply enough time must pass for the children to grow into workers.

Hence, the classical economists believed that population growth was influenced by wage variations; but because demographic effects take considerable time to be felt on the labour market, they did not see population changes in response to wage variation as affecting the adjustment of the labour market in a given normal position of the economy (in contrast with the changes in labour supply in response to wage changes appearing in modern neoclassical theory). Changes in the population (or its growth rate) in response to changes in wages were seen rather as a factor that might affect wages and other economic variables in the course of the accumulation process – that is the 'secular' movements of the economic system. Moreover, as I shall argue, the classical economists did not see the relation between wages and population growth as one in which the signs and magnitudes of the parameters are known and sufficiently stable for it to be expressible in mathematical form. On the contrary, they generally held (except for Malthus) that wage variations could induce effects on the population that were variable in size and even in sign, quite unlikely to be determinable *a priori*.

For the classical economists, in a given normal position of the economy the labour supply, like the demand for labour, was not a 'curve' but a determinate quantity: the population belonging to the wage-earning classes. Changes in wages may influence what Marshall called the 'gradual' or 'secular' movements of the labouring population.

There are obvious historical reasons why the classical economists identified the population belonging to the labouring classes with the supply of labour. Very low income levels, poverty and the customs of the time meant that in general all members of those classes – including children, old people and women – were willing to accept a paid job whenever they had a chance, to provide for their own subsistence and contribute to that of their families.

The theoretical views of the classical economists, however, may also have had a role in this identification. In their theoretical framework, which does not involve a tendency to full employment of labour, labour supply as currently defined could not be regarded as independent of the demand for labour. It would be impossible to rule out the existence of a potential supply of labour, not expressed in the active search for a job because of discouragement at the lack of opportunity.

UNEMPLOYMENT

The unemployed, as currently defined, are people out of work and actively seeking it.

The possibility of unemployment was contemplated by the classical economists, but it was often indicated by other terms or circumlocutions: the unemployed were referred to as 'idle' (as opposed to 'industrious', but without the moral connotations now implicit in these words), or as people who 'want employment'. They included not only people actually seeking jobs and underemployed labourers wanting to work more days or hours, but also those who had become vagrants, beggars or criminals. They also included sections of the population such as women or children, who might or might not be actively seeking jobs but who would readily offer their services whenever the opportunity arose. Although these people would not always be 'unemployed' according to the current definition, they were regarded by the classical economists as 'wanting employment' and as part of the labour supply. This evidently reflects the analytical problem mentioned at the end of the foregoing section. If the rate of unemployment, as defined today, is to be considered a significant indicator of the state of the labour market, one must presuppose that the number of people seeking work can be considered independent of actual opportunities of finding it. This supposition is legitimated by the conclusion, inherent in contemporary neoclassical economic theory, that the normal operation of economic forces always tends to ensure the full employment of labour, and that unemployment may only be due to 'frictions' or to temporary fluctuations of the level of output and employment around full employment. As the possibility of widespread persistent unemployment is ruled out, so is the discouragement from the active search for work that would plausibly follow from it. The absence of a tendency to full employment in the theoretical perspective common to the classical economists may thus explain why, to describe the state of the labour market, they refer not only to the number of unemployed workers, but also to the variations in the ratio between demand for labour (employment in the market sector of the economy) and the population belonging to the working classes.

In the light of the above considerations, in the following pages I shall use terms like 'unemployment' or 'excess labour supply' in a broad sense, to indicate not only people who are actively seeking jobs, but also the potential labour supply consisting of people who are underemployed, employed in non–market activities (such as housework and production for home consumption), or self-employed with low incomes, and who if they had the opportunity would be willing to accept a job, or to work more hours.

2. Wages in the English Economic Literature of the Late Seventeenth and Early Eighteenth Centuries

INTRODUCTION

Historians and economists dealing with the English economic literature in the last quarter of the seventeenth century and the first half of the eighteenth,[1] when discussing wages, employment and other labour problems, have focused mainly on the normative aspects of that literature, especially the different views about the most appropriate level of wages.[2]

Normative elements are indeed very prominent in the literature of the period, whose main aim was to indicate what economic policies should be followed to enhance the wealth of the nation, its competitive advantage on international markets, and its economic development. One aspect of such policies is the regulation of the

1. Many of the authors discussed in this chapter can be described as mercantilists, whether this is defined – as it is by most scholars – in terms of their views on foreign trade and state intervention in the economy (a protectionist position, favouring the maintenance of a positive balance of payments and state intervention in general), or in terms of Marx's criterion whereby the typical feature of mercantilism is that the origin of profit is seen in exchange rather than production (cf. below, Chapter 3, p. 29, n. 1). I have chosen, however, to adopt a chronological criterion, including authors like Petty and Cantillon who are not mercantilist in terms of the above definitions. This follows from the question under investigation– the determination of wages – for which a distinction based on the above criteria was not immediately relevant. The authors included were chosen simply on the basis of the presence, in their writings, of analytical elements – however limited – related to the question at issue.
2. These aspects are focused upon by Wiles (1968, pp. 113 ff) and Coats (1958, pp. 35–51). Furniss (1920) also gives space to the analytical aspects of this literature in connection with the determination of wages, but these have a limited importance compared to the reconstruction of the normative debates and economic policy. The latter are also at the centre of Heckscher's study (1935, Chapter 6) on the mercantilists' view of problems of unemployment, work and wages.

labour market; and throughout the period one of the major themes of discussion was the effect of English wage levels on the competitiveness of the nation's manufactures in international markets. The prevailing attitude was one of concern lest higher wage levels in England might endanger exports. But there were also other views: some argued that higher wages did not necessarily imply higher production costs if accompanied by more advanced production techniques and greater skills on the part of the workers – in short, a technical and organizational superiority of English manufacturing over that of competing countries (Wiles, 1968, pp. 122–6).

Another recurrent theme in these normatively oriented debates was the controversy over the effects of high wages on the industriousness of workers. Today this question is again the object of attention on the part of economists, particularly in the literature on 'efficiency wages'. Of course the English economists of the seventeenth and eighteenth centuries dealt with the matter in a very different way: they were concerned not so much to identify the spontaneous forces determining wages, as to indicate the advantages and disadvantages of fiscal and pricing policies or regulation of the labour market aimed at manipulating the level of real wages. The commonest view, at least in the early part of the period, was that high wages would discourage hard work and diligence. The workers sought consumption levels that depended on prevailing customs; therefore if higher wages enabled them to obtain those goals by fewer hours of work they would work less, and in general would be more undisciplined. This view was opposed throughout the period – but most strongly after the mid-eighteenth century – by the idea that higher wages would encourage industriousness in the workers by giving them a taste for improved consumption, and hence stimulating them to earn more by working harder. This position was later shared by Smith.[3]

3. The first position, whereby an increase in wages induces a reduction in workers' industriousness, is illustrated in Seligman (1899, p. 30 ff), with numerous quotations; for a broad illustration of the other position see Furniss (1920, p. 178 ff). Among the passages quoted by the latter is the following from Berkeley, who rhetorically asks 'Whether the creating of wants be not the likeliest way to produce industry in a people? And whether if our peasants were accustomed to eat beef and wear shoes, they would not be more industrious? Whether comfortable living doth not produce wants and wants, industry and industry, wealth?' (Berkeley, 1735, p. 3). With

Although the debates on these questions were mainly policy oriented, there were also some analytical and descriptive comments on the forces that determine wages and their variations over time or in different countries. It is these aspects that will be dealt with in the following pages. In the writings of the period they were not treated systematically, but appeared in fragmentary form. Many of the ideas found in these writers, however, also appear in later, more mature and advanced economic analyses; and most of them come together in the *Wealth of Nations*.

One element that differentiates the early writers from those discussed in the next chapter is the absence of an explicit distinction between the normal or average wage and the wage actually observed at any moment on the market, which may be subject to fluctuations around that average value. This distinction is also missing from the works of Cantillon, though he elaborated it rather clearly with regard to the prices of goods. However, when dealing with the determination of wages these writers are concerned with their normal rate, taken as a known element of the economic system in a certain time and place. This normal wage was not regarded as immutable – for example it may change in different historical periods or stages of economic development – but it was considered as an economic magnitude endowed with a certain persistence.

WAGES, HABITUAL LEVEL OF CONSUMPTION, AND TAXES ON LABOUR INCOMES

Subsistence and consumption habits
In the literature of this period, as in the whole subsequent classical tradition, the real wages of unskilled labour and the relative wages in different occupations are taken as given data of the economic system, in the sense that they are known before the determination of commodity prices. This is particularly clear in the writings of Petty and Cantillon, who tried to formulate a theory of relative prices based on the 'units of land' necessary for the production of commodities. In doing so they treated the real wage for each type of work as a known quantity, measured in terms of the units of land

regard to Smith, cf. Smith, 1776, I.viii.44.

necessary for its production.[4]

The wage level was generally taken as equal to the subsistence of the labourer and his family, but this level was clearly not defined in biological terms; it included customary elements.[5] It was regarded as varying among countries according to their different ways of life and consumption habits. Sir W. Harris, for example, advised the establishment of manufacturing firms in Ireland, where labour costs less because the Irish 'are a people that live on a coarser and cheaper dyet, nearer the manner of France, than the English do or can; and therefore they can afford their work cheaper' (Harris, 1691, p. 71). Similarly Cantillon, after calculating that in order to bring up children waged workers must be given double the amount they need for their own maintenance, argues that

> I have not determined to how much land the labour of the meanest peasant corresponds [...] because this varies according to the mode of living in different countries. In some southern provinces of France the peasant keeps himself on the produce of one acre and a half of land [...]. But in the County of Middlesex the peasant usually spends the produce of 5 to 8 acres of land [...]. (Cantillon, 1755, p. 39)[6]

The dependence of wages on habitual consumption, including 'conveniences' not strictly necessary for survival, was clearly affirmed in a Parliamentary speech reported in 1737 in the *Gentlemen's Magazine*: 'In all countries [...] wages [...] must depend on the price of those provisions which are necessary for their convenient support, for even the poorest workmen must and will have some of the conveniences of life' (cited in Furniss, 1920,

---

4. Petty, 1899, p. 181 ff; Cantillon, 1755, pp. 25–30. On this point see also Roncaglia, 1977, pp. 110–21.
5. This is also the interpretation given by Furniss, 1920, p. 172.
6. A passage similar to that of Cantillon, and probably taken from his *Essai*, is found in Postlethwayt, 1757, p. 144. At this point it may be useful to say something about the chronology and propagation of Cantillon's work. Cantillon, born in 1697, was a businessman of Anglo–Irish origin, who travelled widely in Europe and resided for some years in Paris. He died (or escaped to avoid legal suit) when his London house was destroyed by arson in 1734; his writings also perished in the fire. His *Essai*, in a French translation probably by Cantillon himself, was published in France in 1755 by Mirabeau, who had come into possession of the manuscript. The English version of the *Essai*, probably written in the last years of the author's life, has not survived. However substantial parts of the *Essai* (about 6000 words) were incorporated (without reference to Cantillon's work) in Postlethwayt's *Dissertation on the Plan, Use and Importance of the Universal Dictionary of Trade and Commerce*, London, 1749 – hence before the French publication (Higgs, 1931; Walsh, 1987).

p. 172).

Vanderlint, in defining the necessary consumption for labourers, introduces the idea that this level must be appropriate to their (low) social position. The necessary level of consumption is thus defined in relation to the particular social rank to which the worker belongs, and his wages must be sufficient, 'suitably to his low rank and station as a labouring man, [to] support such family as is often the lot of them to have' (Vanderlint, 1734, p. 15). This idea of a relation between social position and the level of consumption considered indispensable was later developed in an interesting way by Steuart.

Effects of taxation

As can be seen from some of the cited passages indicating that money wages must adjust to changes in the prices of wage goods, many of the economists of this period held that real wages could not be persistently affected by price changes, and therefore that taxes on necessaries would not be borne by the workers.

This idea was not universally accepted, and some proposed using indirect taxation as an instrument of economic policy to reduce workers' income and thus stimulate hard work and discipline (Seligman, 1899, pp. 30 ff). But the majority view was that real wages could not be reduced through taxation and price increases (Cannan, 1893, p. 233), and this was later accepted by outstanding economists such as Smith and Ricardo.

Concerning this question (the incidence of indirect taxation) Locke argued:

> Let us see now who, at long–run, must pay this quarter, and where it will light. [...] The poor labourer and handicraftsman cannot: for he just lives from hand to mouth already, and all his food, clothing and utensils costing a quarter more than they did before, either his wages must rise with the price of things, to make him live; or else, not being able to maintain himself and family by his labour he comes to the parish (Locke, 1692, V, p. 57).

The same opinion, that a tax on wage goods could not possibly reduce real wages, was expressed by various authors throughout the period,[7] and it was also shared by those who thought the real wages

7.   See the following assertions: 'Neither are these heavy contributions so hurtfull to the happiness of the people, as they are commonly esteemed: for as the food and rayment of the poor is made dear by excise, so does the price of their labour rise in proportion;

of English workers were too high: 'Augmenting taxes on consumption has not brought our workmen to the sobriety or frugality of a Frenchman or to the thriftiness of a Dutchman: and when our workmen cannot raise the price of their labour and workmanship to the degree they would, they have recourse to the parish or robbery' (Postlethwayt, 1757, p. 160). Tucker, after condemning the 'viciousness' of English workers, meaning their high level of consumption ('[v]ice is attended with expence, which must be supported either by a high price for their labour, or by methods still more destructive'), nonetheless declares that 'the taxes upon the necessaries of life are in fact so many taxes upon trade and industry' (Tucker, 1750, pp. 36, 38).

The adjustment of wages paid to workers and artisans in response to price changes caused by taxation is for the most part treated by these writers as a matter of fact, something which apparently requires no explanation.

In any case it must be emphasized that it is the habitual level of workers' real wages that cannot be reduced, even when this is well above a physiological minimum. This is shown by the fact that the opinion described above on the effect of indirect taxation may go hand in hand with the condemnation – so frequent in the literature

whereby the burden (if any be) is still upon the rich [...]' (Mun, 1664, p. 154); 'High excises [...] are utterly destructive [...] for if malt, coals, salt, leather and other things bear a great price, the wages of servants, workmen and artificers will consequently rise, for income must bear some proportion to the expence' (Davenant, 1699, p. 45; similar remarks also appear on p. 145); 'One necessary consequence that attends raising the annual supplies by taxes laid on the necessaries of life is raising the price of labour' (Anon., 1738, p. 18). Vanderlint expresses a similar view with regard to the effects of a reduction of prices on money wages: 'the plenty may be increased so much as to make victuals and drinks half the price that they are at now; which will make the price of the labour of working people much lower; for the rates are always settled and constituted of the price of victuals and drinks' (Vanderlint, 1734, p. 6). Finally, even Petty, whom Seligman includes among the authors who held that indirect taxes would fall on all consumers without distinction, affirmed that wages would adjust to changes in prices of goods consumed by the workers: 'England, sometimes prohibiting the commodities of Ireland and of Scotland, as of late it did the cattle, flesh and fish, did [...] make food and consequently labour, dearer in England' (Petty, 1676, p. 299). Petty, however, maintained that wages should be regulated by law; thus he does not seem to express a view about the spontaneous forces of the system which are supposed to determine wages (Roncaglia, 1977, pp. 95–7). Furniss (1920, pp. 190–97) discusses the position we have illustrated on the effects of taxation, linking it to the existence of a 'subsistence theory of wages', where subsistence is understood not as a physiological minimum but as a historical and social fact; he also cites other authors, apart from those mentioned here, who share the same view.

of the period – of the luxury and vices of the workers, in other words of their high wages.

THE INFLUENCE OF INSTITUTIONAL, CULTURAL AND ECONOMIC FACTORS

Institutions and culture

We have seen that habits and customs play a part in determining the 'subsistence' level of workers' consumption which must be ensured by wages. Along with these elements, in the authors of this period we find a few passages indicating that wages were seen as the result of a combination of economic, institutional and cultural factors.

According to Locke, cultural factors, rooted in the material living conditions of the workers, were partly to blame for their weakness in bargaining and their marginal role in the conflict between social groups over the distribution of income.

Speaking of the conflict over income distribution following a reduction in the quantity of money, Locke declares:

> This pulling and contest is usually between the landed man and the merchant; for the labourer's share, being seldom more than a bare subsistence, never allows that body of men time or opportunity to raise their thoughts above that, or struggle with the richer for theirs, (as one common interest) unless when some common and great distress, uniting them in one universal ferment, makes them forget respect, and emboldens them to carve to their wants with armed force; and then sometimes they break in upon the rich, and sweep all like a deluge. (Locke, 1692, p. 71)

Locke explains here that, in general, the workers will not play an active part in this conflict, both because of their habit of 'respect' for the upper classes (which they forget only in extreme situations), and because their hard and deprived conditions of life rob them of the 'time and opportunity' to struggle for their share of income, in defence of a common interest. Both poverty and cultural factors ('respect') block the workers from taking collective action in defence of their interests.

The importance of workers' collective actions in determining income distribution is also recognized, more or less implicitly, by other authors of the period.

Tucker, who favoured wage restraint, discussed a proposal made by a 'great manufacturer' to impose a tax on necessary goods in order to reduce real wages and thus motivate workers to work harder for survival. As we have seen he criticised such taxes as bearing 'upon trade and industry', and suggested instead that wages would be lowered by allowing the immigration of foreign workers, partly because this would prevent 'combinations' of workers:

> Foreigners can never get rich in a strange country, but by working cheaper or better than the natives. And if they do so, though individuals may suffer, the publick is certainly gainer [...] Not to mention that by this means the price of labour is continually beat down, combinations of journeymen against their masters are prevented, industry is encouraged, and emulation excited. (Tucker, 1750, p. 42)

The fact that foreigners must work better and at lower cost than native workers in order to 'get rich' (this should perhaps be understood as 'to accumulate enough to reach a standard fitting their social position') must obviously depend on social or institutional factors: foreigners may suffer various forms of discrimination and they lack certain rights implicitly or explicitly granted to the native population. That is why it is specifically the competition of foreign workers that can lower wages – by forcing local workers to compete with them and thus preventing the emergence of organizations uniting all waged workers, which are implicitly recognized as capable of modifying wages.

Hume, in one of his *Political Discourses*, argues that the political system of a country plays an important part in determining wages, as does the 'turn of thinking' which accompanies its changes:

> The poverty of the common people is a natural, if not an infallible effect of absolute monarchy; though I doubt, whether it will be always true, on the other hand, that their riches are an infallible result of liberty. Liberty must be attended with particular accidents, and a certain turn of thinking, in order to produce that effect (Hume, 1752, p. 16).

Hume then develops his analysis further: the level of wages depends on the workers' habits of life and the influence of these habits on their capacity for collective action; but an 'arbitrary government' can allow the rich, through fiscal policy, to impose a reduction of real wages even where the customs of the workers would be such as to favour a relatively high standard of living:

Where the labourers and artisans are accustomed to work for low wages, and to retain but a small part of the fruits of their labour, it is difficult for them, even in a free government, to better their condition, or conspire among themselves to heighten their wages. But even where they are accustomed to a more plentiful way of life, it is easy for the rich, in an arbitrary government, to conspire against them, and throw the whole burthen of the taxes on their shoulders. (Ibid.)

Here too it is interesting to note the importance given to the workers' capacity for common action, for example in pursuit of wage increases. In this passage the idea emerges that in general the distribution of income between wages and profits and the redistributive role of fiscal policy are determined by the action of social groups with conflicting interests.

Thus a range of institutional and cultural elements, including the capacity for collective action on the part of workers, is considered, at least by some authors, as capable of modifying the distribution of income.

Labour market conditions

Others find the causes of differences in wage levels, at various places or historical periods, in circumstances of a more strictly economic nature. In particular, they indicate the state of backwardness or economic prosperity of a country, and the existence of unemployment or a shortage of manpower.

According to Child, 'Wherever wages are high universally throughout the whole world, it is an infallible evidence of the riches of that country, and wherever wages for labour runs low, it is a proof of the poverty of that place' (Child, 1693, *Preface*). The idea of a connection between high wages and a thriving condition of commerce and industry is also found later in an anonymous *Pamphlet* published in 1738: 'High wages are indeed a sure sign of a flourishing people' (p. 18).[8]

Manley seems to believe that economic prosperity may lead to high wages because of the conditions prevailing on the labour market. He maintains that the high level of wages in England (which he complains about) is not caused by 'quickness of trade and want of hands (as some do suppose) which are justifiable reasons' (Manley, 1699, p. 19); and he also remarks, 'I know that want of

8.   Similar expressions appear in Davenant (1696, p. 73) and Defoe (1728, pp. 51–2).

imployments and very low wages are the common makers of a poor nation' (ibid., p. 20). These passages appear in the context of a comparison between societies which experience different economic conditions and different rates of accumulation. This suggests that Manley's observations on the role of the 'want of hands' or 'want of imployments' should not be interpreted as concerning transitory phenomena that cause wages to deviate from their usual level. It would seem rather that he is referring to different conditions of the labour market which characterize thriving economies or poor and stagnant ones, and sees them as factors which determine a difference between the habitual (normal) wage levels in the two situations.

The role of unemployment in determining wage levels – or, more precisely, in making them coincide with the subsistence of the worker and his family, is also mentioned in the following passage by Postlethwayt :

> We may regard labour as a commodity, which every man will purchase as cheap as he can; and therefore the poorer sort, whose commodity it is, are obliged continually to undersell each other, 'if there is not full employment for the whole. They who sell cheapest must live, and they who must sell only to live, being unfortunately in all countries the greater number, they will therefore fix the price of the commodity. The price of a day's labour will be at lowest a day's subsistence. (Postlethwayt , 1757, p. 144)

Here subsistence is indicated as a minimum, with which wages tend to coincide through the effect of competition between labourers in conditions of unemployment or underemployment. It is worth noting that just after the above passage Postlethwayt defines subsistence in relation to the habits of life of the workers in different countries, and not as a physiological minimum (ibid.).[9]

The role of 'want of employments' in determining wages is consistent with the fact that the existence of widespread and persistent unemployment was broadly recognized throughout the period, and its causes and remedies constituted an important object of debate, as we shall see in the next section.

Cary suggested another element that might explain the connection between a country's economic prosperity and relatively high wages: increased productivity and technological progress. He maintained

---

9.   The passage in which Postlethwayt defines subsistence is almost identical with that of Cantillon, cited earlier in this chapter (see note 6 above).

that the high English wages would not harm the competitiveness of the country's goods, thanks to great progress in the productivity of manufacturing. This progress, according to Cary, would reduce the number of workers employed and 'make room for better wages to be given those who are imployed' (Cary, 1695, p. 148).

Lastly, the association between economic prosperity and relatively high wages is seen by some authors from another point of view – that of the positive effects of workers' higher wages and consumption for the prosperity of commerce and agriculture. Take for example the following passage by Defoe: 'If their wages were low and despicable, so would be their living; if they got little, they would spend but little, and trade would presently feel it; as their gain is more or less, the wealth and strength of the whole kingdom would rise or fall' (Defoe, 1704, p. 10).[10]

The passages cited above indicate that some economists of this period considered unemployment as an element that could play a part in the determination of wage levels. In this connection, as I have said, it must be remembered that the existence of persistent forms of unemployment is generally recognized and very often discussed as an important and serious problem calling for the intervention of economic policy measures, whose nature depends on each author's analysis of the causes of the phenomenon.[11]

The central importance of this problem in the economic debates of the period has been underlined by Furniss in his classic study of labour in the mercantilist literature. This writer holds that in the late mercantilist period the preoccupation with a positive balance of payments and the increase in the stock of money, which characterize all mercantilist literature, assumes new meanings. Increased net exports and an increased quantity of money are seen as instrumental

---

10. Other passages on this subject appear in Defoe, 1728, p. 102; Vanderlint, 1734, p. 69; Braddon, 1717, p. 18. This aspect of the mercantilist literature is discussed by Wiles (1968, pp. 119–22). The positive effects of relatively high wages on demand and hence on the level of production are not seen as a possible element for explaining the wage level, but only as its consequence.

11. The causes of unemployment most frequently indicated are the decline of productive activity (see e.g. Fortrey, 1673, pp. 12 and 21; Haynes, 1715, pp. 1–4; Manley, 1677, p. 2), or an insufficient quantity of money which depresses productive and commercial activity (Law, 1705, pp. 213–14 and 217–20). Many solutions are suggested, but the most common proposal is that the unemployed should be put to work in manufacturing, especially in the production of goods imported by the country (this is proposed, for example, by Petty, 1676, p. 269).

in promoting the development of productive activities, and consequently as favouring increased employment (Furniss, 1920, pp. 41–73; Heckscher, 1935, pp. 121–30; Coats, 1958, p. 104).

The extent to which unemployment was considered as a normal feature of a market economy is revealed by a passage of Hume which I think is very significant. Comparing the respective merits of production by slave labour and waged labour, Hume, opposed to the former, sought to show that it was economically inferior by means of the following argument: 'the fear of punishment will never draw so much labour from a slave, as the dread of being turned off and not getting another service will from a freeman' (Hume, 1752, pp. 116–17).

Thus the fear of unemployment, for Hume, is what ensures the discipline of wage earners, and this is an inherent feature of the system of production based on the use of such workers.

MIGRATORY MOVEMENTS OF THE POPULATION

In the literature of this period[12] the relation between wages and population changes caused by migratory movements is mentioned with regard to two separate themes, which are conceptually distinct and are discussed in very different contexts.

The first theme is that of the possibility that when real wages fall below their habitual level (e.g. through a persistent increase in the price of subsistence goods without a compensating increase in money wages) the workers, rather than accept such conditions, will choose to move to other places where they can earn more. This possibility is generally mentioned in connection with the impossibility or inadvisability of cutting real wages because of the negative effects of their reduction; as Locke writes, 'it endangers the drawing away our people, both handicrafts, mariners, and soldiers, who are apt to go where their pay is best' (Locke, 1692, V, p. 50). Similarly Child

12. In Chapter 4, I shall discuss Cantillon's population theory together with that of Steuart, because its approach is more systematic than the ideas of his contemporaries whom I discuss more briefly here, and also because it presents an analysis of population changes based not only on migratory movements, as in the authors here examined, but also on the effects of workers' living conditions on the birth and death rates, in a manner similar to that of later authors.

maintains that 'if we retrench by law the labour of our people, we drive them from us to other countries that give better rates' (Child, 1693, *Preface*).

With regard to the theory of wages, adjustments of population figure analytically as one of the elements that may prevent wages from falling below the habitual level. This happens because emigration may be an alternative to a fall in workers' living standards. A similar argument holds with regard to the possibility that when wages become unacceptably low, workers will throw themselves on the parish, or will engage in illicit activities (Locke, 1692, V, p. 57, quoted in p. 17 above; Postlethwayt, 1757, p. 160). The possibility of emigration makes it unwise to lower wages or adopt any policies leading to that effect, because this may be harmful to the nation.

In some authors we find a second theme, distinct from that of the effect of low wages on emigration: a link between the size of the labouring population and the pattern of accumulation and employment. According to Fortrey, 'if the manufactures and other profitable employments of this nation were rightly improved and encouraged, there is no doubt but the people and riches of the kingdom might be greatly increased and multiplied, both to the profit and honour of the Prince' (Fortrey, 1673, p. 12). Still more explicit in this sense is Child's assertion that 'Such as our employment is for people, so many will our people be; and if we should imagine we have in England employment but for one hundred people, and we have born and bred amongst us one hundred and fifty people, I say the fifty must away from us, or starve or be hanged to prevent it' (Child, 1693, pp. 186–7). This is echoed by a very similar statement by Law: 'the increase or decrease of people depends on trade, if they have employment at home they are kept at home, and if the trade is greater than serves to employ people, it brings more from places where they are not employed' (Law, 1705, p. 33).[13]

13. The same problem is discussed later in the works of A. Young, who refers also to the effects of economic well–being on marriage and birth rates: 'It is employment that creates population [...] all industrious countries are popolous, and proportionably to the degree of their industry. When employment is plentiful, and time of value, families are not burthens [...] marriages are early and numerous [...]' (Young, 1771, IV, pp. 410-11; see also I, pp. 173 ff)

The growth of the population through migratory movements appears to be directly linked with opportunities for work: the absence of such opportunities forces workers to move away or starve; their increase induces workers to migrate from places where they are scarce. Only Child, in this period, also refers to the possibility that a scarcity of labour due to excessive emigration to the colonies might bring about the necessary adjustment of the population through variations in wages:

> if we have evacuated more of our people than we should have done [...] that decrease would procure its own remedy, for much want of people would procure greater wages, and greater wages [...] would procure us a supply of people without the charge of breeding them, as the Dutch are, and always have been supplied in their great extremities. (Child, 1693, p. 187)

Increased opportunities for work, and according to Child also the effect of this increase on wages, lead to changes in the labouring population sufficient to meet the increased demand for labour. No role seems to be ascribed to this adjustment when explaining the tendency for real wages to coincide with habitual or subsistence consumption. As already noted, population adjustments are discussed in the context of the relation between accumulation and availability of labour. The recognition of a tendency for the population to adjust to the demand for labour during processes of economic development (or decline) does not seem to imply the idea that wages are immutable over time, rigidly fixed at a subsistence level that cannot change. As we have seen, in this period it was widely believed that the habitual wage may vary not only between countries but also within the same country, in relation to economic prosperity. This idea can also be found in authors like Child, who at the same time maintained that the population tends to adjust to the demand for labour.

The general admission that unemployment exists, and that it plays a part in determining wage rates, suggests that the tendency of population to adjust to opportunities for work should not be interpreted rigidly: it should be understood as a tendency of the two magnitudes to move in the same direction, which does not preclude the existence, even for long periods, of considerable disequilibria between employment and the labouring population.

SUMMARY

In this chapter we have examined the ideas on the forces behind the determination of wages which appear, though not yet in systematic form, in the English economic literature between the mid-seventeenth and the mid-eighteenth century.

The writers of this period generally connected the wage level at a certain place and historical period with the subsistence level of consumption, determined by prevailing habits and customs; thus wages can vary from one country to another, and within one country at different historical moments. Numerous authors believed that this wage level could not be reduced: an increase in the prices of labourers' 'necessaries', due for example to indirect taxation, would induce a proportional increase in money wages, even though workers' habitual consumption was considered relatively high, and certainly above a biological subsistence minimum.

Some authors point to other factors that may influence the normal level of real wages: the capacity for organization and collective action by workers, the political system, and the economic condition of the country, in particular its prosperity or poverty and the associated shortage of labour or of employment.

Population changes caused by migratory flows are brought into the analysis of the labour market in relation to two different questions. The first is that of the possible effects of a reduction in wages below their habitual level: in this context the possible choice of emigration expresses the refusal of workers to accept lower pay than they are accustomed to. This refusal may also be expressed in other forms: for example by recourse to illicit activities or begging. Thus the possibility of emigration appears as one element among others that may contribute to the maintenance of the habitual level of wages.

The second question is that of how the availability of workers tends to adjust to employment opportunities: in an economy where the latter are ample there will be immigration from other countries, and when they are insufficient there will be emigration. Wage variations are not generally considered (except by Child) as an element in this process: workers are induced to move by the possibility of finding work, not necessarily because wages are higher somewhere else.

But this tendency for the size of the labouring population to adjust to opportunities for work should not be seen as a mechanism capable of ensuring equality between the quantity of labour demanded and that supplied. The possibility of persistent unemployment and underemployment was generally recognized, and indeed this was a central concern in the debates on economic policy. Hume considered unemployment as an inherent feature of the system of production based on the use of waged labour: it is the fear of unemployment which, in his view, guarantees the discipline of waged labour and makes it economically superior to the use of slaves.

3. The Theory of Wages in Adam Smith and his Contemporaries

INTRODUCTION

In this chapter we shall follow the development of the theory of wages over a period of about twenty years, centred around the publication date of Adam Smith's *Wealth of Nations* (1776).

James Steuart, whose treatise on the principles of political economy was published only nine years before the *Wealth of Nations*, may be considered as the last great mercantilist. His theory of profit as originating in exchange ('profit upon alienation') belongs to that tradition, as does his insistence on the need for state interventions to regulate and promote the economic development of the nation.[1]

---

1. Steuart (1713–80) was a Scotsman, educated as a lawyer. His economic studies began in France where he was exiled after his involvement in the attempt by the Pretender, Prince Charles Edward, to seize the throne in 1744. In Paris he met Mercier de la Rivière, Montesquieu and probably Mirabeau. After France, he spent time in Belgium, Germany and Holland, where he continued his economic studies. In 1763 he returned to Scotland, where in 1766 he published his *Inquiry*: the first important attempt to give a systematic structure to political economy. The importance of Steuart's work was obscured by the subsequent publication of Smith's *Wealth of Nations* (in which Steuart is never cited) – but not completely, for Ricardo mentioned him among the principal 'authorities' of the economic discipline in the preface to his *Principles* (Ricardo, 1821, I, p. 5). According to Marx, Steuart was a 'scientific' exponent of the point of view (shared by the pre-Physiocratic economists) that the surplus, identified with profit, results from exchange – i.e. the sale of commodities for more than their value. He considered Steuart 'scientific' because, unlike his mercantilist predecessors, he did not share the illusion that when an individual capitalist makes a profit by selling his own goods above their value he is creating new wealth. He held that the increase of wealth (or 'positive profit' in Steuart's words) derives only from an 'increase of work, industry or skill'. He maintained that the profit of the individual capitalist originates from exchange; but he saw this profit as a 'relative' profit since a gain on the part of one implies a loss on the part of another (Marx, 1861–63, pp. 41–3).

The work of Turgot, on the other hand, can be seen as the most mature expression of Physiocratic economics.[2] The characteristic feature of this system is the identification of agricultural production as the source of the surplus. That is to say, agriculture is seen as the only sector of production in which there is an excess of production over and above the necessary reintegration of the means of production and the wages paid to the workers. In Turgot some interpreters have even seen an advancement beyond that position – a recognition that a surplus is also produced in the manufacturing sector.

Unlike Steuart, and similarly to the Physiocrats and Smith, Turgot was an advocate of 'laissez-faire'; this orientation inspired the reforms he attempted during his political and administrative career.

Necker, a contemporary of Turgot, was Minister of Finance during the years immediately before and during the French Revolution.[3] He has not been generally thought of as a major figure

2. Turgot (1727–81) was educated for a career in the church, but entered the civil service. In 1761 he was appointed *Intendent* (general administrator) of the District of Limoges, and continued in that post until 1774 when he was appointed Minister of the Navy. Shortly afterwards he became Minister of Finance, an appointment that lasted 20 months. He sought to carry out anti-feudal reforms and to encourage free trade; he abolished the guilds and the *corvées*, and liberalized the grain trade (which was then subject to administrative controls and restraints that impeded the free movement of grain within French territory and its export to other countries). Most of Turgot's ideas on distribution are found in his writings on the grain trade. The subject is discussed in seven letters (of which only four survive) which he wrote in 1770 to the Abbé Terray, then *Contrôleur général* (Minister of Finance) in the effort to persuade him to abandon a plan to impose new restrictions on the grain trade and rescind the partial liberalization that had been in force since 1764. These very long letters form an important part of Turgot's economic works. He intended to publish them, but they were not published until after his death (the exact date is not known) by Du Pont de Nemours (Groenewegen, 1977, p. xxxii). Turgot was in very close touch with Quesnay and the other *économistes* (as the Physiocrats were called), especially Du Pont de Nemours, and he wrote for the Physiocratic journal *Ephémerides*. However, though he was often thought of as an *économiste* by his contemporaries, Turgot never wished to be considered as a Physiocrat. As he explained in his correspondence, he disapproved of the Physiocrats' sectarian attitudes and their excessive conformism with regard to the ideas of Quesnay, without the ability to develop them in new directions (Faure, 1961, pp. 276–81, and the correspondence quoted there).
3. Necker (1732–1804), a successful banker, was Minister of Finance for the first time from 1776 to 1781, when he was forced to resign; he returned to the same position in 1788 and held it until 1790. In his first economic work, *Sur la législation et le commerce des grains* (1775), he opposed the liberalization of the grain trade, favoured by the current minister Turgot. Necker's other main work was the treatise *De*

in the history of economic thought.[4] However Marx (1861–63, pp. 305–7) discusses with obvious interest and appreciation his ideas on the origin of profit and rent, which Necker found in the surplus labour performed by wage earners, and on the effects of accumulation on social inequality. Necker's economic writings had a wide circulation in his time, and his name is mentioned with approval in Smith's *Wealth of Nations*.[5] His works were primarily concerned with major political and economic issues of the time, for example whether or not to liberalize the grain trade, a question on which Necker's views differed from those of Turgot. These two economists had no relationship of collaboration, friendship or mutual esteem, but interestingly enough they had very similar ideas about the determination of wages. On that subject, evidently, there was a common ground of opinions extending beyond individual authors or intellectual circles.

There is no need to stress the importance of Adam Smith's *Wealth of Nations*,[6] both as a great synthesis of earlier contributions to the construction of political economy and as a fundamental text of that discipline, a constant reference point for later developments. Smith

l'administration des finances de la France (1785), which had great success, selling 80,000 copies in a few months. He also wrote a *Compte rendue au Roi* (1781), a summary of the events of his first ministry, and after the second, *De l'administration de M. Necker par lui même* (1791).

4. Necker's name does not even appear, for example, in Schumpeter's *History of Economic Analysis* (1954).

5. Smith cites Necker for his studies on population, and his library contained all Necker's economic works mentioned in note 3 above (Mizuta, 1967). Necker's influence on Smith's thought concerning wages has been recently mentioned by Bharadwaj (see above, Introduction, p. xiv, n. 10).

6. Smith (1723–90), a Scotsman, was educated at the University of Glasgow, where he was influenced by Francis Hutcheson, his teacher of Moral Philosophy. He then spent six years at Balliol College, Oxford. In 1751 he obtained the chair of Logic, and the following year that of Moral Philosophy, at the University of Glasgow. His academic success was sealed by the publication of the *Theory of Moral Sentiments* in 1759. Between 1764 and 1766 he spent about two years in France. In that period, thanks also to his friendship with Hume, he had the opportunity of meeting Voltaire, d'Alembert, Holbach and Helvetius. Smith, who had already developed an interest in economics, also met the economists Quesnay, Mirabeau and Turgot. Quesnay had by then published several editions of his *Tableau économique*, and Turgot was working on his *Réflections sur la formation et la distribution des richesses*. In the following years, until its publication in March 1776, Smith's energies were concentrated on the writing of his *Wealth of Nations*. This work had great success and was reprinted many times. Its third edition was published in 1784, and the sixth edition of the *Theory of Moral Sentiments* appeared in 1790.

went beyond the Physiocratic point of view: he saw the surplus as consisting of profits and rents, understood as deductions from the overall product of labour in both agriculture and industry.[7] This nature of the surplus, however, is obscured by his 'additive' theory of value, whereby the natural price of goods is determined by the sum of the natural rates of return on labour, capital and land used in their production. Later, of course, this theory, and the associated idea that an increase in the natural wage can be translated into an increase in prices with no reduction in the profit rate, formed a central element in Ricardo's critique of Smith.

Despite the differences in their approaches, the economists here examined show strong similarities in their discussion of wage theory.

For them, as for earlier writers, real wages are taken as a known quantity at the moment when relative prices are determined. They saw this quantity as being determined in turn by historical and economic circumstances, which they defined and examined with greater breadth and articulation than their predecessors had done.

In their writings we also find a clearer distinction between the normal rate of wages (what Smith calls the natural wage) and the 'market' wage (the wage actually observed at a given moment); the latter can differ from the normal value through the continual action of accidental and transitory events.[8] The normal wage rate emerges as an average or normal value of the actual or market wage, because it results from the action of systematic and persistent forces. For this reason it is the main object of enquiry.

It will be seen that some interpretations of the classical theory of

---

7. Hollander (1987, pp. 74 ff) criticizes the attribution to Smith of the idea that profit and rent are subtracted from the product of labour, on the grounds that according to Smith capital and land also contribute to production. This, however, is not the point: for Smith distribution is not explained by the respective 'contributions' of capital, labour and land to production of wealth. In the institutional context of capitalism, wages (determined in the way we shall see) are less than the whole product; thus part of the latter is made available for the owners of capital and land (on this point see Cannan, 1893, pp. 200–202).
8. The term 'market price of labour' was introduced and defined by Ricardo; here, however, we shall use it to indicate, by analogy with the market price of a commodity, the wage actually observed at each moment on the labour market, whose fluctuations around and relationship with the natural wage are discussed by these writers.

wages appear incorrect, particularly the one whereby the wage rate is said to be fixed at subsistence by population adjustment mechanisms.[9] What emerges, rather, is the role of power relations between the parties involved in wage negotiations, and the influence of social, economic and institutional factors.

THE DEFINITION OF SUBSISTENCE

For the pre-Smithian economists the minimum subsistence consumption was already seen as influenced by the habits and tastes prevailing in different countries and regions. Now it was further enriched by historical-social connotations.[10]

Turgot, while he does not give an explicit historical-social definition of subsistence, very clearly sees it as something different from a physiological minimum. For example in 1770, discussing the impossibility of wages falling below the level of subsistence he specified:

> It is certain that competition, as it drives wages down, reduces those of simple labourers to what is necessary for their subsistence. It must not be thought, however, that this means only what is necessary to keep from starving so as to leave these men with no means of procuring a few small pleasures, or, if they are thrifty, to accumulate some personal savings.[11]

James Steuart equates the normal rate of wages – which enters the determination of the 'real' or 'intrinsic' value of goods – with the subsistence of the labourer. Subsistence at one stage is identified with the full satisfaction of the physiological requirements of survival, determined, as Steuart says, by the 'animal oeconomy' of man. Thus

9. See Schumpeter, 1954, pp. 266 and 269; also above, Introduction, p. xv.
10. Bowley (1976) takes Smith's subsistence wage as a physiological minimum. This allows her to explain the fact that the natural wage does not fall below that level even in the presence of unemployment, with the immediate effects on the population of a reduction of wages (p. 189, n. and pp 191–2). In what follows I shall give a different interpretation of the forces that prevent wages from falling below subsistence.
11. 'Il est certain que la concurrence, en mettant les salaires au rabais, réduit ceux des simples manoeuvres à ce qui leur est nécessaire pour subsister. Il ne faut pas croire cependant que le necessaire soit tellement réduit à ce qu'il faut pour ne pas mourir de faim, qu'il ne reste rien au delà dont ces hommes puissent disposer, soit pour se procurer quelques petites douceurs, soit pour se faire, s'ils sont économes, un petit fond' (Turgot, 1770, III, p. 288).

defined, subsistence comprises the goods Steuart calls the 'physical necessaries'. But in Steuart's analysis this definition has an essentially normative role: it represents the level at which wages should be maintained by government intervention to promote the industriousness of workers and the nation's ability to compete on international markets. But when we move from the normative to the analytical/descriptive level, we find that necessary consumption was regarded as including not only the 'physical necessaries' but also what Steuart calls 'political necessaries':

> The nature of man furnishes him with some desires relative to his wants, which do not proceed from his animal oeconomy, but which are entirely similar to them in their effects. These proceed by the affection of his mind, are formed by habit and education, and when once *regularly established*, create another kind of necessary, which for the sake of distinction I shall call *political*.
> [...] The *political necessary* has for its object, certain articles of physical superfluity, which distinguishes what we call *rank* in society. *Rank* is determined by birth, education, or habit. A man with difficulty submits to descend from a higher way of living to a lower; [...] the common consent of his fellow citizens prescribes a certain *political necessary* for him, proportioned to his ambition; and when at any time this comes to fail he is considered to be in want. (Steuart, 1766a, pp. 270–71)

Such needs, acquired through education and habit, are associated with membership in a particular social group, and are rigidly defined by the social conventions prevailing in that group. They become a sort of second nature, with effects that Steuart says are quite similar to those of physiological needs. The force of these socially induced needs is so strong that sometimes individuals sacrifice physiologically necessary goods to satisfy them:

> The desires which proceed from the affection of his mind are often so strong as to make him comply with them at the expense of becoming incapable of satisfying those which his animal oeconomy necessarily demands. (Steuart, ibid.)

The definition of necessary consumption which is analytically relevant for Steuart's wage theory includes 'political necessaries'. This will emerge more clearly below in connection with his analysis of how in time high earnings become an integral part of the normal price of goods, and his view of the effects of taxation on goods consumed by workers.[12]

Smith also gives a historical-social definition of workers' necessary consumption. This depends on the habits and customs of the country, which set the generally accepted norms of decorum and respectability to which even the lowest classes must conform:

> By necessaries I understand, not only the commodities which are indispensably necessary for the support of life, but whatever the custom of the country renders it indecent for creditable people, even of the lowest order, to be without [...] Under necessaries, therefore, I comprehend not only those things which nature, but those things which the established rules of decency have rendered necessary to the lowest rank of people. (Smith, 1776, V.ii.k.3)[13]

Hence, when the subsistence of the worker and his family is seen as a threshold below which the natural wage cannot fall, this must be understood with reference to norms and habits that are socially and historically determined, not merely in terms of the bare necessities of survival.

FACTORS DETERMINING THE NATURAL WAGE AND ITS CHANGES

The writers under discussion held that the normal wage rate tends to coincide with subsistence, a minimum below which real wages could fall only temporarily, if at all. This tendency results from a combination of social, economic and institutional factors – 'social laws', as Necker calls them – that determine the workers' weakness and the employers' advantage in the process of wage bargaining. Yet any modification of those factors in favour of the workers may cause a persistent rise in wages, above subsistence level. Thus the normal wage does not necessarily coincide with bare subsistence: in particular circumstances it may be higher.

---

12. See below, pp. 66–8 and 71–3.
13. Sen (1985) emphasizes the importance, in Smith, of cultural norms and socially acquired habits in the definition of the 'standard of living'. He also claims that Smith's definition, shared by other classical economists, still holds good for current economic policy issues such as the specification of a poverty line (pp. 17 and 38).

Turgot

Bargaining and subsistence

In a letter written to Hume in 1767, Turgot illustrates his point of view about the role of workers' subsistence in determining wages. He distinguishes, for both commodities and labour, two prices: the 'current' price or value, and the 'fundamental' price.[14] The latter, in the case of wages, corresponds to the subsistence of the labourer. This fundamental price of labour is defined as a minimum below which the current value of wages can never fall:

> As far as the wage of the worker is concerned, the fundamental price is the cost of his subsistence. [...] Now, while the fundamental price is not the immediate regulator of the current value, it is still a minimum below which that value cannot fall.[15]

This shows that Turgot did not believe that wages necessarily coincided with the labourer's subsistence, but only that subsistence was the minimum possible level. In other writings, however, he

14. For Turgot, as for Quesnay and the Physiocrats, the 'current price' was the price observed on the market; the 'fundamental price' was defined by Turgot as: 'what the thing costs to him who sells it, that is, the raw material costs, the wages of his labour, and the profits of his stock' [ce que la chose coûte à celui qui la vend, c'est-à-dire les frais de matière première, intérêt des avances, salaires du travail et de l'industrie] (Turgot, 1767c, 2, pp. 655–6, n., cited in Groenewegen, 1970, p. 181). Turgot describes the relation between 'current price' and 'fundamental price' in the following way: '[t]he fundamental value is fairly stable and changes less frequently than the exchange value. The latter is ruled by supply and demand; it varies with needs, and often opinion alone suffices to produce very considerable and sudden fluctuations. It is not in any essential proportion to the fundamental value, but it has a tendency to approach it continually and can never move far away from it permanently.' [La valeur fondamentale est assez fixe et change beaucoup moins que la valeur vénale. Celle-ci ne se règle que sur le rapport de l'offre à la demande; elle varie avec les besoins, et souvent la seule opinion suffit pour y produire des secousses et des inégalités très considérable et très subites. Elle n'a pas une proportion nécessaire avec la valeur fondamentale, parce qu'elle dépend immédiatement d'un principe tout différent; mais elle tend continuellement à s'en rapprocher, et ne peut guère s'en éloigner beaucoup d'une manière permanente] (ibid.). With regard to wages, however, it is the 'current price' of labour, not the 'fundamental price', whose level in real terms cannot be persistently affected by variations in taxes or prices. It will appear that the 'current value' can differ rather persistently from subsistence as a consequence of a lasting change in the ratio of employment to labour supply, and is itself treated as a normal value.

15. 'Pour le salaire de l'ouvrier, le prix fondamental est ce que coûte à l'ouvrier sa subsistance. [...] Or, quoique le prix fondamental ne soit pas le principe immédiat de la valeur courante, il est cependant un minimum au-dessous duquel elle ne peut baisser' (Turgot, 1767a, 2, p. 663).

suggested that there was a tendency for the normal wage rate to coincide with this minimum: 'it is well known that the daily wage of a man who has nothing but his hands is commonly reduced to what he and his family need to live'.[16]

The view that the worker's wage tends to coincide with subsistence is argued in Turgot's best-known work, the *Réflexions sur la formation et la distribution des richesses*:

> The simple Workman who possesses only his hands and his industry, has nothing except in so far as he succeeds in selling his toil to others. He sells it more or less dear; but this higher or lower price does not depend upon himself alone; it results from the agreement which he makes with the man who pays for his labour. The latter pays him as little as he is able; since he has a choice between a great number of Workmen, he prefers the one who works most cheaply. Thus the Workmen are obliged to vie with one another and lower their price.. In every kind of work it is bound to be the case, and in actual fact is the case, that the wage of the Workman is limited to what is necessary in order to enable him to procure his subsistence. (Turgot, 1766, para. VI, translation by Meek, 1973, p. 122)[17]

Like Smith later, he saw wages as the result of bargaining between the parties, in which the competition of workers fixes them at the minimum possible level, i.e. subsistence. Two elements are introduced to explain this result: the fact that the worker has no other resources except what he can get for his labour, and the large number of workers among whom the employer can choose.

The workers have no resources but their labour
The reference to the lack of resources other than one's own labour is clear enough: for workers who live on wages and have no property, who in Turgot's time were undoubtedly close to poverty, selling their labour power was essential for immediate survival, and this

16. 'On sait que la journée de l'homme qui n'a que se bras est communement réduite à ce qu'il lui faut pour vivre avec sa famille' (Turgot, 1770, 3, p. 287).
17. 'Le simple ouvrier, qui n'a que ses bras et son industrie, n'a rien qu'autant qu'il parvient à vendre à d'autres sa peine. Il la vend plus ou moins cher, mais ce prix plus ou moins haut ne dépend pas de lui seul: il résulte de l'accord qu'il fait avec celui qui paye son travail. Celui-ci le paye le moins cher qu'il peut; comme il a le choix entre un grand nombre d'ouvriers, il préfère celui qui travaille au meilleur marché. Les ouvriers sont donc obligés de baisser le prix à l'envi les uns des autres. En tout genre de travail, il doit arriver et il arrive, en effet, que le salaire de l'ouvrier se borne à ce qui lui est nécessaire pour lui procurer sa subsistance'.

weakened their ability to bargain with the employer. Turgot mentions this situation of need, for example, in explaining why when food prices are very unstable the wage rate is too low to give workers a margin of protection against increased prices in years when the harvest is poor:

> In good years as well as bad, wage earners have no resources to live on except their labour [...] [the worker] will not predict and calculate the possibility of a bad harvest to force his employer to raise his wages; for whatever may happen in that distant future, he must live now, and if he makes too much trouble his neighbour will take the job at a lower wage.[18]

The bargaining power of the workers is thus negatively influenced not only by their position as wage earners with no resources other than their work; but also (as it did for Locke)[19] by their income level. Turgot observed, for example, that when variations in the prices of subsistence goods impoverish the workers, for a certain time[20] this reduces their bargaining power: 'the greater his distress, the less the journeyman can impose his own conditions'.[21]

This is because the poorer a worker is, the less able he is to live without working. This is very well brought out by a passage of Necker that seems worth quoting in this context. Necker expresses himself with more clarity than Turgot:

> As bread becomes dearer the power of the proprietor increases, because the artisan or labourer, when he has no more reserves, can no longer bargain; he must work today or starve tomorrow, and in this conflict of interests between proprietor and workman, the latter stakes his life and that of his family, while the former only a delay in the increase of his luxury.[22]

---

18. 'Le peuple salarié n'a, dans les bonnes années comme dans les autres, des ressources pour vivre que le travail [...] Il n'ira pas prevoir et calculer la possibilité d'une disette pour obliger celui qui le paye à hausser son salaire; car, quel que ce soit cet avenir éloigné il faut qu'il vive à present, et s'il se rendait trop difficile, son voisin prendrait l'ouvrage a meilleur marché' (Turgot, 1770, 3, p. 336–7)
19. See above, Chapter 2, p. 19. Turgot knew Locke's economic writings: cf. Groenewegen, 1970, p. 195.
20. That is, until their wages adjust to the change if the latter is persistent, and thus resume their normal value in real terms. See below, pp. 73–4.
21. '[L]e journalier fait d'autant moins la loi qu'il est plus mal à son aise' (ibid., p. 287).
22. 'A mesure que le pain renchérit, l'empire du proprietaire augmente, car dès que l'artisan ou l'homme de travail n'ont plus de réserve, ils ne peuvent plus disputer; il faut qu'ils travaillent aujourd'hui sous peine de mourir demain, et dans ce combat d'interêt entre le propriétaire et l'ouvrier, l'un met au jeu sa vie et celle de sa famille, et l'autre un

The possibility of having 'reserves', resources to call upon for sustenance – which is obviously linked with the income level of working families – is thus one of the elements that affect the outcome of bargaining between workers and employers. This might appear to make the argument a vicious circle (whereby income depends on the wages which the worker's bargaining power allows him to obtain, while the bargaining power depends on income), but that is not the case. The income level of working families does not depend exclusively on the level of wages, it also depends on the proportion of employed people in the population as a whole. Moreover, the effect of income level on bargaining power can be seen as one of the ways in which past history influences the determination of wages in a certain period. Workers who in the past have enjoyed favourable conditions and higher income levels will have an advantage in negotiating current wages, partly because they can call upon 'reserves'.

The 'great number' of workers

The other element mentioned by Turgot to explain the tendency of wages to coincide with subsistence is the 'great number' of workers from whom the employer can choose, which forces them to compete against one another. The 'great number' of workers, like the absence of other sources of income, is thus seen as a specific element weakening the bargaining power of the workers. This, together with the explicit reference to competition among workers, suggests not just that in general wages are determined by a competitive process, but that they are fixed at a level equal to subsistence because of an excess supply of workers.

In the economic literature of the period, references are often made to the 'great number' of workers competing amongst themselves, or to the 'small number' of employers, as causes of weak bargaining power on the part of wage earners; the same idea appears in Smith and Necker as we shall see.

A passage of Postlethwayt cited in the last chapter, which has considerable similarities with the one in Turgot's *Reflexions*, provides support to my interpretation. In that passage the tendency

simple retard dans l'accroissement de son luxe' (Necker, 1775, I, p. 74)

of the wage rate to settle at subsistence was explicitly associated to the existence of unemployment, taken as a normal feature of the economy. Because of it workers undercut each other, fixing the wage at its minimum.

Cantillon too uses an expression similar to that of Turgot in a different context (i.e. when analysing the market for a commodity), giving it the meaning we have supposed. He speaks of a number of sellers greater than the number of buyers, to indicate that the quantity of goods offered is greater than the quantity demanded, and vice versa.[23]

The proposed interpretation is further supported by the fact that Turgot considers unemployment and underemployment as being quite possible in ordinary conditions of the economy.

Describing the effects of a rise in demand for labour due to increased investments, Turgot says: '[i]f this offer of jobs to the class of workmen of all sorts fails to raise wages, this proves that there is a crowd of unemployed hands trying to get them'.[24] And he goes on to describe what follows an increase in opportunities to find work:

> Here [...] regardless of any rise in wages, we see an increase in well-being for the people: there is work where before there was none; those who before could find work and earn money only for two thirds or three quarters of the year can now find it every day; women and children can find work suited to their strength, that was formerly done by men. Hence the workman is better off and can consume more, extend his enjoyments and those of his family, eat better, dress

23. '[T]he real and intrinsic value of the corn will correspond to the land and labour which enter into its production; but as there is too great an abundance of it and there are *more sellers than buyers* the market price of the corn will necessarily fall below the intrinsic price or value. If on the contrary the farmers sow less corn than is needed for consumption there will be *more buyers than sellers* and the market price of corn will raise above its intrinsic value' (Cantillon, 1755, Higgs's translation, pp. 29–31, italics added).

24. 'Si cette offre d'ouvrages proposés à la classe des ouvriers de toute espèce n'augmente pas les salaires, c'est une epreuve qu'il se presente pour le faire une foule des bras inoccupés' (Turgot, 1770, 3, p. 320). In this letter Turgot illustrates the advantages for the nation of a liberalization of trade. One of these is an increase in the income of landowners and agricultural entrepreneurs (*cultivateurs*). According to Turgot this income will be wholly or partially invested in the extension and improvement of cultivation, leading to an increase in production and employment that benefits wage earners as described in the passages cited in the text. Moreover, the part which is not invested will be spent by the landowners to purchase goods, thus increasing production and the incomes of artisans and wage earners in the manufacturing sector.

better, bring up his children better.[25]

This gives us a precise picture of a labour supply consisting of unemployed workers in the narrow sense, plus women and children not formerly employed and underemployed workers, which is immediately available to satisfy the increased demand for labour following an increase in investments and production. At the end of the discussion from which the above passage is taken, Turgot sums up the advantages for wage earners of an increase in productive investments in agriculture, listing first of all 'a greater assurance of finding employment and, for each workman, a greater number of useful days'.[26]

Another indication that Turgot refers to unemployment when he states that competition among workers drives wages down to their minimum level, is his claim that an increase in employment may cause a rise in wages above the minimum of subsistence.

According to Turgot the increased employment described in the above passages must ultimately also lead to higher wage rates. This rise is not immediate if the increased demand is met by a large number of formerly unemployed workers, but it must occur sooner or later:

> For the mere fact that workmen are more sought after means that wages must gradually rise, as workers will become rare in proportion to the jobs [*salaires*]

25. 'voila [...] abstraction faite de toute augmentation du prix des salaires, une augmentation d'aisance pour le peuple, en ce qu'il a de l'ouvrage lorsqu'il n'en avait pas; en ce que tel qui ne trouvait à s'occuper et à gagner de l'argent que pendent les deux tiers ou les troi quarts de l'année, pourra trouver à en gagner tous les jours; en ce que les femmes, les enfants, trouveront à s'occuper d'ouvrages proportionnés à leur forces, et qui était auparavant exécutés par des hommes. De là un surcroit d'aisance pour l'homme de travail qui lui procure de quoi consommer d'avantage, de quoi étendre ses jouissances et celles de sa famille, se nourrir mieux, se mieux vêtir, élever mieux ses enfants' (ibid.).
26. 'une plus grande assurance de trouver du travail et, pour chaque travailleur, un plus grand nombre de journées utiles' (ibid., p. 321). Turgot's thesis that the liberalization of the grain trade would favour wage earners by reducing unemployment had already been advanced by the Physiocratic school, and had been used as an argument in defence of liberalization against critics who considered it dangerous for the workers' living conditions (Weulersse, 1968, vol. 2, pp. 556 and 570). Some of the opponents of the Physiocrats held that, on the contrary, the improvements in agricultural production would cause unemployment in two ways: they would reduce the demand for labour in the large farms and at the same time turn many small producers into landless wage earners. But the Physiocrats maintained that progress would increase overall production and hence also employment (ibid., pp. 546–53).

offered. It is well known that after some years of intensive building in Paris bricklayers are paid higher wages.[27]

Wages increase 'because of the competition between cultivators and proprietors, who will bid against each other to raise wages and thus attract workers'.[28]

When workers gradually become more 'rare' compared with demand, the employers have to compete among themselves by raising wages, just as when labourers are in excess supply their competition lowers them.

Higher than subsistence wages

Turgot sees the rise in wages following an increase in employment not as a transitory event, but as a persistent change. He argues that the increase in population, which will tend to occur as a consequence of workers' improved conditions, will not necessarily cause wages to return to their previous levels. The effects of a population increase on the labour supply are very slow, and in the meantime production will have been able to increase further:

> The greater number of jobs [*salaires*] offered and the wellbeing of the people lead to an increase in population; but by nature this increase is much less rapid than the growth of production. [...] It takes twenty years to form a man, and in those twenty years production could grow more and more, if its progress were not slowed and constrained by the limits of consumption.[29]

27. 'Car, de cela seul que le travail est plus recherché, les salaires doivent augmenter par degrés, parce que les ouvriers deviendront rares à proportion des salaires offerts. Depuis quelques années qu'on bâtit beaucoup à Paris, il est notoire qu'on y donne aux maçons des salaires plus forts' (ibid., p. 320). With regard to the beneficial effects on wages of an increase in employment, Turgot returns to the subject further on in the context of a description of the situation of wages in the district of Limoges, of which he was governor: 'l'augmentation du revenu des propriétaires [...] les a mis en état de faire travailler davantage, et l'augmentation du travail a fait hausser les salaires. La construction des plusieurs grand édifices à Limoges et le parti que j'ai pris depuis plusieurs années de supprimer les corvées et de faire les chemins à prix d'argent, y ont aussi eu quelque part' (ibid., p. 343).
28. '[P]ar la concurrence des cultivateurs et des propriétaires qui enchériront les uns sur les autres pour attirer les travailleurs' (ibid., p. 321).
29. 'La plus grande quantité de salaires offerts et l'aisance du peuple augmentent la population: mais cette augmentation est, suivant l'ordre de la nature, bien moins prompte que celle des productions. [...] avant qu'un homme soit formé il faut vingt ans, et avant que ces vingt ans fussent écoulés, la production aurait eu le temps de s'accroître de plus en plus, si ses progrès n'étaint ralentis et restreints par les bornes de

It is true, Turgot says again, that the population might be increased very rapidly by immigration of workers from other places, but he believes that even this source of population growth will not tend to cancel the advantages of accumulation for the working classes. This is because 'men are too attached to their homeland for this emigration ever to become too great',[30] and because whether the increase in population is caused by the multiplication of the species or by immigration, 'it will always be the effect of the well-being of the people, and will always presuppose it'.[31]

A wage increase following a non-transitory increase in employment may thus be seen as a rise in the normal rate of wages above subsistence level. This is confirmed by the fact that, as we shall see later in this chapter, Turgot held that real wages, if disturbed for example by price variations, tend to return towards a level (thus taken as the normal level) which does not necessarily coincide with the subsistence of the worker and his family, but may be higher.

This conclusion – i.e. the possibility that in an economy with a sufficiently high level of employment in relation to the working population, the normal wage will be above subsistence – contradicts the usual interpretation of Turgot, which attributes to him a subsistence theory of wages based on population adjustment, a first formulation of the so-called 'iron law of wages'.[32]

---

la consommation' (ibid.). Note Turgot's reference here to consumption as a possible constraint on growth. This can be related to his idea that increases in real wages favour an expansion in demand and production of agricultural goods (see below, p. 76).

30. 'Les hommes tiennent par trop de liens à leur patrie, pour que cette émigration soit jamais trop forte' (ibid.).

31. '[E]lle sera toujours l'effet de l'aisance du peuple, et la supposera toujours' (ibid.). This argument also was shared with the Physiocratic school: some critics maintained that the growth of the population would eliminate the benefits which free trade would bring to wage earners; the Physiocrats denied this, claiming that an increase in population would take place only after the increase in incomes and wages, and that population increase is slower than the increase in employment (Weulersse, vol. 2, pp. 543, 545, 553–4).

32. See Schumpeter, 1954, p. 266; see also the interpretation proposed by Wermel, claiming that '[i]n Turgot's work we find the first presentation of the "iron law" of wages. His law was based upon the conception of the territorial movements of population as a factor in the levelling out and reduction of wages to the minimum of the means of subsistence' (1939, p. 61). In a more recent study by Lancry it is asserted that Turgot's theory can be seen as a forerunner of the 'iron law of wages' (whose definitive formulation is attributed to Ricardo), on the basis of which population always pushes wages towards minimum subsistence level. Lancry

In support of this interpretation some critics have cited a passage written before those quoted above, in which Turgot argues that the increase in landowners' incomes would lead to an increase in employment and wages, and that: '[h]igh wages encourage the population; and abundant yields attract foreigners, multiply men; and the multiplication of men in turn makes wages fall, because of the competition amongst them.'[33]

This passage may seem to contradict those previously cited, but the contradiction is probably only apparent: first of all because Turgot is not saying that the increase in population, by lowering wages, will necessarily bring them back to the level preceding the improvement; and second, because the passage just cited can be interpreted as a description of 'secular' movements of wages, associated with slow, gradual changes in the population offering its services on the labour market ('it takes twenty years to make a man'). Hence such changes would not prevent the average wage level from staying above subsistence for long periods of time – indeed long enough for it to be considered the normal level. Lastly, we should say that, as will be shown better in the next chapter, in this period the theory of population was rather flexible and open to the possibility of different outcomes, depending on circumstances, of the reciprocal influences of wages on population and vice versa. We may note in this connection that Turgot associated wages persistently higher than subsistence with a situation of continual growth of production and employment, more rapid than the growth of population.

On the other hand, when Turgot argues that wage rates tend to approach subsistence he refers not to a 'law' based on population change, but to certain factors that negatively influence workers' bargaining power: their condition of need and the existence of a surplus supply of workers.

recognizes, however, that Turgot's 'subsistence' cannot be interpreted as the physiological minimum, and that Turgot's view of the effects of a population increase is not pessimistic like that of Malthus (Lancry, 1981, pp. 104, 107). On the question of attributing an 'iron law of wages' to the classical economists, see the conclusions of Chapter 4 of the present study.

33. 'Les forts salaires [...] encouragent la population; et la fécondité appelle les étrangers, multiplie les hommes; et la multiplication des hommes fait à son tour baisser les salaires par leur concurrence' (Turgot, 1767b, 2, p. 634).

Implications of Turgot's analysis

In the preceding discussion we have seen how, in Turgot's view, the conditions of the labour market influence the determination of wages. Turgot's recognition of unemployment as one of the elements that determine the *normal* wage rate, making it coincide with subsistence, clearly has interesting implications for our picture of the way the classical economists dealt with the determination of wages.

The view that wages remain at their normal rate even when there is unemployment is in striking contrast with the notion that as long as there is unemployment competition must keep reducing wages indefinitely, which characterizes later economic theory. In Turgot's view there is a definite lower limit for wages: the subsistence of the worker and his family. Turgot did not provide an accurate explanation of why wages could not fall below that level – this opinion was common in the literature of the period, and so probably did not seem to require specific analyses. However, where he discusses the effects on money wages of persistent changes in the prices of subsistence goods we find some explanation of why real wages cannot fall for any length of time below their normal level. Such an explanation can also help us to understand what forces prevent wages from falling below subsistence level in the presence of unemployment (see below).

Necker

Conflict of interests and disparity of power

With regard to the reasons why wages tend to be fixed at subsistence level, Necker's ideas are substantially similar to those of Turgot; however, he places more emphasis on the vast disparity of power between employers (identified with the class of 'propriétaires') and waged workers, and he is more inclined to stress the existence of a conflict of interests:

> Such power in the hands of proprietors is based on their very small numbers compared to the number of men without property, and on the great competition among the latter. Most of all, it is based upon the enormous inequality between those who sell their labour to live today, and those who buy it simply to increase their luxuries and comforts: the former are always under immediate pressure, the latter are under no pressure at all; one group will always give the law, the other

will be forced to accept it.[34]

Necker also refers to the 'small number' of proprietors as compared to the number of workers competing among themselves, as strengthening the bargaining power of the employers. Here, as we have seen in Turgot's case, the implication is that the supply of workers exceeds the demand for labour. Necker too, though he does not deal with the subject extensively, sees unemployment as a not exceptional feature of the economic system. Among the economic policy interventions that might generally improve workers' living conditions, he suggests measures for creating employment through public works, 'which sustain the price of a day's work'.[35]

In the preceding quote taken from his work *Sur la législation*, Necker stresses the role of the vast economic inequality, and hence inequality of power, between labourers and proprietors. This is a recurrent theme in his writings. In the same work he writes that workers' pay depends on the 'respective degrees of need and power existing between the proprietors who are served and the men without property who serve them'.[36] In his later work *De l'administration des finances de la France* Necker expresses himself in similar terms:

> The class of society whose fate is fixed by the effects of social laws, is composed of all those who, living by their labour, are forced to submit to the conditions imposed by the proprietors, and must content themselves with a wage proportioned to the mere necessities of life: their competition and the urgency of their needs constitute their state of dependence.[37]

34. '[C]e pouvoir entre les mains des propriétaires est fondé sur leur très petit nombre, en comparaison de celui des hommes sans propriété, sur la grande concurrence des ces derniers, et principalement sur la prodigeuse inégalité qu'il y a entre les hommes qui vendent leur travail pour vivre aujourd'hui, et ceux qui l'achètent pour augmenter simplement leur luxe ou leurs commodités: les uns sont pressés par l'instant, les autres ne le sont point; les uns donneront toujours la loi, les autres seront toujours contraints de la recevoir' (Necker, 1775, 1, p. 137–8).
35. '[Q]ui soutiennent le prix des journées' (Necker, 1785, V, p. 334).
36. '[D]egrés respectif de besoin et de pouvoir qui existent entre les propriétaires qui se font servir et les hommes sans propriété qui les servent' (Necker, 1775, I, p. 68)
37. 'La classe de la société dont le sort se trouve comme fixé par l'effet des lois sociales, est composée de tous ceux qui, vivant du travail de leur mains, reçoivent impérieusement la loi des propriétaires, et sont forcés de se contenter d'un salaire proportionné aux simples nécessités de la vie: leur concurrence et l'urgence de leurs besoins constituent leur état de dépendance' (Necker, 1785, V, p. 323)

Circumstances favourable to the workers

Despite his emphasis on the profound inequality between workers and proprietors as the cause of the workers' poverty and dependence, Necker maintained that there are circumstances that can improve the workers' lot. While, as we have seen, he held that increased employment might help to sustain wage levels, he did not share the opinion of Turgot, and later Smith, regarding the favourable effects of economic development on workers' living conditions. With regard to the processes of accumulation, Necker highlights factors that work against wage earners: the tendency for social inequalities to increase and for wealth (and hence power) to be concentrated in the hands of the few; and the possibility that accumulation will not bring an increase in employment.[38] According to Necker, the workers' living conditions may be improved by certain forms of government and by the acquisition of political rights on the part of the working classes. The latter can improve the 'consideration' and respect they enjoy in society, and their ability to 'resist' the domination of the upper classes:

> [t]here is no relief from this sort of slavery, except in that small number of states where the form of government leaves in the hands of the people some political rights which influence the consideration which they enjoy, and give them some means of resistance.[39]

The importance of political conditions is underlined again in Necker's explanation of the superior living conditions of English workers:

---

38. According to Necker, workers do not benefit from the enormous increase in labour productivity in both agriculture and industry arising from discoveries and improvements in production techniques, because their wages are fixed at subsistence by 'social laws' (i.e. by their low bargaining power). Hence the benefit goes entirely towards increasing the wealth of landowners (1785, V, p. 325). Moreover, since the luxury goods which accumulate in the hands of the rich often last longer than one generation, according to Necker their accumulation over time competes with the current production of the workers and reduces the demand for the fruits of their labour, or in any case makes them less necessary to the employers and hence further reduces their bargaining power (ibid., pp. 326–9; 1775, I, pp. 138–9).
39. 'Il n'y a d'adoucissement à cette espèce d'esclavage, que dans le petit nombre d'états où la forme du gouvernement laisse entre les mains du peuple quelque droit politique, dont la jouissance influe sur sa considération; et lui procure quelque moyen de résistence' (ibid.). Although the generic term 'peuple' is used here, the context leaves no doubt that Necker is speaking of the economic conditions of waged workers.

England is the country where the situation of the people appears to be the best,
[...] the cause of this must be sought in the nature of the government, which
grants the people a degree of strength and resistance which influences the level of
wages.[40]

Further on, speaking of Switzerland in which, unlike in England,
'the people count for nothing', Necker maintains that wage earners
do not live better than elsewhere, 'even though the competition
between them is reduced by the continual emigrations due to foreign
service'.[41] Thus for Necker political circumstances have a profound
influence which may be more important than conditions of the
labour market such as low unemployment in Switzerland. In his
overall treatment of the forces determining wages, Necker gives
particular weight to social and political-institutional factors that
affect the workers' bargaining power, and stresses the importance of
a country's overall institutional and historical conditions in
determining income distribution.[42] This influence also works
through unwritten rules, the prevailing conventions of a society:
different forms of government affect not only the workers' capacity
for direct resistance, but also in the 'consideration' accorded to
them.

Competition and the subsistence floor

Thus for Necker, as for Turgot, the workers' subsistence level
constitutes a 'minimum' which wages approach because of economic
and social factors that place the workers in a weak bargaining

---

40. 'L'Angleterre est le pays du monde où la condition du peuple paroît la meilleure, [...]
    il faut plutôt en chercher la cause dans la nature du gouvernement qui donne au peuple
    un degré de force et de résistance qui influe sur le prix de ses salaires' (id., 1775, I,
    p. 313).
41. '[D]ans les parties de la Suisse [...] où le peuple n'est rien, les hommes qui vivent de
    leur travail n'ont pas un sort plus heureux qu'ailleurs; et cependent, leur concurrence
    est diminuée par les émigrations continuelles qu'occasionne le service étranger' (ibid.).
42. The influence of forms of government on workers' remuneration had been discussed by
    Hume (see above, Chapter 2), and was taken up later by Malthus in the chapter 'On
    wages' in his *Principles* (1820, V, p. 184). Nor should we forget that Smith attached
    great importance to legislation favourable to the capitalists in determining wages
    (below). Even Ricardo, in some passages which I shall discuss (Chapter 4) maintains
    that, in principle, changes in the political system might permanently modify the
    living conditions of the workers. Thus the theme of the role of political-institutional
    factors in determining income distribution, strongly emphasized by Necker, is in fact
    widespread among the economists of this period.

position. But wages do not fall below this minimum level, even though it is not a physiological minimum. If circumstances change in favour of the workers following an increase in employment (Turgot) or as a consequence of a changed political–institutional setting (Necker) the normal wage can become established at a level higher than that of minimum subsistence.

It should be noted that throughout the arguments of Turgot and Necker, the constant reference to the importance of bargaining power on both sides for determining the *normal* wage rate – which both writers emphasize by continually referring to the capacity of the parties to impose their own conditions (*faire la loi*) – does not exclude, but actually accompanies the view whereby wages are determined by a process of competition. Moreover, the existence of competition does not prevent these writers from considering the presence of unemployment as completely normal, indeed as a factor that helps to fix wages at a certain level – that of subsistence.

Steuart

In listing the various components of the 'intrinsic' or 'real' value of a commodity, Steuart includes the wages of those who took part in its production; the wage level is taken as equal to 'subsistence'. Thus it would seem that Steuart shares the idea of a tendency for wages to be fixed at that level. But in his work we find no discussion of the causes of such a tendency, except for the observation that:

> In every industrious society, the lowest class is frequently found reduced to the barely necessary. The competition among themselves to obtain employment at any rate, produces this effect. (Steuart, 1776a, p. 401)[43]

43. For the writers of that period the term 'industrious' had multiple connotations: 1) the normal contemporary meaning of the word, an adjective referring to a quality of a person or group; 2) an adjective referring not to a subjective quality but to a state of things: the 'industrious' person or group is one who has the opportunity to produce, for example artisans, labourers etc. for whose services there is sufficient demand; 3) an adjective referring to activities in the 'industrial' sector, i.e. manufacturing. Similar considerations apply to the word 'industry', which may mean 'industriousness' and at the same time 'productive activity', and hence sometimes 'employment', 'work' or 'level of production'. In the context of the passage cited in the text, the adjective 'industrious' should probably be interpreted as indicating the existence of production for the market, carried on through the employment of waged labour – of 'free hands', to use Steuart's term.

In Steuart, as in Turgot and Necker, competition for jobs seems here to be associated with the excess labour supply, which reduces wages to the minimum (subsistence) level. In fact Steuart, as was typical of the mercantilist tradition, acknowledged the existence of unemployment and underemployment. In his discussion of the effects of introducing new machines, for example, he comments that:

> objections have been made against them [invention and introduction of machines], in countries where the numbers of the idle, or triflingly industrious are so great, that every expedient which can abridge labour is looked upon by some as a scheme for starving the poor. (Ibid., p. 256)

Steuart for his part favoured the introduction of machines, which he considered necessary for improving or maintaining the nation's competitiveness on international markets, but he admitted that it might create unemployment (ibid., pp. 121–5).

Smith

Masters' advantage fixes wages at subsistence
In some well-known passages of the *Wealth of Nations*, Adam Smith notes that the natural rate of wages, defined as the 'ordinary or average' rate at a particular place and period (Smith, 1776, I.vii.1), tends to settle at its lowest level – i.e. that which corresponds to the subsistence of the worker and his family. He explains this tendency as the result of the advantage which 'masters' generally have over workers in wage bargaining:

> What are the common wages of labour depend every where upon the contracts usually made between those two parties [the labourer and the owner of stock] whose interests are by no means the same. The workmen desire to get as much, the employers to give as little as possible. The former are disposed to combine in order to raise, the latter in order to lower the wages of labour.
> It is not however difficult to foresee which of the two parties must, upon all ordinary occasions, have the advantage in the dispute, and force the other into compliance with their terms. The masters, being fewer in number, can combine much more easily; and the law, besides, authorizes, or at least does not prohibit their combinations, while it prohibits those of the workmen [...] In all such disputes the masters can hold out much longer [...] though they did not employ a single workman [they] could generally live a year or two upon the stocks which they have already acquired. Many workmen could not subsist a week, few could subsist a month, and scarce any a year without employment. (Smith, 1776, I.viii.11–12)

But though in disputes with their workmen masters must generally have the advantage, there is however a certain rate below which it seems impossible to reduce, for any considerable time, the ordinary wages even of the lowest species of labour.

A man must always live by his work, and his wages must at least be sufficient to maintain him. They must even upon most occasions be somewhat more; otherwise it would be impossible for him to bring up a family, and the race of such workmen could not last beyond the first generation. (Ibid., I.viii.14–15)

In the above passages we find again all the themes we have seen in Necker and Turgot. The determination of wages is the result of bargaining between two parties with opposed interests and very unequal bargaining power. Capitalist employers are at an advantage in bargaining because of the needy condition of the wage earner who must work to survive, and therefore cannot hold out for long in negotiations.

The advantage of the 'masters' is further explained by Smith in terms of the institutional context, in particular the existence of laws that prohibit workers' coalitions and allow judicial intervention in support of the employers' interests against attempts by workers – often desperate and riotous – to organize to obtain better wages. Here Smith is evidently carrying on a polemic against institutions and laws that favour one social sector, to the detriment of the working classes.[44] Of greatest interest for us, however, is the importance he gives to the institutional context, and the implicit admission that the possibility of collective action on the part of workers might alter the distribution of income in their favour.[45] The laws prohibiting workers' associations are mentioned among the causes of the tendency for the natural wage to be fixed at its minimum level – that is, among the causes of the employers' superior bargaining power. On the other hand Smith's later reflections on the very infrequent success of workers' collective actions are based on observation of the particular historical circumstances in which such actions take place (especially those already mentioned: the neediness of the workers and the hostile

44. On this subject see also ibid., I.x.c.61, where Smith again expresses disapproval of the partiality of such legislation.
45. The importance of the capacity for collective action in the conflict over income distribution was indicated earlier by Locke, Hume and others (see above, Chapter 2).

institutional set-up). Thus Smith clearly does not attribute the fact that 'the workmen [...] very seldom derive any advantage from the violence of those tumultuous combinations' (ibid. I.viii.13) to the operation of necessary economic laws; this idea came later with the rise of the wage-fund theory, as the latter implied that any wage increase must bring a proportionate reduction in the number of employed workers (see Chapter 6 below).

Like Necker, Smith regards the 'fewer number' of employers as an explanation of their bargaining advantage: he sees it as the reason why it is easy for employers to 'combine'. As he explains,

Masters are every where in a sort of tacit, but constant and uniform combination, not to raise the wages of labour above their actual rate. To violate this combination is every where a most unpopular action, and a sort of reproach to a master among his neighbours and equals.(Ibid.)

It seems possible that in Smith's case this 'fewer number' of employers actually also denotes a situation of excess labour supply which is advantageous to the 'masters' and thus favours their 'tacit combination'. This seems plausible since, as we shall see, it is precisely the increase of employment linked with rapid economic growth which, according to Smith, leads the employers to break ranks and increase wages – whereas, on the other hand, it is in economies characterized by high unemployment that competition between workers drives wages down to subsistence level.[46]

The reference to 'combinations' of capitalist entrepreneurs to keep wages from rising, in the context of an analysis like Smith's which emphasizes the role of the bargaining advantage of the capitalists, has led some scholars to interpret Smith's theory as a monopsony theory of wage determination whereby wages are fixed arbitrarily by the capitalist entrepreneurs rather than by impersonal market forces.[47] This interpretation, however (as its proponents themselves emphasize), is inconsistent with other elements of Smith's analysis. It conflicts with the central role of competition in his

46. Hollander notes that '[i]t is common for eighteenth-century writers to assume the existence of a reserve of unemployed or underemployed labour', although he maintains that Smith did not emphasize this phenomenon (Hollander, 1973, p. 245).
47. See, among others, Cannan, 1893, p. 235; Knight, 1956, p. 81; Bowley, 1976, p. 190.

treatment of distribution – for example in bringing to uniformity the rate of profit and in equalizing the wages of workers who have the same characteristics in the same profession. Further, the central role of competition among the 'masters' assumes a central role in his explanation of the tendencies of wages in growing economies.

I shall return later to the interpretation of this passage, and particularly the role of the 'tacit combination' between capitalists, and I shall suggest a different interpretation.

'Constant scarcity of employment' and natural wage

The role of the labour market and unemployment in determining the natural wage emerges quite clearly in Smith's analysis of how the latter is affected by a country's economic development or decline. In this context Smith strictly associates the tendency of wages to approach subsistence with the unemployment that characterizes stationary and declining economies. In a stationary economy,

> the number of labourers employed every year could easily supply, and even more than supply, the number wanted the following year. There could seldom be any scarcity of hands, nor could the masters be obliged to bid against one another in order to get them. The hands, on the contrary, would, in this case, naturally multiply beyond their employment. There would be a *constant scarcity of employment*, and the labourers would be obliged to bid against one another in order to get it. If in such a country the wages of labour had ever been more than sufficient to maintain the labourer, and to enable him to bring up a family, the competition of the labourers and the interest of the masters would soon reduce them to this lowest rate which is consistent with common humanity. (Smith, 1776, I. viii. 24, italics added)

In a declining economy:

> Every year the demand for servants and labourers would, in all the different classes of employments, be less than it had been the year before. Many who had been bred in the superior classes, not being able to find employment in their own business, would be glad to seek it in the lowest. The lowest class being not only overstocked with its own workmen, but with the overflowings of all the other classes, the competition for employment would be so great in it, as to reduce the wages of labour to the most miserable and scanty subsistence of the labourer, *many would not be able to find employment* even upon these hard terms, but would either starve, or be driven to seek a subsistence either by begging, or by the perpetratione perhaps of the greatest enormities. (Ibid., I.viii.26, italics added)

In his discussion Smith explicitly considers the possibility of persistent unemployment, which enters as a factor of primary importance in determining the natural rate of wages. It is also interesting to note that neither in these passages nor elsewhere in the book does Smith indicate any spontaneous adjustment mechanisms capable of leading to the full employment of labour.

While in stationary or declining economies unemployment pushes wages to the minimum, when there is sustained economic growth the employers lose their advantage. The continuous increase in employment creates a scarcity of labour that makes the employers compete among themselves by increasing the wage offered to the workers:

> There are certain circumstances however which sometimes give the labourers an advantage, and enable them to raise their wages considerably above this [subsistence] rate; evidently the lowest which is consistent with common humanity.
> When in any country the demand for those who live by wages; labourers, journeymen, servants of every kind, is continually increasing; when every year furnishes employment for a greater number than had been employed the year before, the workmen have no occasion to combine in order to raise their wages. The scarcity of hands occasions a competition among masters, who bid against one another, in order to get workmen and thus voluntarily break through the natural combination of masters not to raise wages. (Ibid., I.viii.16–17)
> The wages of labour [...] are much higher in North America than in any part of England [...] there is a continual complaint of the scarcity of hands in North America. The demand for labourers, the funds for mantaining them, increase, it seems, still faster than they can find labourers to employ. (Ibid., I.viii.22–24)[48]

Smith's view, therefore, is that accumulation, with the consequent growth in employment, leads to a rise in the natural wage rate. Such positive effects are explained by the fact that the 'scarcity of hands' favours the bargaining position of the workers and forces employers to compete with each other; in the same way, the unemployment characteristic of stationary or declining economies tends to lower the natural wage to its minimum level by forcing workers to compete amongst themselves.

Skinner, in line with others,[49] interprets Smith's theory of wages

---

48. Cf. also ibid., IV.vii.b.2–3, where the high wages of North America are attributed to employers' difficulty in finding hands.
49. Cannan, 1893, pp. 235–7; Blaug, 1985, pp. 44–5; Lowe, 1975; Bowley, 1976,

as being based on the wage-fund theory, whereby in a given period wages are determined by the relation between a wage fund, defined in real terms, and the labour supply (i.e. the labouring population), which would thus be fully employed. According to Skinner, subsistence is the long-run supply price of labour, at which the population just reproduces itself, without increase or decrease. The natural (i.e. equilibrium) wage coincides with the subsistence wage. In light of this Skinner then interprets Smith's three 'cases', the stationary, declining or growing economy. The stationary state, he argues, is the equilibrium position at which wages are at subsistence level, and neither the population nor the wage fund change over time. In the declining economy the wage fund diminishes, wages (still according to Skinner) fall below subsistence, and this makes the population decrease. In a growing economy the increase in the wage fund raises the wage rate until the population has adjusted to the increased 'fund'. If this fund is continually increasing, however, the wage rate will constantly remain above subsistence (Skinner, 1979a, pp. 164–6). The above passages from the *Wealth of Nations* must immediately suggest difficulties in Skinner's interpretation. For the stationary economy (Skinner's state of 'equilibrium') is characterized by a 'constant scarcity of employment', and this is why wages tend to be fixed at subsistence level. By contrast, according to the wage-fund theory unemployment can only be a transitory condition of disequilibrium in which wages continue to decrease until full employment is reached. Similarly, the case of the declining economy appears to conflict with the wage-fund approach to wage determination. Also in this case we have large-scale unemployment and underemployment. But despite this, and in contrast with Skinner's interpretation, wages do not fall below subsistence, and the impossibility of finding work, rather than reduced wages, is cited as the cause of a fall in population ('many would be unable to find employment even upon these hard terms, but would [...] starve').

It might be suggested that unemployment in stationary and declining economies is due to rigidity or to stickiness of the real wage rate (Bowley, 1976, p. 203–4). Yet Smith did not envisage

pp. 201–4, who however discusses in some details the difficulties in reconciling the passages just quoted with the wage fund interpretation.

potential equilibrating mechanisms based on an inverse relation between employment level and real wage rate. He never argued that if wages were flexible higher levels of employment might be reached.[50] This suggestion, therefore, appears to reflect the influence of modern ways of thinking on the interpretation of past economists.

In describing the conditions of the labour market in economies characterized by stagnation, decline or growth, Smith always compares the supply of labour with the demand, both understood as given quantities. Terms like 'the number wanted' or 'the number employed' are used interchangeably with the term 'demand for labour'. This is given in each period, and its variations over time depend on the progress of accumulation: [t]he demand for those who live by wages therefore, naturally increases with the increase of national wealth, and *cannot possibly increase without it*. (Smith, 1776, I. viii. 21, italics added). This, together with the admission of unemployment and underemployment, works against the temptation to represent Smith's analysis in terms of the wage-fund theory, and hence in terms of the inverse relation between wages and employment which characterizes that theory (like the modern marginalist theory, though on different analytical grounds).

The possibility, maintained by Smith, that in rapidly growing

50. Commenting on the consequences of a tax on wages Smith writes: 'If direct taxes upon the wages of labour have not always occasioned a proportionable rise in those wages, it is because they have generally occasioned a considerable fall in the demand for labour' (1776, V.ii.i.3). The possible negative impact on employment in these circumstances is due to the rise in the price level that follows that of the money wages and diminishes the aggregate demand for national product: 'Taxes upon necessaries, by raising the wages of labour, necessarily tend to raise the price of all manufactures, and consequently to diminish the extent of their sale and consumption'(ibid., V.ii.k.9). This appears to be the case because of the worsened position of the country in international trade: 'that degradation in the value of silver which, being the effect either of the peculiar situation, or of the political institution of a particular country, takes place only in that country, is a matter of very great consequence [...] The rise in money price of all commodities, which is in this case peculiar to the country, tends to discourage more or less every sort of industry which is carried on within it, and to enable foreign nations [...] to undersell them, not only in the foreign, but even in the home market' (IV. v.a.17). The adverse effect on employment therefore follows the rise in the price level, and is due to international competition. It has nothing to do with a 'demand schedule' for labour as supposed by wage-fund and neoclassical theory, whereby the inverse relation between the real wage and the employment level holds in general in an economic system, be it closed or open to international trade, and does not depend on changes in the general price level.

economies wages will exceed the level of subsistence, has been interpreted by Skinner and others as the possibility of a divergence (though a rather persistent one) of the actual wage from the natural wage (identified with subsistence).[51] This contrasts with the interpretation suggested here, whereby different conditions of the labour market, associated with different accumulation trends, produce changes in the *natural* wage. The following arguments support the latter interpretation.

First, Smith states that the natural rates of return which make up the price of commodities (wages, profit and rent) vary in each society 'according to their circumstances, according to their riches or poverty, the advancing, stationary or declining state of the society' (ibid., I.vii.33 and I. vii. 1). The object of enquiry in his chapter on wages, he declares, is precisely the effects of economic stagnation, decline or progress on the circumstances that determine the natural wage.

In addition, the natural wage rate is identified by Smith with the 'ordinary or average' rate observable in 'every society or neighbourhood' and regulated by the 'general circumstances of the society' (i.e. 'their advancing, stationary or declining condition'). Thus if wages remain long enough above subsistence, this higher level will by definition be the natural rate of wages in the changed social context.

Lastly, when the purchasing power of money wages is disturbed by persistent changes in the prices of wage goods, they tend to readjust so as to preserve the real value they had before the price increase, even if (as in growing economies) this is above subsistence.[52]

---

51. See for example Skinner, 1979a, p. 166; Pivetti, 1987, p. 873. Bowley, however, is in agreement with my interpretation on this point (1976, pp. 123, 186–7). Skinner maintains that the 'ordinary or average' wage, which Smith takes as given for the determination of the natural prices of commodities, is the wage determined in any given situation by the relation between the 'wages fund' and the population, which may in general differ from the natural (subsistence) wage. But this obviously conflicts with Smith's argument whereby the 'ordinary or average' rate of wages, taken as given in the determination of prices, is by definition the natural wage.
52. See below, pp. 81--3.

Summing up

Thus the natural wage rate, for Smith as for Turgot and Necker, is determined by the bargaining power of the parties. When circumstances are unfavourable to the workers their wages tend to fall to subsistence level; and according to Smith this is generally the case, because of their conditions of need, the unfavourable institutional context, and the existence of an excess of workers over the available jobs. In rapidly growing economies, however, competition between employers may improve the bargaining position of the wage earners, making the natural wage rise above subsistence level.

It should be emphasized, however, that according to Turgot and Smith the natural wage rate can be affected by changes in labour market conditions only if these are of a persistent nature – for example changes in the pace of accumulation which are not matched by population growth.

Temporary fluctuations in employment level, such as those caused by good or bad harvests, can only induce transitory oscillations in the market wage around the natural wage; and these will cease with the end of the accidental circumstances that caused them (Smith, 1776, I.viii.46–7 and 53–5; I. vii. 19; Turgot, 1770, III, pp. 336–7).

COMPETITION AND CONVENTIONS: THE VIEW OF HUMAN BEHAVIOUR IN THE *THEORY OF MORAL SENTIMENTS*

Role of social norms and conventions

In Smith's argument the growth of employment and the 'scarcity of hands' lead to an increase in the natural wage, raising it above subsistence; but it does not imply a continuous and indefinite increase in wages. Symmetrically, unemployment brings the natural wage to coincide with subsistence, which is repeatedly indicated as the 'minimum level consistent with common humanity'. Although this minimum may to some extent be eroded in declining economies (where it is 'miserable and scanty') it does set a limit to the fall of wages. This is the case even where unemployment assumes vast proportions which, as Smith says, are such as to force many into beggary, crime or starvation.

Of course Smith's mention of the role of common humanity in maintaining wages at subsistence when there is unemployment has aroused some perplexity in his interpreters (Cannan, 1893, p. 235; Bowley, 1976, p. 189, n.), for in today's prevalent economic theory such a sentiment has no role in the functioning of labour markets, and could not prevent the fall of wages brought about by the competitive behaviour of workers and employers. The role of this common sense of humanity is still more difficult to interpret if one imagines a situation of monopsony, as has been done by some interpreters in the effort to rationalize the role Smith attributes to the 'advantage' and 'tacit combination' of the employers.

It seems possible to give a unitary explanation of both the 'tacit combination' among capitalists, which tends to prevent wage increases, and the 'common humanity' which prevents wages from falling below subsistence level: an explanation based on the role of social norms and conventions in determining individual behaviour, or at least in defining the limits within which it may vary.

The 'combination' between employers is defined as 'tacit' and as being maintained by the disapproval which its violation would provoke among their 'neighbours and equals' – that is in the social community important to them. Clearly this does not describe a 'cartel' in the strict sense: not a monopsonistic market but a form of social control over individuals.[53] It is made possible by the fact that the employers belong to a community, within which norms develop that lead to moral sanctions against those forms of behaviour that might damage the community itself.[54]

Similarly, through social interchange and historical experience,

---

53. When Smith wants to describe a monopsonistic agreement between employers, in the chapter where he discusses the obstacles to free competition, he uses different, very precise terms: 'When masters combine toghether in order to reduce the wages of their workmen, they commonly enter into a private bond of agreement, not to give more than a certain wage under a certain penalty' (Smith, 1776, I.x.c.61). Here he is speaking neither of tacit agreements nor of disapproval, but of precise penalties associated with the breaking of a formal agreement.

54. An interpretation of both the nature of the 'tacit combination' among capitalists and the 'common humanity' that sets the lower limit of wages, explaining these by the existence of social norms of behaviour, has been advanced by Garegnani (1990, pp. 119–21). The importance of norms of behaviour in defining the limits within which competition operates in Smith's thought is mentioned also by O'Brien (1975, pp. 31–2; see also below, p. 62)

widespread opinions form as to what is the decorous level of consumption even for 'the lowest rank of people', which the wages of an adult worker should be able to provide. Thus any attempt to reduce wages below that level might be perceived as contrary to social and moral norms – to 'common humanity'.

These conventions and norms, even when they are not reflected in a particular institutional se-tup (for example legislation setting minimum and/or maximum wage levels), sets limits to the pursuit of individual self-interest and competitive behaviour. Impersonal market forces are not absent, but they work within a space defined not only by laws and institutions but also by opinions and conventions that are widely shared in society.

This interpretation is consistent with Smith's general view of the determinants of human behaviour, expounded in his *Theory of Moral Sentiments*.

View of human behaviour

In the *Theory of Moral Sentiments* Smith explicitly rejects the utilitarian view which explains behaviour as the result of individual rational calculation, entirely based on considerations of self-interest.[55] Instead he emphasizes the nature of man as a social being, whose actions are determined by a complex of motives. Among these individual interest, or 'self-love', as Smith called it, certainly plays a very important part. But individual interest is not the only cause of human action, and its pursuit in any case is regulated by man's innate desire for the approval of his fellows:

> Nature, when she formed man for society, endowed him with a desire to please, and an original aversion to offend his brethren [...] She rendered their approbation most flattering and most agreeable to him for its own sake, and their disapprobation most mortifying and most offensive. (Smith, 1790, III. 2. 6)

This strong desire for approbation is an important factor in inducing

---

55. In connection with Smith's position on utilitarianism, it is interesting to note O'Brien's observation, according to which '[t]here is little justification for according utilitarianism a major independent role in relation to the development of classical economics' (1975, p. 25). According to this writer only the two Mills were influenced by it; whereas the main influence on Smith and the later tradition was that of natural law. On Smith's anti–utilitarian view see also Coase, 1976, pp. 529, 545; Skinner, 1979b, pp. 60–65; Sen, 1987, pp. 22–8.

individuals to respect the norms of moral behaviour which they have acquired through experience and social interaction.[56]

Other people's judgement is extremely important in motivating behaviour also in the economic sphere of activity – so much so that, according to Smith, the very objective of accumulation of wealth is strongly associated with a desire for approval and admiration in the social community to which one belongs:

> It is chiefly from this regard to the sentiments of mankind, that we pursue riches and avoid poverty. For to what purpose is all the toil and bustle of this world? What is the end of avarice and ambition, of the pursuit of wealth, of power, and pre–heminence? [...] what are the advantages we propose by that great purpose of human life which we call bettering our condition? To be observed, to be attended to, to be taken notice of with simpathy, complacency, and approbation, are the advantages which we can propose to derive from it. (Ibid., I.iii.2.1)[57]

But if even the pursuit of wealth and power must in the end be ascribed to a desire for admiration and approval, it is no surprise that competition is constrained by that desire:

> In the race for wealth, and honours, and preferments...[he] may run as hard as he can, and strain every nerve and every muscle, in order to outstrip all his competitors. But if he should justle, or throw down any of them, the indulgence of the spectators is entirely at an end. It is a violation of fair play, which they cannot admit of. (Ibid., II.ii.2.1)

Since even in the economic sphere individual behaviour can be determined by other motivations than those suggested by the utilitarian view, the operation of competition itself will be kept within bounds by the prevailing opinions and social norms, whose violation arouses disapproval.

Continuity between 'Theory of Moral Sentiments' and 'Wealth of Nations'
Scholars have long disagreed as to whether there is inconsistency and

---

56. On the content of the *Theory of Moral Sentiments*, in relation to the motivations of human behaviour and the process of formation of social norms, see: Raphael and Macfie, 1976, pp. 15–20; Morrow, 1969, pp. 83–4; Anspach, 1972, pp. 438–42; Macfie, 1967 pp. 45–8.
57. On this passage Skinner and Campbell comment: 'it is indeed one of Smith's most striking achievements to have recognized the social objective of many economic goals' (1976, p. 9).

conflict between the views of human behaviour expressed in the *Theory of Moral Sentiments* and in the *Wealth of Nations* – in particular, between the emphasis in the *Theory* on social interaction and moral norms dictated by the sense of justice and benevolence, and the view of human behaviour as entirely motivated by individual self–interest which some interpreters attribute to the *Wealth of Nations*.

But this contrasting view of the two works has been rejected by major contemporary scholars. Another kind of interpretation, which has also been criticized, considers the two books as complementary rather than contradictory, dealing with distinct spheres of human action; thus the economic sphere, treated in the *Wealth of Nations*, would be characterized by motivations and behaviour founded solely on individual interest.[58]

Critics of both the above interpretations have stressed the fact that Smith saw the *Wealth of Nations* as developing the social theory set out in the *Theory of Moral Sentiments*. Proof of this is provided by Smith himself, who says in the 'Advertisement' to the sixth edition of the *Theory* (1790) that his promise to continue what he began in that work with another book about 'law and government' has been partially satisfied with the publication of the *Wealth* (Macfie and Raphael, 1976, p. 24). In addition, between the 1759 and 1790 editions of the *Theory* there are no changes that can be linked with the development of Smith's economic theory in the meantime (ibid., p. 20).

O'Brien, after underlining the close links between the two works, asserts that '[the *Theory*] offers a theory of the way in which both public and private laws limit the operation of individual interests where these may conflict with social interests.[The *Wealth*] offers a theory of the way in which individual interests thus limited produce

---

58. Both these positions – the one that considers the two works to be contradictory and the one that considers them complementary, but concerned with entirely distinct aspects of human behaviour – are criticized by Macfie and Raphael in their Introduction to the *Theory of Moral Sentiments*. See also Coase 1976; Anspach, 1972. Hollander also finds a continuity between Smith's two works, but he sees it in the accent on the importance of the pursuit of individual self-interest. He admits, however, that in the *Theory of Moral Sentiments* Smith firmly rejects the idea that the motivations of human behaviour are entirely reducible to the pursuit of individual interest (Hollander, 1977, n. 32).

optimal resource allocation' (1975, p. 31).[59] The same author also stresses that for Smith there is a conflict of interests between social classes over the distribution of income. Accordingly, it could be argued that this is a sphere in which the unrestrained pursuit of individual and group interests might generate social tensions undermining the stability and viability of the system, and would therefore conflict with the interest of society as a whole. In these cases, according to O'Brien's interpretation of Smith's position, the corrective action of private rules of behaviour or state laws is essential.[60] These considerations support the interpretation I have suggested regarding the role of 'common humanity' in sustaining the minimum wage level.

The view that there is a substantial continuity in Smith's conception of human behaviour in the two works does not seem necessarily to conflict with his famous assertion that 'it is not from the benevolence of the butcher, the brewer or the baker that we expect our dinner, but from their regard to their own interest' (Smith, 1776, I.ii.2).

This has often been taken to indicate a utilitarian conception of human behaviour in the economic sphere, but it does not really seem sufficient to sustain such an interpretation.[61] The quotation simply indicates that profit maximization is what ensures that the amount produced of each good will correspond to the 'effectual demand' for it. But this is fully compatible with a non-utilitarian view of human behaviour, even in the economic sphere – as emerges from the passages of Smith previously cited. Most important, it does not rule

59. The assertion that there is 'optimal allocation of resources' in Smith's economic theory is inexact, however, as it is incompatible with the existence of unemployment. Rather, one should speak of an appropriate production to satisfy the 'effectual demand' for each commodity, which is realized through competition.

60. Cf. Also Halévi, who in his discussion of Smith's economic theory argues that the idea of a natural harmony of interests, while present in other parts of Smith's writings, is absent from his theory of distribution (1934, pp. 100–101). Morrow, though he attributes to the *Wealth of Nations* an individualistic point of view unlike that of the *Theory of Moral Sentiments*, admits that even in the *Wealth of Nations* Smith at some points recognizes that society is not composed of individuals each pursuing his or her own ends, but expresses the view that 'society is composed of individuals who belong to various groups, and whose sentiments and interests are moulded by those groups, and that 'in the actual social order there are associations of individuals which would seek to impose their class interest' (1969, pp. 85–6).

61. See Sen (1987, p. 23–5) for a similar view.

out the existence of areas such as that of income distribution, where the pursuit of individual interest must be in some degree regulated by unwritten rules of conduct, or by laws and institutions.

Social conventions in the labour market

To sum up, Smith explicitly brings in the role of what we may call 'social conventions' in the operation of the labour market. These conventions not only define the content of the minimum necessary subsistence consumption, but also sustain the minimum wage level even amid general conditions of bargaining weakness on the part of workers, and even in the presence of unemployment. These conventions also underlie the collusive behaviour of the capitalists, their 'tacit combination' to avoid raising workers' wages.

The role of socially determined rules of behaviour in defining the range within which competition takes place – a role which also seems to be present, though sometimes only implicitly, in the works of other authors[62] – in Smith is consonant with the ideas on motivations of human behaviour developed in the *Theory of Moral Sentiments*.

It is not surprising that those ideas, stressing the importance of social judgement and moral norms in determining individual behaviour, should re-emerge particularly in Smith's analysis of the labour market. In the *Wealth of Nations* we find no adjustment mechanisms for the demand for labour based on a decreasing relation with respect to wages; while on the other hand the adjustment of the quantity of labour supplied (i.e. the labouring population) is necessarily slower and more uncertain for labour than for other commodities. Consequently, within Smith's theoretical approach (as in that of the other authors discussed), ruling out conventional and institutional limits to competition would lead to the unrealistic conclusion that when unemployment occurs wages will continue to fall indefinitely (or vice versa to rise indefinitely if the

---

62. This aspect will emerge later on, see pp. 71-83 below. In any case, the classical economists seem generally attentive to interdependence in the behaviour of individuals and social groups. Such interdependences are very much taken into account, for example, in the discussion of the formation of habits of consumption (see pp. 65-70 below). Indeed the economists of this period, including Smith himself, typically consider the behaviour of individuals as broadly determined by the economic and social context.

demand for labour exceeds the number of available workers). In the context of the classical economists' analysis the role of institutional and conventional factors thus appears essential to give stability and continuity to the distributive variables. At the same time, precisely because these factors are so important in regulating the labour market, a change in the institutional context, laws or common ways of thinking may have an independent role in explaining changes in those same variables.[63]

CHANGES OVER TIME IN HABITS OF CONSUMPTION

Natural wage and subsistence

The discussion in the foregoing sections suggests that the notions of the natural wage and of subsistence consumption must be considered as conceptually distinct, although in the analysis of the classical economists the two magnitudes often tend to coincide and therefore the terms are sometimes used as synonyms. Subsistence, historically defined, is a 'minimum' which wages tend to approach as a result of the weak bargaining position of the workers. This view of subsistence is explicitly indicated in Turgot's work, where he defines subsistence as the 'fundamental price' of labour, which is precisely the minimum price. Smith too speaks repeatedly of the wage sufficient to maintain the labourer and his family as the lowest level below which wages cannot fall 'for any considerable time' (Smith, 1776, I.viii.14). Both these writers, as well as Necker and Steuart, also admit the possibility that the average or normal rate of wages might rise above subsistence level. For example, in his chapter on wages Smith explains at length that the wage normally paid to English workers does not coincide with subsistence (ibid., paras 28–36).

The two concepts, then, can be distinguished as follows: the natural wage is the central or average value around which the wages actually observed on the labour market gravitate. Subsistence, in a

---

63. On the other hand, observation has continually brought to the attention of scholars the importance of institutions and social conventions in the actual working of the labour market, even after the classical approach was abandoned.

given time and place, represents the minimum possible level of the natural wage.

However, as I have argued at the beginning of this chapter, subsistence is defined in historical and sociological terms. Thus it is possible that subsistence in turn is to some extent dependent on the natural wage rate. Changes in that rate, in the course of time, might actually induce a modification in consumption habits, and thus to an upward shift in the minimum threshold of consumption which is regarded as indispensable.

Steuart on changes in habits

The most interesting contribution to the analysis of changes in consumption habits over time is that of James Steuart, derived from development of his analysis of the 'political necessaries' and his theory of 'consolidated profits'. He argues that because of the changes induced in habits of life, exceptionally high earnings, if prolonged in time, become normal (or 'consolidated'), and hence an integral part of the 'real' or 'intrinsic' value (i.e. the normal price) of goods.

I have already said that Steuart considers necessary consumption as dependent on 'habit and education', and as associated with membership of a particular social group (p. 34 above). These elements also help to explain how necessary consumption changes as time goes by: this happens as a consequence of increases in income sufficiently prolonged as to allow new habits to form, and widespread enough so that these habits take root in the whole social group involved.

According to Steuart, in a situation where demand is in continual growth and so the quantity of goods supplied keeps lagging behind, prices remain above the normal level and profits are high. In such circumstances:

> in a little time not only the immediate seller of the goods, but also every one who has contributed to the manufacture, will insist upon sharing these new profits. Now [...] the mischief is that, in consequence of this wide repartition, and by such profits subsisting for a long time, they insensibly become consolidated or as it were, transformed into the intrinsic value of the goods. This, I say, is brought about by time; because the habitual extraordinary gains of every one employed induce the more luxurious to change their way of life insensibly, and fall into the habit of making greater consumpion [...] When therefore it happens that large

profits have been made for a considerable time, and that they have had the effect of forming a taste for more expensive way of living among the industrious, it will not be the cessation of the demand, nor the swelling of the supply, which will engage them to part with their gains (Steuart, 1766a, p. 192–3)

Elsewhere Steuart argues that the 'consolidated profits' make prices 'sticky',

> because the workmen, having long enjoied [higher profits] will have bettered their way of living; and as they are many, and live uniformly, anything which obliges them to retrench a part of their habitual expence, is supposed to deprive them of necessaries. (Steuart, 1766b, III, p. 11)[64]

According to Steuart these new needs cannot be retrenched, even if the economic circumstances that initially favoured their acquisition cease – because everyone would feel that giving up the new level of consumption, once it was broadly established, represented a loss of status, a demotion to a lower social class. This is something which, Steuart says, individuals are very unwilling to accept (Steuart, 1766a, pp. 270–71, quoted on p. 34, above).

Nor should it be imagined that the importance of particular consumer goods as signs of membership in a social group, which one cannot or does not intend to give up, is unique to the upper and middle classes:

> The moment a person begins to live by his industry, let his livelihood be ever so poor, he immediatly forms little objects of ambition, compares his situation with that of his fellows who are a degree above him, and considers a shade more of ease, as I may call it, as an advancement, not of his happiness only, but also of his rank. (Ibid., p. 272)

Thus even among the lower classes social imitation helps to set a limit below which consumption cannot be reduced. Steuart believes

---

64. Note that while in his definition of the 'real price' Steuart correctly distinguishes wages and profit as the incomes accruing to labour and capital respectively, at other points in the argument as in the passage just quoted (perhaps because he is thinking of small independent producers) he calls 'profits' also labour incomes in excess of subsistence. The acquisition of improved habits of consumption described in this passage is also part of the process of nations' rise and decline, which is one of the themes of Steuart's analysis. The more economically advanced countries develop higher habitual consumption levels, even among the working classes, which gradually make it more difficult for those countries to compete on international markets; less advanced countries may then supplant them despite their inferior skills in production.

that a rise in necessary consumption generally follows sufficiently long periods of sustained economic growth, involving a rise in earnings which allows higher levels of consumption to become habitual.[65]

Thus in Steuart we find a detailed analysis of changes in habits of consumption, showing a relationship of mutual causation between them and the normal wage rate. In none of the other economists is this subject dealt with so broadly and clearly.

Other classical economists on changes in habits
Smith frequently describes and compares the consumption habits of the lower classes in different regions, countries and historical periods. These passages also suggest an association between economic development and improvements in workers' habitual living standards. The definition of subsistence in essentially historical and sociological terms, emphasizing the habits and customs acquired over time, also seems to imply such an association arising from the positive effect (according to Smith and others) of economic growth on the natural wage. That is, the improved natural wage rate may in turn enhance consumption habits and subsistence requirements. This might explain Smith's idea of different levels of subsistence ('liberal, moderate, or scanty') associated with different rates of accumulation in a country.

In the context of a comparison between the habitual consumption of the popular classes in Scotland and England, Smith says it is higher in England because for over a century it has enjoyed a much higher rate of accumulation, which has allowed the workers to obtain higher pay. Smith goes on to argue:

> This difference, however, in the mode of their subsistence is not the cause but the effect of the difference in their wages; though, by a strange misapprehension, I have frequently heard it represented as the cause. (Smith, 1776, I.viii. 33–34)

Thus he emphasizes only one direction of causality, whereby higher wages, due to economic growth, in time induce better habits of

65. One cannot but note the numerous affinities between Steuart's analysis and the one proposed almost two centuries later by Duesenberry (1949), based on data and observations on American society. This could be an indication of the present relevance of the classical approach.

consumption. Later Malthus commented on this passage, showing that he saw a reciprocal influence, acting over time, between consumption habits and the normal rate of wages. Referring to Smith's observation cited above, he wrote:

> It must be allowed, however, that this correction of common opinion is only partially just; the effect in this case as in many others certainly becomes in its turn a cause. (Malthus, 1820, V, p. 183)

Among Smith's successors the idea of a reverse effect of relatively high wages on necessary consumption, and hence on the subsequent historical evolution of the natural wage, appears not only in Malthus's *Principles* but also in Barton, who argued that the effects of a change in wages on the population are so slow that in the meantime the workers acquire new habits of consumption, more consonant with their new level of wages (Barton, 1817, p. 40). Ricardo too, in passing, mentions that wage increases might induce an increase in the level of habitual consumption (rather than in the population) (Ricardo, 1821, I, pp. 406–7). Among Smith's predecessors, in Cantillon we find an analysis of consumption which may show some affinities with that of Steuart, in that he suggests that periods of prosperity induce an increase in consumption which later becomes difficult to reverse:

> When a large number of the inhabitants have acquired considerable fortunes from this money, which enters the State regularly and annually, they will, without fail, increase their consumption and raise the price of everything. Though this dearness involves them in a greater expense than they at first contemplated they will for the most part continue so long as their capital lasts; for nothing is easier or more agreeable than to increase the family expenses, nothing more difficult or disagreeable than to retrench them. (Cantillon, 1755, Higgs's translation, pp. 168–9)
>
> I conclude that an increase of money circulating in a State always causes there an increase of consumption and a higher standard of expence. (Ibid., p. 181)

Cantillon also describes the tendency of the middle classes to imitate the consumption models of the upper classes.[66] Yet in Cantillon we

---

66. 'The owner, who has at his disposal the third of the produce of the land, is the principal agent in the changes which may occur in demand. Labourers and mechanicks who live from day to day change their mode of living only from necessity. If a few farmers, master craftmen or other undertakers in easy circumstances vary their expense

do not find the analysis that leads Steuart to conclude that downward rigidity in consumption habits (and hence irreversibility of improvements) results from the association of these habits with membership in a particular social group.

EFFECTS OF TAXATION AND CHANGES IN THE PRICES OF SUBSISTENCE GOODS

The authors under discussion believed that real (disposable) wages cannot be persistently modified by changes in the prices of subsistence goods, even when they are caused by indirect taxation, and by direct taxes on wages. I shall try to clarify the reasons why they held that actual real wages cannot diverge for long from the level of consumption corresponding to the natural wage.

To understand the position of the classical economists on the adjustment of wages to changing prices or taxes, one must bear in mind the distinction between the natural and market prices of goods, and that between the natural wage and the market wage.

The market prices of goods consumed by workers, especially the agricultural products which are their main component, are subject to continuous fluctuations. However frequent and, in the case of agricultural goods, wide, these are transitory and accidental phenomena, which result in temporary variations in the workers' real wages. It is persistent changes in prices of consumer goods – i.e. changes in their natural price – that affect the natural (money) wage so as to leave its purchasing power unchanged.

On the basis of this distinction it is possible to clarify the seemingly contradictory arguments regarding the consequences of variations in the prices of agricultural wage goods. Indeed we often find, along with the assertion that the price level for subsistence goods regulates the money wage, the opposite claim that the latter does not vary with the price of subsistence goods. But these two ideas are not really inconsistent: the first concerns the relation between money wages and the natural price of goods consumed by

and consumption they always take as their model the lords and owners of the land. They imitate them in their clothing, meals, and mode of life' (Cantillon, 1755, Higgs's translation, p. 63).

workers, while the second has to do with the oscillations of the market prices of those goods.

Steuart

At some points in his argument Steuart states that money wages do not vary with the price of subsistence goods.[67] But, as I have said, these passages should be interpreted in the light of the distinction between oscillations in market prices and changes in the normal prices of labour and goods. Steuart himself argues that although wages are regulated at any moment by the quantities demanded in proportion to those supplied, they still reflect the *average* price of subsistence goods:

> The price of the market [...] may in great measure be influenced by the price of subsistence [...] A high demand for work will raise the price of wages in years of plenty: a low demand will sink the price of wages in years of scarcity. When therefore it is said, that the price of subsistence influences the rate of markets, we only mean, that the average price of subsistence, when good and bad years are taken toghether, have a certain influence in regulating prices. (Steuart, 1766a, p. 696)[68]

Moreover, wages adjust to indirect taxes on necessary consumer goods in such a way as to leave the workers' purchasing power unchanged:

> This class of taxes which I have now been describing [taxes upon alienation] never can fall either upon, or affect any person but the idle, that is to say, the not industrious consumer. (Ibid., p. 683)

67. For example in the following passage: 'the rate of demand for their labour will constantly regulate [the rate of wages], independently of the price of subsistence' (Steuart, 1766, p. 400; see also pp. 188, 694–5).
68. See also the following: '[t]his augmentation of the value of subsistence must necessarily raise the price of all work' (ibid., p. 197). In the passage quoted in the text, Steuart wants to bring out the possibility that actual market wages may move in the opposite direction to prices of agricultural subsistence goods because of conditions on the labour market: in years of abundance employment increases and hence wages rise while the price of agricultural goods tends to fall, and vice versa (Smith also takes up this theme in the last pages of his chapter on wages). The 'rate of the market' or 'price of the market' of which he speaks in the text is the price of the products of labour in manufacture. The price of the product, however, moves together with that of labour. As for Steuart, a rise in wages due to variations in the average price of agricultural subsistence goods causes a proportional rise in the prices of manufactured goods.

With regard to taxes on workers' 'superfluous' consumption, Steuart says the workers must be considered in the same way as 'rich and idle consumers'. But the superfluous consumption comprises only those goods whose consumption is not widespread among the working classes: 'if the shoemaker's subsistence should happen to include tavern expenses [...] he will not draw these back: because other shoemakers who do not frequent the tavern [...] will undersell him' (Steuart, 1766b, quoted in Seligman, 1899, p. 118). Steuart admits at once that when goods that are 'superfluous' to physiological survival are consumed in a general and habitual way by the working classes (i.e. when they have become what Steuart elsewhere calls 'political necessaries'), money wages will adjust to indirect taxation on those goods. And, he continues, the only way to prevent money wages from rising in response to taxes on goods that are not strictly necessary for survival (according to a physiological definition, though clearly they have become so from a social point of view), is to introduce 'fresh and untainted hands', into the labour market through immigration (Steuart, 1766a, p. 684).

It is interesting to note that the measure suggested is not simply the introduction of new hands, which would obviously increase competition for jobs, but the introduction of 'fresh and untainted' workers who have not yet acquired those habits of consumption (bad habits, in Steuart's view) common to the workers already present on the market.[69] This shows the importance of social conventions – in this case relative to workers' habitual consumption – in setting the limits within which competition operates. The mere increase in the number of workers looking for jobs might not suffice to reduce real wages, if they aim to share the habits of consumption already enjoyed by the other workers in the market. Steuart's affirmation also implicitly gives some indications as to what forces make wages adjust to events like price changes or taxation. Such forces are (in the last analysis) the bargaining power of the parties on the labour market and the social habits and conventions affecting the level of consumption considered essential by the workers. It was on these two fronts that Steuart proposed to intervene to change real wages: increasing the supply of hands – thus worsening the workers'

---

69. A similar position was adopted by Tucker (see above. Chapter 2, pp.19–20)

bargaining power – and also introducing workers with different habits who are prepared to accept conditions which the others would find unacceptable, even if confronted with the risk of unemployment.

Turgot

Interdependences in the economic system
Among the authors under examination, Turgot is perhaps the one who gives most indications as to what forces guarantee the adjustment of real wages towards the normal rate.

This problem is discussed in relation both to the effects of taxation and to the effects of increased prices of agricultural subsistence goods. The latter point is of particular importance for Turgot since it is related to the discussion on the liberalization of the grain trade, which Turgot favoured. It was widely believed that such liberalization would raise the average level of food prices, and hence it was relevant to assess the consequences of such an increase on the living conditions of the working classes. Turgot always strongly supported the idea, shared by the Physiocrats, that the normal real wage rate could not be reduced by an increase in prices. He did specify, however, that this only applied to persistent changes in price levels; while temporary fluctuations would affect the workers' purchasing power (Turgot, 1770, III, p. 338). For that reason such fluctuations were most to be feared, and the stabilization of prices of subsistence goods was seen as the main objective to be pursued: according to the Physiocrats and Turgot, through the liberalization of trade, according to Necker and other economists, through administrative control of prices and trade.

Turgot also maintained, as did the Physiocrats, that the only disposable income (as distinct from that necessary for reproducing the economic system) on which taxes can be levied is that of landowners. Both direct taxation on wages and indirect taxation of goods consumed by workers must ultimately fall on the landowners, that is on rent, without permanently modifying real wages.

Turgot argues that an indirect tax on consumer goods may cause only a transitory reduction in real wages: '[b]efore the tax wages had a certain level in relation to the usual price of provisions. This relation, which results from numerous causes that combine and balance each other, must tend to re-establish itself'.[70] The combination of factors that fix real wages at a certain level must bring them back to the level preceding the introduction of the tax, even when that level does not coincide with subsistence but allows the workers a margin beyond it:

> Following a sudden decrease in wages or rise in the cost of living, the workman may endure being reduced to the strict necessaries of life. But the same causes that raised wages yesterday above the cost of these necessaries are still at work, and will raise wages again until they stand in the same relation to today's cost of necessaries.[71]

What are these 'causes' which by continuing to operate determine the adjustment of wages? The use of expressions like 'host of causes', often repeated in similar contexts, suggests the existence of a multiplicity of factors. However, it is possible to work out what Turgot means through other passages, and his opinion on the effects on real wages of price changes or taxes:

> In a nation where commerce and industry are free and lively, competition fixes this profit at the lowest possible level.[72] A sort of equilibrium is established between the value of all agricultural product of the earth, the consumption of various kinds of food, the different sorts of jobs, the number of men employed to do them, and their wages. Wages cannot even be fixed, or remain constant at a certain level, except by virtue of this equilibrium and the reciprocal influences of all parts of society and all branches of production and commerce.[73]

70. 'Les salaires ont pris avant l'impôt un niveau avec le prix habituel des denrées, et ce niveau, qui est le resultat d'une foule des causes combinées et balancées les unes par les autres, doit tendre à se retablir' (Turgot, 1770, III, p. 288).
71. 'Si par une diminution subite du salaire ou une augmentation de dépense, l'ouvrier peut supporter d'être réduit à l'étroit nécessaire, les mêmes causes qui avait forcé les salaires de se monter un peu au delà du necessaire d'hier, continuant d'agir, les feront remonter encore jusqu'à ce qu'ils atteignent un taux plus fort dans la même proportion avec le necessaire d'aujourd'hui' (ibid.; see also Turgot, 1767a, II, p. 664).
72. Here the French term 'profit', as is clear from the preceding passage, indicates the amount the workers receive above the strict individual subsistence, 'to be able to afford accidents, to bring up his family' [pour subvenir aux accidents, pour élever sa famille] (Turgot, 1767a, p. 663).
73. 'Dans une nation où le commerce et l'industrie sont libre et animés, la concurrence fixe ce profit au taux le plus bas qu'il soit possible. Il s'etablit une espèce d'equilibre entre la valeur de toutes les production de la terre, la consommation des differentes espèces des denrées, les differentes genres d'ouvrages, le nombre d'hommes qui y sont occupés, et le prix de leurs salaires.
Les salaires ne peuvent même être fixés et demeurer constamment à un taux determiné, qu'en vertu de cet equilibre et de l'influence qu'ont les unes sur les autres toutes les

Here, and in other passages of similar content,[74] Turgot refers to the link between different economic variables: the value of agricultural production, the composition of consumption, employment, money wages, population and net income (*revenu*). What I have already said about Turgot's ideas on the determination of wages permits us to interpret certain aspects of the relations between these variables.

The level of employment ('the amount of work to be done') in relation to the size of the labouring population ('the number of workers') affects the bargaining power of the parties and hence the real wage. Employment depends in turn on the level of production and on its composition, which is determined by the composition of consumption. The prices of subsistence goods, for a given real wage, determine the money wage.

Alongside the influence of the relationship between employment and population on real wages, and the influence of agricultural prices on money wages, another kind of link is suggested between real wages and consumption, and between consumption and the income of landowners and agricultural entrepreneurs.

---

parties de la société, toutes les branches de la production et du commerce' (Turgot, 1767a, p. 663). Because of this passage Turgot has been interpreted as a forerunner of Walrasian general equilibrium theory (Hollander, 1987, pp. 54–5). But the interdependence of several economic magnitudes, and normal or 'equilibrium' positions, are not features of marginalist theory alone. However, in classical economic theory they fit into an analytical framework very far from that of modern general equilibrium. As I shall argue, Turgot's analysis suggests that the relationships among the magnitudes indicated in the quoted passage should be interpreted as very different from those suggested by the theory of general equilibrium. The latter, among other things, is incompatible with Turgot's view concerning the possibility of widespread unemployment or underemployment in normal positions of the economy (see above, pp. 39–42)

74. 'The money price of provisions, revenue, the price of labour, the population – these things interact to produce a spontaneous equilibrium'. [La valeur vénale des denrées, le revenu, le prix des salaires, la population, sont des choses liées entre elles et qui se mettent d'elles mêmes en équilibre, souivant une proportion naturelle] (Turgot, 1767b, II, p. 634); the same passage appears in the later *Letters on the grain trade* (ibid., III, p. 334). Again we find the following remarks in the *Observations sur le mémoire de M. Graslin:* [b]etween the wealth produced, revenue and wages there is a natural proportion that spontaneously establishes itself [...] the natural proportion [...] depends on the amount of wealth, the value of subsistence goods, the amount of work to be done and the number of workers. [il y a entre les richesses produites, le revenu, les salaires, une proportion naturelle qui s'etablit d'elle même [...] la proportion naturelle [...] dépend de la quantité des richesses, de la valeur des denrées de subsistence, de la quantité des travaux à faire et du nombre des travailleurs] (Turgot, 1767b, II, p. 634–5).

Workers are the main consumers of agricultural products. A fall in real wages, and hence in their consumption, cannot but affect the demand for agricultural goods, causing first their prices and then their production to fall. This in turn will lead to a fall in landowners' incomes: '[i]f the fall in the price of provisions due to the reduced consumption were to persist, [...] the profits of the cultivator would diminish, and this would force him to reduce his investments, and hence his production'.[75] Note that a reduction in real wages ultimately leads to a drop in production (and employment). This is in sharp contrast with the conclusions of contemporary marginalist theory, and hence contradicts the interpretations that try to associate Turgot with the modern general equilibrium theory (see above, note 73). Similarly, it denies the common interpretation in terms of wage fund notions. Indeed, if there is an association it is between the views of Turgot and many mercantilist economists, who held that sufficiently high wages would increase demand and hence favour production and development (see above, Chapter 2, p. 23).

Let us return to the question of how the relation between real wages and production helps to sustain the real wage level. According to Turgot, landowners as a group have no interest in reducing real wages as this might cause a fall in the value of agricultural production. In the *Observations sur le mémoire de M. Graslin* Turgot, after asserting that there is an inverse relationship between wages and profit rate, argues that even so

> Neither the entrepreneur nor the proprietor have any interest in a fall of wages below this [natural] proportion [between commodity prices and money wages]. Apart from the fact that the underpaid workman, who does not earn enough to live comfortably, works less well, there is the fact that if the worker earns less he consumes less, and if he consumes less the money value of agricultural production is lower.[76]

---

75. 'si la baisse du prix des denrées occasionnée par la diminution de la consommation se soutenait, [...] ayant diminué les profits du cultivateur, l'obligerait de diminuer ses dépenses productives et, par conséquent, la production' (Turgot, 1770, III, pp. 288–9). But as we have just seen Turgot held that this does not generally happen, because money wages would be rapidly adjusted to the increased cost of living, leaving the real wage unchanged.

76. 'Ni l'entrepreneur ni le propriétaire n'ont l'interêt que les salaires baissent au-dessous

Thus, according to Turgot, the awareness of a link between wages and the income of landowners, owing to the links between income distribution, consumption, prices, and level of agricultural production, would favour the stability of distribution variables. This awareness implies a recognition of a common interest on the part of the landowning classes, and it gives rise to a form of 'regulation' of competition, which if unchecked would lead each capitalist anarchically to cut the wages of his own workers, ignoring the possible negative consequences if all the other employers did so at the same time.

However, as in the case of the 'tacit combination' of Smith's entrepreneurs not to raise wages, this tacit consensus of Turgot's landowners not to force real wages down for fear of a common disadvantage should not be understood too rigidly. Turgot also tells us that when real wages are initially reduced by a tax on subsistence goods, as employers' incomes are negatively affected by the reduction of workers' expenditure, they become more unwilling to raise money wages than they would otherwise have been (Turgot, 1770, III, p. 288). In other words, if the perception of a possible common interest works to set limits to competition, the pursuit of that interest may cease when it requires proprietors individually to meet an increase in costs in a difficult and uncertain situation.

Finally, Turgot mentions the positive influence of wages on the quality of the work done. As mentioned in the introduction to the last chapter, the existence and direction of that influence were vigorously debated throughout the period, but the suggestion that it might help to keep wages at their normal rate is peculiar to Turgot.

Role of population changes

In one of his letters on the grain trade Turgot argues that if all the factors that normally restore real wages to their former level should fail, emigration might reduce the labouring population and thus again enable the workers to impose their own conditions in wage bargaining. Turgot, after describing the 'host of circumstances'

de cette proportion. Outre qu'en tout genre l'homme mal payé, et qui ne gagne pas par son travail une subsistance abondante, travaille moins bien, l'homme salarié, s'il gagne moins, consomme moins, s'il consomme moins la valeur vénale des productions du sol est moindre' (Turgot, 1967b, II, 634)

whose continued operation must re-establish the real wage at its normal rate, goes on to say that if the landowners refused to grant the necessary increases in money wages to compensate for a tax on wage goods, then:

> the workman would look elsewhere to find the well-being he considers necessary; the population would decrease, and this would go on until the reduced number of labourers diminished competition among them and enabled them to impose their conditions and force the proprietors to raise wages.[77]

Emigration represents the possibility of refusal, on the part of workers, to accept real wages below the level required to maintain the consumption which has become necessary to them. Changes in the labouring population, brought about by emigration, may restore wages to their normal level by reducing competition among workers; that is by reducing the excess labour supply and thus improving their bargaining position.

In Turgot's analysis changes in the population through emigration play a role similar to the one we have seen in some mercantilist writers – the role of keeping wages up when there are forces working to reduce them. In general, however, other forces bring about the adjustment of wages following variations in prices or taxes, while emigration is regarded as an adjustment mechanism of last resort, only operative when all the usual ones fail.

Summing up

At this point we can try to summarize the forces and circumstances which, according to Turgot, make wages adjust to variations in the prices of consumer goods or taxes on those goods. First, we have the relative dimensions of employment and the labouring population, which determine the bargaining power of the workers. Second, there is the employers' awareness of the link between real wages, workers'

---

77. 'L'ouvrier irait chercher ailleurs une aisance dont il ne peut se passer; la population diminueraient, et cela jusqu'au point que la diminution du nombre des travailleurs en restreignant leur concurrence, le met en état de faire la loi et de forcer les propriétaires à hausser les prix' (Turgot, 1770, III, p. 288). See also the *Letter to Hume* where he states that the worker's subsistence is a minimum below which wages cannot fall, because 'if a worker cannot live by his work, he either becomes a beggar or he emigrates' [si un ouvrier ne peut vivre de son travail, il devient mendiant ou s'expatrie]. (Turgot, 1767a, II, 663).

consumption and agricultural production. This awareness helps to stabilize the distributive variables inasmuch as the employers see that it is not in their common interest to press for a reduction in real wages below their normal rate. Last, but not least are the elements of custom that determine the level of consumption which the workers cannot or will not give up. The refusal of the workers to accept a reduction in their habitual consumption may also result in emigration, which reduces the population until the improved bargaining position of the workers restores wages to their normal level.

As Turgot says, then, 'the *same causes* that raised wages yesterday above the cost of these necessaries are still at work, and will raise wages again' (see above, p.74). Thus the same circumstances that determine the normal wages level make the actual real wage return to that level when it is altered by external events.

Necker

The difference between Necker's position and that of Turgot with regard to the desirability of liberalizing the grain trade does not arise from differing views about the adjustment of money wages following persistent changes in price levels. The difference lies in Necker's stress of the advantage for the owners and the distress of the working classes in the lapse of time between the price rise and the adjustment of money wages:

> the constantly high price of corn does not improve the situation of the land proprietors, because the price of labour conforms to it. But the price increase, that is, the transition from low to high price, and the initial period of high price give these same proprietors a real advantage [...] the proprietors profit from all the sufferings of the labourer.[78]

78. 'Le haut prix constant des blés n'améliore point le sort des propriétaires des terres, parce que le prix du travail s'y conforme; mais le renchérissement, c'est-a-dire, le passage du bas prix au haut prix, et les premiers temps de cherté, procurent un avantage réel à ces mêmes propriétaires [...] les propriétaires profitent de toute la souffrance de l'homme de peine'(Necker, 1775, I, p. 72). The main reasons for the difference between Necker and Turgot regarding the effects of free trade in cereals, in particular on the living conditions of the popular classes, are: 1) Necker's greater emphasis on the sufferings of the workers in the phase of rising prices that would follow the liberalization, before they stabilized at the new level and wages had time to

However, in the end money wages must adjust to the new level of prices: 'but this advantage disappears gradually as the workman manages to raise the price of his labour time, and the old relations are re-established'.[79]

Necker never doubts that the real wage will ultimately return to its former level, despite his emphasis on the disparity of power between proprietors and workers in favour of the former, and despite the fact that this disparity increases as prices rise and the workers are further impoverished.

In describing what happens when prices rise, Necker refers to the conflict between the parties: 'when the proprietors raise the price of provisions, and refuse to increase the price of the workmen's labour, a sort of hidden but terrible struggle sets in between these two classes of society'.[80]

Since Necker believes that real wages are determined by the 'respective degrees of need and power of proprietors and workers' (ibid., p. 68; see above, p. 46) it might be thought that in his view an event which does not alter these power relations cannot affect real wages either. In another passage, also concerning the effects of changes in grain prices, Necker attributes the adjustment of money wages directly to the behaviour of the proprietors: 'in general the fate of the people will not change at all, whatever may be the constant price of corn, because the proprietors will always correspondingly regulate the price of labour'.[81]

That is all there is to be found in Necker's works on the causes of adjustment. The above passages suggest, on the one hand, the idea of conflict and bargaining that restores real wages to their former level

---

adjust; for this reason Necker doubted, among other things, the social and political feasibility of such a reform; 2) Necker's opinion that the objective of price stability, which like Turgot he considered of primary importance, would be better achieved through careful policies of administrative control than through liberalizing the market (see also ibid., pp. 74–6 and Chapter 8, part IV).

79. 'Mais cet avantage disparoît à mesure que l'homme industrieux parvient à renchérir le prix de son temps, et que les anciens rapports se rétablissent' (ibid., p. 72).

80. 'Lorsque les propriétaires haussent les prix de denrée, et se defendent de hausser le prix de la main d'oevre des hommes industrieux, il s'établit entre les deux classes de la société une sorte de combat obscur, mais terrible' (ibid., pp. 74–5).

81. 'Le sort du peuple, en général, ne sera point changé, quel que soit le prix constant des grains, parce que les propriétaires régleront toujours en conséquence celui de la main d'oevre' (ibid., pp. 304–5).

and on the other hand, perhaps, the idea of customary elements on the basis of which employers regulate real wages.

Smith

Smith's view with regard to the adjustment of money wages following a rise in the prices of subsistence goods was similar to that of the other economists. This does not contradict his long digressions, in the chapter on wages, in which he explains that in Great Britain wages are not immediately regulated by the prices of subsistence goods and do not vary with them. These assertions should be interpreted according to Smith's own clear suggestion:

> The money price of labour, as I shall endeavour to show hereafter, does not fluctuate from year to year with the money price of corn, but seems every where accommodated, not to the temporary or occasional, but to the average or ordinary price of that necessary of life. (Smith, 1776, I.v.16)

Smith also held that money wages would rapidly adjust following the imposition of a tax on necessary goods or on wages:

> the wages of the inferior classes of workmen are every where regulated by two circumstances; the demand for labour, and the ordinary and average price of provisions. [...] While the demand for labour and the price of provisions, therefore, remain the same, a direct tax upon the wages of labour can have no other effect than to raise them somewhat higher than the tax. (Ibid., V.ii.i.1)
> a tax upon the necessaries of life, operates exactly in the same manner as a direct tax upon the wages of labour. (Ibid.,V.ii.k.5)

Smith does not give any general explanation of the causes for this adjustment, but simply states that real wages are regulated by the state of demand: if demand does not change, money wages must readily adjust to variations in prices or taxation so as to leave real (disposable) wages unaltered. But at one point where he deals with the theme of adjustment, in distinguishing between the effects of taxes on luxuries and necessaries, Smith argues that a reduction in consumption of luxuries has no negative effect on the worker's ability to maintain his family, and hence no effect on the population. But it is different with subsistence goods:

> Any rise in the average price of necessaries, unless it is compensated by a proportionable rise in the wages of labour, must necessarily diminish more or less the ability of the poor to bring up numerous families, and consequently to

supply the demand for useful labour; whatever may be the state of that demand, whether increasing, stationary, or declining; or such as require an increasing, stationary, or declining population. (Ibid., V.ii.k.8)

This has suggested to some interpreters that Smith had in mind a mechanism of adjustment for wage levels through a change in population; the initial reduction in wages would lead to a fall in the rate of growth of the population, which would then be inadequate to meet the demand, and thus would induce a rise in wages.[82]

Even though the passage may suggest this interpretation, Smith's position regarding the speed with which wages adjust does not seem compatible with the long process that would be necessary for a change in the rate of population growth to be felt on the labour market. Smith declares, as we have just seen, that taxation 'can have no other effect' than to raise wages, and shows that he considers the adjustment to be almost immediate: the adverb 'soon' is often used in connection with the theme of wage adjustment in the *Wealth of Nations*, and in his lectures Smith had spoken of the time required in terms of 'a few months'.[83] Thus we face a choice. Either we must accept the coexistence of contradictory elements in Smith's theory where this problem is concerned, or we can interpret the changes in the rate of population growth as having a role rather similar to that found in Turgot for emigration – a last line of defence for the wage level, which under normal conditions does not enter the process of adjustment.

Indeed in the above passage Smith appears to conflate two distinct temporal and logical dimensions. On the one hand, there is the time lag required for the adjustment of actual (market) wages to their natural level. This must be short enough to allow him, for example, to treat real wages as given at their natural level when he analyses the effect of taxes on natural prices. Deviations in real wages from their natural level can be neglected only in so far as they are regarded as strictly transitory phenomena. On the other hand, there is the influence on wages of changes in population size or growth

---

82. Hollander, 1987, pp. 158–60. According to this author 'an increase in the "price of provisions" influences the money wage [...] to assure against a reduction in the growth rate of population' (ibid., p. 158). Hollander's subsequent discussion, however, reveals some difficulties in this interpretation (see Chapter 4, n. 31 below).
83. Smith, 1766, pp. 375–6.

rate. This takes a relatively long time, and has to do with the 'secular' evolution of the (natural) wage rate.

Thus, in conclusion, I believe that Smith's position must be interpreted like that of the other authors we have examined: the adjustment of the natural money wage to maintain the workers' purchasing power is generally rapid, and does not depend on changes in the rate of population growth. This is because the same forces that determine the natural level of real wages, i.e. the conditions of the labour market and the workers' habitual living standards, will tend to restore that level when external events, which do not modify the workers' bargaining position, cause a (transitory) fall in real wages.

SUMMARY

The concepts of subsistence consumption and the normal wage rate do not strictly coincide, though they are closely related and are often used interchangeably by these economists.

Subsistence consumption does not coincide with physiological needs; rather, as Steuart and Smith argue with particular clarity, it is determined by historical and social forces.

The tendency for the natural wage to coincide with subsistence is explained by specific historical and social conditions, in particular poverty and need on the part of the workers, unemployment, the institutions and the political system. But there are circumstances which may allow the normal wage rate to rise above that minimum level. Smith and Turgot, in particular, emphasize the role of high rates of accumulation, which reduce unemployment and produce a 'scarcity of hands' forcing employers to compete. Necker emphasizes the role of changes in the 'forms of government', which modify the socio-political position of the workers.

Thus, the natural wage is a centre of gravitation, an average value of the actual wage, while subsistence consumption represents the minimum level for the natural wage at a given time and place.

The relation between subsistence and the normal wage rate is further complicated, however, by the possibility that after a sufficient length of time changes in the latter will in turn induce a change in the level of consumption considered necessary for the workers. This possibility, which arises immediately from the classical economists' historical and sociological definition of subsistence goods, is discussed in detail by James Steuart. He brings out the role of social imitation, and of consumption levels as signs of membership in a certain social group, in determining the irreversible rise of the minimum necessary consumption which follows a lasting and widespread improvement in living standards.

The interaction between subsistence consumption and the natural wage helps to explain occasional ambiguities in the use of these concepts: Smith, for example, argues that high rates of accumulation lead the natural wage to rise above subsistence level, but elsewhere he speaks of different subsistence levels ('moderate, liberal or scanty') associated with different rates of accumulation.

Often these authors do not deal specifically with the question of what forces guarantee the adjustment of real wages to the normal rate after price changes or taxation. But in general this does not occur through variations in the quantity of labour (population) or of employment. Rather, and this is explicitly stated by Turgot, the forces that guarantee the adjustment of wages are the same as those that determine its natural level in real terms: employment in relation to population, the institutional context, the social norms that define subsistence consumption, and, for Turgot, also the employers' awareness of the relation between real wages, consumption, and their own incomes.

From the analytical point of view one of the most interesting elements emerging from the foregoing discussion is that unemployment is regarded as a non–transitory phenomenon, and has a role in determining the normal rate of wages.

This explains why competition among workers is indicated as one of the reasons for the tendency of the natural wage to approach its minimum, subsistence level: when there is unemployment competition among workers weakens their bargaining power. And this explains why, on the other hand, in rapidly growing economies competition among employers due to 'scarcity of hands' is seen as increasing the workers' bargaining power, so that the natural wage may be fixed above the subsistence level. In other words, since it is possible for persistent disequilibria to exist between the quantity of labour demanded and its supply, the existence and the size of such disparities are factors that enter the determination of the natural wage, by influencing the bargaining power of the parties.

It follows that competition among workers (when there is unemployment) or among employers ('scarcity of hands') does not lead respectively to an indefinite reduction or increase of wages; rather, such competition influences the level of the normal wage rate in relation to the subsistence minimum. This implies that competition is conceived as a process that works within definite limits, which in the case of wages are set by social conditions and opinions as to what is the decent and necessary level of consumption for workers.

The above arguments show that the analogy between labour and commodities (based on the fact that labour is bought and sold on the market, and that its quantity can vary in response to demand), often mentioned by these economists, does not hold up in all respects. While the market price of goods coincides with the natural price when the quantity produced is equal to the effectual demand,[84] the same is not true for the natural price of labour. The latter, as we have seen, is determined among other things by the size of the differences between supply and demand, when these differences are persistent in nature, i.e. when they are associated with the economy's capacity for development and accumulation trends.

This has to do with the special nature of the commodity labour, i.e. the fact that its 'production', which the classical economists saw as dependent on demographic processes, cannot be adjusted to demand as rapidly as the production of commodities; moreover, as we shall see in the next chapter, the adjustment cannot be ensured by equally reliable mechanisms. The consequence is that the natural price of labour, unlike the natural price of a commodity, is also determined by the relative sizes of supply and demand, that is of population and employment.

---

84. 'When the quantity brought to market is just sufficient to supply the effectual demand and no more, the market price naturally comes to be either exactly or as nearly as can be judged of, the same with the natural price' (Smith, 1776, I.vii.11).

4. Theories of Population from Cantillon to Ricardo

INTRODUCTION

Studies and controversies on the subject of population had an important place in the economic debates of the period under discussion. These dealt with numerous aspects: the problem of estimating population size (without the benefit of census data, which were first collected in the 19th century), the demographic evolution of different countries or even of the whole world, and the attempt to discover what laws govern that evolution, especially in connection with economic development.

Here we shall consider only those aspects that are most relevant to this study: the ideas about the relation between population growth and particular economic circumstances (accumulation, employment, wages); and the implications of these ideas for the analysis of the labour market and distribution.

I shall begin by looking at the views of Cantillon and James Steuart. Their ideas about the explanation of population size and the role of population changes in the functioning of the labour market can be taken as representative of opinions then shared by many other economists.

One of their central concerns was the relation between economic development or decline (and hence increasing or declining employment) and population. In particular, there is a clear effort to identify the forces which ensure that the available labour force tends to be commensurate with the requirements of accumulation.

Next, I shall discuss the role of population theory in Smith's analysis, showing how he, more than the earlier authors, connected population theory with the theory of wages. This connection has led some economists to see Smith's theory as based on the role of wages in adjusting the rate of population growth to the rate of increase of the demand for labour; these interpretations will be critically examined.

The largest section of this chapter will be devoted to Malthus's ideas on the implications of the 'principle of population' for the living conditions of the working classes, as set out in his famous *Essay on the Principle of Population*. My aim is to bring out, along with elements of continuity, certain points of considerable difference between Malthus's analysis and the earlier tradition.

These distinctions suggest that the role of the theory of population in connection with the determination of wages has often been misinterpreted. The problems arise from the fact that some of Malthus's ideas, leading to the formulation of the so-called 'iron law of wages', have been attributed to the whole classical and pre-classical tradition. As I shall argue in the last section of the chapter, this is inaccurate: the iron law is properly seen as a feature peculiar to Malthus's theory alone.

THEORIES OF POPULATION IN THE EIGHTEENTH CENTURY: CANTILLON AND STEUART

Earlier, in examining ideas about population in the economic literature of the seventeenth and eighteenthth centuries, we noted the connection that some economists saw between economic development (or decline) and the increase (or decrease) of population. It was then common experience that in the cities and regions where productive activities and employment opportunities arose and flourished, there was also an increase in the available 'hands'. This was usually explained as the effect of employment opportunities on migratory flows, by means of which the labour supply was thought to adjust to the needs of economic development.

The existence of a direct link between employment and population was also envisaged in the more systematic studies of Cantillon and Steuart, which we shall examine below.

Cantillon on population and consumption habits
Cantillon, like other writers on population in this period, draws an

analogy between the propagation of animal and vegetable species and the multiplication of men; this has often led scholars to see Cantillon as a forerunner of Malthusian ideas about population. The passage most often cited in this connection is the statement that 'men multiply like mice in a barn if they have unlimited means of subsistence' (Cantillon, 1755, Higgs's translation, p. 83; see also p. 67).

In reality Cantillon's theory of population is more complex than this suggests. From his argument as a whole it is clear that the 'laws' which he sees as regulating the human population are much less simple than those that regulate the propagation of animal species. In the first place, in the case of human beings he brings out the importance of habits of consumption, rather than physiological needs, in determining the size of the population which can be maintained by a certain amount of available food:

> According to the different manner of living, 400,000 people might subsist on the same produce of the land which ordinarily supports 100,000. A man who lives upon the produce of an acre and a half of land, may be stronger and stouter than he who spends the produce of five or ten acres. (Ibid., p. 81)

Changes in consumption habits can also modify the number of inhabitants of a country. This is what Cantillon says happened in England: 'We see dayly that Englishmen, in general, consume more of the produce of the land than their fathers did, and this is the real reason why there are fewer inhabitants than in the past' (ibid. p. 83).[1] In this passage, Cantillon is so little a 'Malthusian' as to say that an increase in consumption leads to a fall rather than a rise in population. This is because in regulating population he assigns a central role to living standards rather than to a natural impulse to procreate. It is on the basis of these standards that decisions are taken about the formation of new families and the number of

---

1. Nowadays it may seem surprising that Cantillon believed the English population had decreased. But the debates of the period up to the end of the eighteenth century show that there were two conflicting opinions about what was happening to the population: some said it was decreasing in a disturbing way; others saw it as increasing (Gonner, 1912–13). This strong divergence of opinion, apparently, arose not only from the absence of reliable data but also from the different points of view of the exponents of these theses. The idea that the population was decreasing seems to be based on observation of the depopulation of the countryside, while the rapid growth of the cities suggested the opposite view.

children:

> I assumed that most men desire nothing better than to marry if they are set in a
> position to keep their families in the same style as they are content to live
> themselves. That is, if a man is satisfied with the produce of an acre and a half of
> land he will marry if he is sure of having enough to keep his family in the same
> way. But if he is only satisfied with the produce of 5 to 10 acres he will be in no
> hurry to marry unless he thinks he can bring up his family in the same manner.
> (Ibid., p. 77)

Employment and population

As well as bringing out the importance of these cultural and social
elements in regulating population, Cantillon identifies the ways in
which food is made available to the working classes – i.e. to the
largest part of the population.

The area and fertility of the soil and the techniques available to
cultivate it are not the only factors that determine the amount of
food the workers can obtain. In any system other than that of
production for self-consumption, this amount depends crucially on
the level of employment. The waged worker's access to an income,
and hence his ability to buy food, depends on the possibility of
getting work. This in turn determines to what extent the land will be
used to produce food for the workers:

> If a Lord or owner who has let out all his lands to farm, take the fancy to change
> considerably his mode of living; if for instance he decreases the number of his
> domestic servants and increases that of his horses: not only will his servants be
> forced to leave the estate in question, but also a proportionate number of artisans
> and of labourers who worked to mantain them. The portion of land which was
> used to mantain these inhabitants will be laid down to grass for the new horses,
> and if all landowners in a State did the like they would soon increase the number
> of horses and diminish the number of Men.(Ibid., p. 64–5)

> The natural and constant way of increasing population in a State is to find
> employment for the people there, and to make the land serve for the production of
> their means of support. (Ibid., p. 85)

Thus there are two main themes in Cantillon's discussion of the
factors determining population size: 1) the level of employment,
which for a given wage determines the purchasing power of the
working population and hence the actual production of food and its
availability for their use; and 2) the habits of consumption which,
for a given average level of income or resources (quantity of land)

available for the use of workers' families, determine the number of marriages and the number of children per marriage.

In Cantillon's analysis the positive relation between employment opportunities and population not only explains population changes in different regions and countries, but also serves to adjust the supply of labour to the demand for it on the labour market:

> If all the labourers in a village breed up several sons to the same work there will be too many labourers to cultivate the lands belonging to the village, and the surplus adults must go to seek a livelihood elsewhere, which they generally do in cities: if some remain with their fathers, as they will not all find sufficient employment they will live in great poverty and will not marry for lack of means to bring up children, or if they marry, the children who come will soon die of starvation with their parents, as we see every day in France. [..]
> By the same process of reasoning it is easy to conceive that the labourers, handicraftsmen and others who gain their living by work, must proportion themselves in number to the employment and demand for them in market towns and cities.
> [..] Be that as it may, when [the labourers and handicraftsmen] have no work they quit the villages, towns or cities where they live in such numbers that those who remain are always proportioned to the employment which suffices to mantain them; when there is a continuous increase of work there is gain to be made and enough others arrive to share it. (Ibid., p. 23–5)

Thus, Cantillon observes that the working population tends to be proportional to the opportunities of employment, and he explains this through two different mechanisms of adjustment: migratory flows and variations in mortality and fertility. It must be noted, however, that Cantillon fails to distinguish between adjustments in the case of single occupations (farmers, artisans, etc.), which might in principle work through changes from one trade to another, and the adjustment of the aggregate quantities of labour supplied and demanded.

Cantillon tends to consider wages as fixed at the level of customary consumption in a certain place and time. Naturally this level can vary at different times and circumstances, but Cantillon never mentions any influence of a changed level of employment on wages. Thus, the effects of changed employment levels on migratory flows and on the well-being of the working classes – which in turn cause changes in mortality and fertility – must be attributed to changes in the opportunity to find employment.

Implicit in all this is the idea that normally there are underemployed and unemployed labourers who may move from one place to another in search of work, and whose numbers are reduced by an increase in the demand for labour, so that the average per capita income of the working classes depends not only on the level of wages but also on the level of employment.[2] This is explicitly stated in the passage cited above: 'as they will not all find sufficient employment they will live in great poverty and will not marry for lack of means [...], or if they marry, the children who come will soon die of starvation with their parents'.

Steuart on population

Steuart's theory of population has many points in common with that of Cantillon. Like the latter, he begins with the analogy between men and animal species. This is used to affirm the relation between means of subsistence and population, and to illustrate (anticipating some arguments later used by Malthus) the way scarcity of food works to arrest the multiplication of men, or even to reduce their numbers:

> Several kinds of animals, expecially insects, multiply by thousands, and yet the species does not appear annually to increase [...] It is therefore reasonable to conclude, that what destroys such vast quantities of those produced, must be, among other causes, the want of food. Let us apply this to men. [...] certain individuals may become worse fed, consequently weaker, consequently if, in that weakly state, nature should withhold a part of her usual plenty, [...] a disease may take place and sweep off a far greater number than that proportioned to the deficiency of the season (Steuart, 1766a, p. 32)

However, as in Cantillon, while the analogy with the animal world illustrates a general principle governing the relationship between population and food supply, the discussion moves at once to the question of the conditions that allow population growth in a society where there is division of labour and where subsistence goods are objects of production and exchange. In this context any increase in agricultural production over the cultivator's own needs for

---

2. The tendency to ignore the possibility of persistent unemployment and underemployment in the theory of the classical economists has caused difficulties in interpreting this direct nexus between employment and population. See for example Bowley's comment on this aspect of Cantillon's theory: 'Cantillon does not really make it clear how an increase (as distinct from a decrease) of population would be stimulated [...] He does not, I think, anywhere set out the effect of an increase in aggregate demand for labour pushing wages above customary subsistence and, thereby, increasing survival' (1976, p. 182).

consumption must be stimulated by a demand for agricultural goods from workers who have access to an income:

> [...] we may lay it down as a principle, that a farmer will not labour to produce a superfluity of grain relatively to his own consumption, unless he finds some want which may be supplied by means of that superfluity; [...] Here than is one principle: *Agriculture among a free people will augment population, in proportion only as the necessitous are put in a situation to purchase subsistence with their labour*.
>
> If, in any country which actually produces nourishment for its inhabitants, [...] a plan is set on foot for the extention of agriculture; *the augmentation must be made to bear a due proportion to the progress of industry and wants of the people* . (Ibid., p. 40)[3]

It follows that an insufficient development of employment or consumption can prevent the full use of a country's potential capacities for agricultural production:

> Here then will be found a country the population of which must stop for want of food; and which, by the supposition, is abundantly able to produce more. Experience every where shows the possible existence of such a case, since no country in Europe is cultivated to the utmost: and there are many still, where cultivation, and consequently multiplication, is at a stop. These nations I consider as in a *moral incapacity* of multiplying: the incapacity would be *physical*, if there was an actual impossibility of their procuring an augmentation of food by any means whatsoever. (Ibid., pp. 41–2)

Thus Steuart, like Cantillon, saw the limits on the supply of food for the working classes, and hence on population increase, as deriving not from limited natural resources but from an insufficient demand for food. This insufficient demand in turn is caused by lack of opportunities for employment. Cantillon showed how the level of employment depended on the composition of consumption and production, and hence on the decisions of the upper classes on the use of their income. Steuart's analysis, on the other hand, emphasizes the role of economic growth.

Not only does Steuart seem more interested in what he calls 'moral' limits to growth, but considers these limits as the only important ones, because what he calls 'physical' limits appear remote and of no practical relevance:

---

3. The word 'industry' is here used in the sense of 'employment' (see Chapter 3, n. 43 for a discussion of the various meanings assumed by this term in the economic writings of the period).

As to the physical impossibility, the case can hardly exist, because means of procuring subsistence from other countries, when the soil refuses to give more, seem, if not inexhaustible, at least very extensive. A country therefore fully peopled, that is, in a physical impossibility of increasing their numbers, is a chimerical and useless supposition.(Ibid., p. 116)

Thus in this respect Steuart was very far from one of the themes that would later be important in Malthus's analysis.[4]

As was common in the literature of this period, Steuart uses the connection between population and employment to explain the adjustment of the number of workers to the development of productive activities:

While there is a demand for the trade of any country, inhabitants are always on the increasing hand. [...] There never was any branch of trade established in any kingdom, province, city, or even village; but such kingdoms, province etc. increased in inhabitants. (Ibid., p. 196)

Also present in Steuart is the idea that a given supply of available resources can maintain a greater or lesser population, depending on the habits of consumption of the inhabitants: 'The more frugal a people are, and the more they feed upon the plentiful productions of the earth, the more they may increase in their numbers' (ibid., p. 119).

The themes developed by Cantillon and Steuart – the role, in regulating population growth, of employment (i.e. access to an income) and habits of consumption – are prominent in all the eighteenth century works on population theory; they are found in the works of Hume, Necker, Wallace and the Physiocrats, among others.[5]

A characteristic feature in the works of these economists is the existence of a direct link – not mediated by changes in wages – between employment opportunities and population. Such a link was later cited by Smith, as we shall see; and in the nineteenth century it was again introduced by Barton in his famous pamphlet on the effects of machines. Here he states that 'it is the difficulty of finding

4. This contradicts the interpretation of Schumpeter, who considers Steuart a 'Malthusian' (Schumpeter, 1954, p. 225)
5. Hume, 1750, pp. 11–2; see also Rotwein, 1955, p. lxxxix; Necker, 1775, I, pp. 28, 35–40 (Necker enjoyed a certain fame as an expert on population; even Smith cites his estimates of the size of the French population); Wallace, 1753, pp. 15–23; On the Physiocratic literature in this connection see Spengler, 1942, p. 200.

employment, much more than the insufficiency of the rate of wages, which discourages marriage'. (1817, p. 22).

THEORY OF POPULATION AND THEORY OF WAGES IN THE *WEALTH OF NATIONS*

Smith, like his predecessors, believed that there was a relation between population growth and the availability of food for the working classes. He differed from the foregoing tradition in two respects: first, he made no reference to migratory flows as an important factor in the adjustment of the working population to the demand for labour; and second, he stressed the relation between changes in population and changes in the natural wage – an element which, as we have seen, was absent, or of secondary importance, in the earlier literature.

Smith sees the relation between wages and the working population mainly in terms of the effect of wage levels on infant mortality. Where the natural wage rate is higher, he says, working-class families are able to take better care of their children, so that more of them survive beyond infancy and hence the population increases (Smith, 1776, I.viii.38–44). Smith also sees another possible cause of population growth in the increased economic contribution to the family made by children in prosperous nations like the American colonies, where young people have many opportunities for well-paid employment. This leads to a growth in population by increasing the number and fertility of marriages (ibid., I.vii.23).

In pointing out the role of children's contribution to the family, Smith anticipates an element which economists and demographers still today consider very important in explaining differences in fertility at various stages of economic development. In Smith this also implies a direct link between population and employment opportunities. The economic contribution of the children to the family depends not only on their wages, but on the plentiful opportunities to find work in nations like North America where labour is scarce.

Wages and population
In the *Wealth of Nations*, then, Smith lays more emphasis than

previous writers on the link between population and wages. In the following passage, which has had great influence on the interpretation of Smith's wage theory, he suggests that wages tend towards a level which allows the population to grow at the pace required by the growth of the demand for labour:

> The liberal reward of labour, by enabling [the inferior ranks of the people] to provide better for their children, and consequently to bring up a greater number, naturally tends to widen and extend those limits [to the multiplication of human species]. It deserves to be remarked too that it necessarily does this as nearly as possible in the proportion which the demand for labour requires. If this demand is continually increasing, the reward of labour must necessarily encourage in such a manner the marriage and multiplication of labourers, as may enable them to supply that continually increasing demand by a continually increasing population. If the reward should at any time be less than what was requisite for this purpose, the deficiency of hands would soon raise it; and if it should at any time be more, their excessive multiplication would soon lower it to this necessary rate. The market would soon be so much under-stocked with labour in the one case, and so much over–stocked in the other, as would soon force back its price to that proper rate which the circumstances of the society required. It is in this manner that the demand for men, like that for any other commodity, necessarily regulates the production of men; quickens it when it goes on too slowly, and stops it when it advances too fast.(Ibid., I.vii 40)

This argument has led some to interpret Smith's wage theory as based on the existence of a precise quantitative relation between wages and the population growth rate (Hollander, 1973, pp. 157–8 and 1987, p. 157; Samuelson, 1978).

In the next section, I shall first briefly illustrate this interpretation and then assess the affinities seen by some contemporary economists between Smith's theory, thus represented, and the marginalist theory in which wages are determined by 'supply and demand'. Subsequently I shall consider the validity of this interpretation in the light of the overall treatment of the natural wage in the *Wealth of Nations*.

Assessment of interpretations based on a functional relation between wage and population

According to the interpretation in question, as argued by Hollander, the rate of population growth $(dP/dt)/P$ is a positive function of the wage rate (w); taking the rate of employment growth $(dL/dt)/L$ as determined independently of the wage rate by the rate of accumulation, we find that for any rate of growth of employment, the natural wage rate (w^*) is univocally determined as that at which population and employment growth rates are equal.

If the current wage rate is less than w^* there will be a shortage of labour which will make wages rise, and vice versa if it is greater than w^*; thus wages will tend to settle at the natural rate w^*. Of course it is possible to complicate this formulation to bring it closer to Smith's analysis. For example one can introduce a notion of subsistence consumption and make the rate of population growth vary in relation to the difference between it and current wages. In addition, one can introduce adjustment lags and admit that these can lead to a change in habits of consumption (thus producing a parametric shift of the function linking $(dP/dt)/P$ to w).[6] But when all these elements have been added to the model, the quantitative relation between wages and population growth loses any explanatory power because any change in wages may be accompanied by a corresponding parametric shift in the curve. The size of this shift is not plausibly predictable, since it depends on factors such as the way changes occur in workers' habits of consumption and in their behaviour with regard to fertility and marriage.[7]

It has been claimed that Smith's theory, represented in the way described above, comes close to the modern theory whereby wages are determined by 'supply and demand' (Hollander, 1973, p. 157; Samuelson, 1978).

Indeed, even if that view of his theory is accepted, this does not imply the determination of wages by 'supply and demand' in a manner comparable to that envisaged by the marginalist theory. Demand is represented by the rate of growth of employment, realized in the course of a process of accumulation. In each period along the growth path, the demand for labour is treated by Smith as

6. As is suggested by Caravale, 1988, pp. 604–5.
7. In discussing the interpretation of the classical theory of wages as based on the fact that 'in the long-run wages are controlled by a "standard of living" through the tendency of population to increase or decrease whenever they are above or below the workers' psycological requirements which regulate reproduction', Knight observes, I think rightly, that '[a] standard of living, to operate in this way, must obviously itself remain stationary, or at least change slowly in comparison with the population changes which bring the supply of labour into equilibrium with reference to it'. According to Knight 'subsistence', in the works of the classical economists, does not seem to satisfy this condition (Knight,1956, p. 85).

a determinate quantity largely independent of the wage level, not as a function of the latter, as it is in the contemporary theory.

Moreover, as Hollander recognizes, in contrast to some interpretations of the classical theory (Samuelson, 1978), for Smith the rate of expansion of employment over time does not depend on the rate of profit and hence cannot be seen as inversely related to wages:

> The demand for labour increases with the increase of stock whatever be its profits; and after these are diminished, stock may not only continue to increase, but to increase much faster than before. It is with industrious nations who are advancing in the acquisition of riches, as with industrious individuals. A great stock, though with small profits, generally increases faster than a small stock with great profits. (Smith, 1776, I.ix.11)[8]

Thus, on the demand side, we have a rate of growth – growth of employment – which proves to be largely independent of the distributive variables.

On the supply side, we have a relation in which the level of wages is linked not with variations in the labour supply for a given population, as in contemporary theory, but with the long-term rates of increase of the population. In any single period (i.e. in any normal position of the economy), the supply of labour, like the demand for labour, is a given quantity, and it coincides with the working-class population.

The interpretation we have been discussing is based on two main tenets: 1) the existence of a particular quantitative relation between wages and population growth; and 2) the role of this relation in bringing wages to such a level that the growth rates of employment and population are equal. Can such an interpretation be considered sufficiently faithful to the vision of Smith?

The passage cited on p. 96 above undoubtedly offers some support for this view, but other elements in Smith's analysis suggest caution. In his chapter on wages he frequently refers to institutional, social and cultural factors, and he gives a significant role to bargaining power.

8.   Bowley comments as follows on this passage of Smith: '[t]his seems to have been a common view during the eighteenth century. Saving appears to have been regarded as dependent on the habits and outlook of society, on its thriftiness arising from an attitude of mind and on the desire of certain sections to better themselves' (1976, p. 194).

The interpretation in question conflicts particularly with Smith's recognition that 'constant scarcity of employment' or 'scarcity of hands' can exist in normal positions of the economy, and with the role he attributes to these circumstances in determining the natural wage rate.

We have seen, for example, that when the natural wage rises above subsistence level in rapidly growing economies, Smith explains this in terms of a 'scarcity of hands', which 'gives the labourers an advantage' by forcing the employers to compete amongst themselves (Smith, 1776, I.viii.16–17, quoted in Chapter 3, p. 54). To make this assertion compatible with the interpretation proposed by Hollander and others, it would have to be taken as describing only a 'transitory phase'. Once the natural wage reached its new, higher natural level – meaning the level at which the working population and the demand for labour are equal and grow at the same rate – the labour shortage would disappear. This idea is not convincing.

As I argued in the last chapter (pp. 53–7), Smith refers to different 'circumstances of society' associated with varying levels of the natural wage. These circumstances include both the 'scarcity of hands' occurring in rapidly developing economies, and the 'constant scarcity of employment' which in a stationary economy makes wages coincide with the 'lowest rate consistent with common humanity'. Smith sees the 'scarcity of hands' or of employment as situations persistent enough to modify the 'ordinary or average' level of the wage which is its natural rate. What keeps the natural wage above subsistence level is the fact that the demand for labour grows more rapidly than the population (and not that population grows at a positive rate equal to that of labour demand).[9]

If the economic system were generally characterized by conditions of 'dynamic equilibrium' between population growth and the growth of demand for labour, Smith's references to the 'scarcity

9.   The idea that, in Smith's analysis, increased wage levels in growing economies are caused by an increase in the 'demand for labour' more rapid than the increase of population, is maintained, among others, by Cannan, 1893, p. 237; Stigler, 1965, p. 193; Lowe, 1975, p. 418. But these writers interpret Smith's theory as based on the theory of the wages fund; therefore they interpret the term 'demand for labour' as meaning a predetermined 'fund' for the maintenance of the workers. Here, however, the term 'demand for labour' is understood as equivalent to 'employment' (see Chapter 1, pp. 5–7 and Chapter 6, pp. 177–84)

of hands' and to the role of competition among masters in modifying the general tendency of the natural wage towards a minimum subsistence level would make no sense. His indication of a 'constant scarcity of employment' and competition among workers as an explanation of that tendency would be equally meaningless.

There is another reason for caution with regard to the interpretation of Smith's natural wage as the result of a 'dynamic equilibrium' based on a precise quantitative relation between wages and population growth.

Smith's discussion suggests that the relation between wages and population growth is not mechanical, in contrast with the possibility of defining a generally valid quantitative relation between them.

Spengler, for example, points out that when Smith says higher wages lead to a reduction in infant mortality and thus to an increase in population, he is referring to working classes which live in extreme poverty, like that of Scotland. At the other extreme, in the American colonies the high economic contribution made by children to the family favours a rise in the birth rate. Thus, Spengler argues, it does not follow that Smith had in mind a positive relationship between wages and population, valid for all countries and all historical conditions. For example, a rise in working-class incomes might induce a change in habits of consumption in favour of 'conveniences and luxuries', rather than to an increase in population.[10]

The desirability of a less rigid interpretation of Smith's population theory, suggested by Spengler, is also suggested by a passage on the effects of a tax on 'luxuries' consumed by the working classes. Smith observes that the resulting drop in income may actually have favourable effects on the population:

> The high price of such commodities does not necessarily diminish the ability of the inferior ranks of people to bring up families. [...] Their ability to bring up families, in consequence of this forced frugality, instead of being diminished, is

---

10. Spengler, 1959, pp. 6–7. With regard to the role of the population theory in Smith, see also O'Brien, who, while asserting that 'wages were determined by the interaction of population and capital advanced' (1975, p. 36), also writes that 'Adam Smith, like most writers of his time, had recognized some sort of interaction of population, growth, and wage levels, but he did not attach any great significance to it' (ibid., p. 38).

frequently, perhaps, increased by the tax. (Smith, 1776, V.ii.k.7)[11]

Thus, it looks as though Smith's idea of the relation between wages and population growth is much more open to different outcomes than the determination of a 'dynamic equilibrium' natural wage would imply. At the same time a non-mechanical relation between population and working-class income is more consistent with other aspects of Smith's discussion of wages, especially the role of unemployment and labour shortages in determining the natural wage.

In my opinion Smith's statement that wage variations determine the adjustment of population growth to the needs of accumulation can be seen as an attempt to identify the forces favouring a tendency of the supply of labour to increase when the demand for labour rises in the course of economic growth, and to decrease when the demand falls with economic decline. Such a tendency excludes the unlikely occurrence of indefinitely increasing imbalances between opportunities for employment and the available labour force; and it ensures that the lack of hands will not hinder economic development. This view reflects the classical idea of labour as a 'producible commodity' rather than a 'scarce resource', clearly expressed by Smith when he writes that 'the demand for men [...] regulates the production of men'.

But the process whereby the population varies according to the requirements of accumulation must not be interpreted as a tendency to equality of growth rates, based on a determinate and stable quantitative relation between population growth and wages. Persistent imbalances between employment and the supply of labour do normally occur, and they influence the natural wage.

MALTHUS'S *ESSAY ON POPULATION*: ELEMENTS OF CONTINUITY AND CHANGE WITH RESPECT TO THE PREVIOUS TRADITION

The first edition of Malthus's *Essay on the principle of population*

---

11. See also Hollander, who recognizes that 'Smith's allowance that productive workers might choose to enjoy above–subsistence wages in the form of luxury goods plays havoc, potentially, with the automatic population response usually envisaged' (1973, p. 162).

(1798) was a pamphlet which, as its full title declares,[12] was meant as a critique of the egalitarian ideas which certain intellectuals, influenced by the events and ideas of the French Revolution (especially Godwin), were defending in England with some success.[13]

In the preface, Malthus says that the *Essay* owes its origins to a conversation with a friend (actually his father Daniel Malthus) about Godwin's essay *Avarice and Profusion* – a conversation which then went on to consider the more general question of the possible future improvement of society. In the first chapter of the essay Malthus observes that the great recent discoveries in the field of 'natural philosophy' and still more that 'tremendous phenomenon in the political horizon, the French revolution', had caused many people to think they were living in a historical period full of very important changes that would somehow be decisive for the future of humanity. With regard to the possibilities for social improvement, while some saw prospects for progress to a degree formerly inconceivable, others defended the existing state of things. Malthus, for his part, declared: 'I ardently wish for such happy improvements. But I see great, and to my understanding, unconquerable difficulties on the way to them' (Malthus, 1798, I, p. 7).

The aim of the *Essay*, then, is to examine, in the light of the 'principle of population', the possibility of realizing egalitarian social systems. In dealing with this question, Malthus also considers measures aimed at a redistribution of income in favour of the working classes, and in this connection he discusses the effects of current legislation on poor relief.

12. *An essay on the principle of population as it affects the future improvement of society, with remarks on the speculations of Mr Godwin, M. Condorcet and other writers.* Malthus (1766–1834) came from an intellectual family: his father, for example, corresponded with Rousseau, Hume and Godwin. T.R. Malthus was educated at home and then at Cambridge, where he studied mathematics at Jesus College. In 1788, after obtaining his degree, he took religious orders. He became a fellow of his college, and in 1805 professor of modern history and political economy at the college recently founded at Haileybury by the East India Company, where he remained for the rest of his life. He is best known for his *Essay on the principle of population,* which had numerous editions. His other main work was the *Principles of political economy,* whose first edition dates from 1820; he also published many other essays on economic questions.

13. Cf. K. Smith, 1951, who attributes the great success of this work largely to the fact that it discusses the ideas of Godwin, who was then very fashionable among young intellectuals.

Before Malthus, Wallace (1761) and Townsend (1786) had already used the idea of a pressure of population on scarce resources in a similar context. Wallace, however, saw the shortage of food that would occur 'when the whole earth is cultivated like a garden' as an obstacle to the viability of egalitarian social systems at some distant and hypothetical future time.

Townsend more closely anticipated the ideas of Malthus: he used the principle of population to interpret the current situation and to criticize legislation on the poor. But his *Dissertation* did not have the same wide circulation or impact on public opinion as Malthus's *Essay*, which for many years continued to be the object of polemics whose echoes are still evident, for example, in the writings of Marx and Engels.

Except for Townsend's work, the conclusions Malthus drew from his theory of population were new. The novelty is associated with the presence in the essay of certain analytical differences from the preceding tradition. These differences are in some ways sharper in the first edition of the *Essay*, whose content we shall examine below; but they remain in Malthus's later works on population theory.

The 'Essay on Population'

The thesis of the *Essay* is that the potential capacity for population growth is greater than the capacity for increasing the production of the food necessary for human survival.

When the population is not limited by the scarcity of resources, says Malthus, it increases in a geometrical progression; whereas the production of food increases arithmetically. These potentially divergent rates of growth must be kept equal by men's need for food to survive. This involves 'a strong and constantly operating check on population from the difficulty of subsistence. This difficulty must fall somewhere; and must necessarily be severely felt by a large portion of mankind' (Malthus, 1798, I, p. 9).

The difference between the growth rates of the population (unless somehow checked) and the food supply is argued in the following way. In the American colonies, it is maintained, the population had doubled in 25 years. This is taken to be the rate of population growth when unconstrained by scarcity. According to Malthus, in the historical experience of all known types of society from the primitive to the contemporary, rates of population growth were lower than that of North America, and this proves the 'constantly operating check on population'.[14]

This argument is accompanied by another, which is simply a statement – not based on any historical or empirical observation – that in countries which have been inhabited for a long time agricultural production cannot be increased at the same rate at which the population could potentially increase. That is to say it cannot be doubled in 25 years, or even if this were possible once it could not be repeated afterwards.

Thus the pressure of population on resources is the cause of poverty, and it rules out any possible improvement of living conditions for the working classes:

> [...] there is a constant effort towards an increase of population. This constant effort as constantly tends to subject the lower classes of the society to distress and to prevent any great permanent amelioration of their condition. (Ibid., p. 14)

The argument regarding the different rates of progression – geometrical and arithmetical – remains the keystone of Malthusian theory through all the later editions of the *Essay*,[15] though the arithmetical progression was later replaced (or accompanied) by the law of diminishing returns on land.[16]

14. This growth of population in the American colonies, according to both Smith and Malthus, was independent of the increased numbers resulting from immigration. Of course this assertion, like all those concerning population in that period, is an estimate of doubtful accuracy; but here we are mainly interested in examining the analytical aspects of Malthus's theory rather than the validity of its empirical foundations. It may be observed that the rapid increase of population in North America could be attributed not to the absence of constraints, as Malthus says, but (as had been argued by Smith) to the exceptional stimulus to procreation owing to the shortage of labour, which meant that children could make a high economic contribution to the family.

15. With regard to the consequences of this difference in (potential) rates of growth between the population and the means of subsistence, two distinct possibilities have been noted: 1) in a more or less distant future, when the productive capacities of the earth have been fully and intensively exploited, the further growth of the population will be prevented by the impossibility of further increasing the means of subsistence; 2) the population constantly tends to increase more rapidly than resources and this pressure on available resources constantly generates widespread poverty. This causes illness, high death rates and occasional famines, thus preventing a more rapid growth of the population (Cannan,1893, pp. 135–6). The first proposition, largely accepted even by critics of Malthus, had already been formulated, as we have seen, by Wallace (1761). What characterizes the position of Malthus is the second proposition (in addition to the passages quoted in the text, see Malthus, 1798, I, p. 53)

16. Meek notes, in this connection, that 'the "arithmetical progression" was in fact purely

According to Malthus, population can be checked not only by the poverty caused by the pressure of population on resources, but also by 'vice', by which he means the practice of abortion and contraception as well as sexual relations outside marriage or not aiming at procreation. While this 'vice' might in principle reduce poverty by limiting the expansion of the population, Malthus condemns such practices on moral grounds and declares that even in the 'most vicious societies' the population tends to grow faster than the means of subsistence (ibid. p. 14). To the restraints imposed by poverty and vice, in later editions Malthus adds a third possible preventive obstacle to population growth – that of prudent abstention from marriage. The possibility of such a control on population growth is also discussed in the first edition of the *Essay*, but there it is dismissed as not very realistic and hence irrelevant to the analysis.

Because poverty is the consequence of natural laws governing population growth and agricultural production, it cannot be overcome through changes in the institutions and human laws that regulate present-day society. Thus the principle of population could not only be used to deny the hopes for progress raised by egalitarian theories, but could also show the ineffectiveness and harmfulness of the existing poor laws in England – a source of constant anxiety because of the increase in pauperism and the funds required for poor relief.

According to Malthus, attempts to abolish (or diminish) inequality in the distribution of wealth and income would only reduce everyone to the same poverty: 'no possible form of society could prevent the almost constant action of misery upon a great part of mankind, if in a state of inequality, and upon all, if all were equal'(ibid.,

chimerical. Recognizing this Malthus's followers began to substitute another allegedly 'natural law', the so called 'law of diminishing return' for the discredited 'arithmetical ratio' and Malthus himself laid increasing emphasis upon this law in successive editions of the *Essay*. But this does not save the 'principle of population' from collapse. The "law of diminishing returns", in fact, is just as chimerical as the "aritmetical ratio"(1954, p. 177). In support of this assertion Meek then quotes the criticisms of that 'law' made by Marx and Engels, who give great importance to the role of scientific and technical progress in increasing the productivity of land (ibid., pp. 184–5). Robbins also brings out the importance, in Malthus's writings on population, of the 'law of diminishing returns', which he, unlike Meek, sees as an indication of the importance of Malthus's contribution to the history of economic thought (1970, pp. 85–91).

pp. 16–17). And this is because 'The superior power of population cannot be checked without producing misery and vice' (ibid.).

This conclusion crucially depends not only on the rapid growth of the population that would result from redistribution of income, but also on the difficulty of adjusting agricultural production to the increased demand (Cannan, 1893, pp. 238–40). This emerges clearly in Malthus's discussion on the ineffectiveness of transferring monetary income from the rich to the working classes:

> Suppose that by a subscription of the rich the eighteen pence a day which men earn now was made up five shillings, it might be imagined, perhaps, that they would then be able to live comfortably and have a piece of meat every day for their dinners. But this would be a very false conclusion. (Malthus,1798, I, p. 30)

The reason initially put forward by Malthus is that the total available quantity of meat is fixed and cannot be increased; the price would increase and the pattern of consumption would remain unchanged in real terms. He then considers the possibility that the increased price of meat, if persistent, would increase production; but this, he again observes, would not be advantageous because it could happen only at the expense of production of other agricultural subsistence goods; while the overall supply of these goods is something that cannot be changed by the distribution of income:

> when subsistence is scarce in proportion to the number of people, it is of little consequence whether the lowest members of the society possess eighteen pence or five shillings. They must at all events be reduced to live upon the hardest fare and in the smallest quantity. (Ibid., p. 31)

This view, however, is clearly in conflict with the then established economic theory, which held that a change in the normal quantity demanded for a commodity (owing to changes in tastes, income distribution or accumulation) would lead to a corresponding change in its production. Malthus was aware of this, as he finally addressed the possible objection that an increased demand for food would induce their production to increase:

> It will be said, perhaps, that the increased number of purchasers in every article would give a spur to productive industry and the whole produce of the island would be increased. This might in some degree be the case. But the spur that these fancied riches would give to population would more than counterbalance it,

and the increased produce would be to be divided among a more than proportionably increased number of people. (Ibid.)

In the end, Malthus's argument is that the production of food tends to increase more slowly than the population. But he often also inclines to the view that the supply of food for the workers is given, independent of the existing demand for it and of variations in that demand.[17] To support his assertions on the inefficacy of increasing the workers' money income, Malthus also has to exclude another element of possible flexibility of the food supply in response to changing demand: the importation of food from other countries. He does this by arguing that only in a very small country could such imports suffice to meet the needs of consumers, and anyway the price of the food would rise substantially (ibid., p. 109).

Lastly, we may observe that the argument about the difficulty and slowness of adjustment of agricultural production is particularly hard to sustain if this adjustment can be made simply by changing the use of the already cultivated land in favour of food typically consumed by the working classes. This possibility did not escape Malthus himself, and it leads him to admissions that seem to contradict his thesis on the inefficacy of income redistribution:

> I cannot help thinking, that the present demand for butchers' meat of the best quality, and the quantity of good land that is in consequence annually employed to produce it, toghether with the great number of horses at present kept for pleasure, are the chief causes that have prevented the quantity of human food in the country from keeping pace with the generally increased fertility of the soil and a change of custom in these respects would, I have little doubt, have a very sensible effect on the quantity of subsistence in the country, and consequently on its population. (Ibid., p. 112)

17. In this connection consider the following passage: 'The constant effort towards population, which is found to act even in the most vicious societies, increases the number of people before the means of subsistence are increased. The food therefore which before supported seven millions must now be divided among seven millions and a half or eight millions. The poor consequently must live much worse, and many of them be reduced to severe distress. [...] During this season of distress, the discouragement to marriage, and the difficulty of rearing a family are so great that the population is at a stand. In the mean time [...] cultivators employ more labour upon their land [...] till ultimately the means of subsistence become in the same proportion to the population as at the period from which we set out. The situation of the labourer being then tolerably comfortable, the restraints to population are loosened, and the same retrograde and progressive movements with respect to happiness are repeated' (Malthus, I, pp. 14-15; see also ibid., p. 109)

But such a change, which he admits would significantly affect the supply of food, is attributed by Malthus simply to a change in 'custom'. He ignores the possibility that it might result from a redistribution of income among social classes with different habits of consumption.

Malthus's denial of the efficacy of a transfer of money income from the upper classes to the working classes suggests that for a given total food supply in the economy he considers the proportion allotted to the workers as fixed. Indeed, he rules out the possibility that the workers' income might be increased by reducing the consumption of the upper classes. At the level of economic analysis, this attitude leads to another important consequence, i.e. the principle that any improvement of the living conditions of one section of the working classes can be realized only at the expense of other workers. From this derives his position on the Poor Laws and their effects of 'redistributing' income from the industrious and independent poor to the assisted poor through increased food prices. Not only did the Poor Laws lead to increases in the working-class population by allowing the otherwise not economically independent poor to survive and reproduce, but they did so 'without increasing the food for its support' (ibid., p. 33).[18]

Malthus and earlier writings on population

Malthus's conclusions concerning the causes of poverty and the impossibility of amending it (for example by redistributing income), represent a novelty with respect to population theory and economic theory as developed until then.

Of course, there are also elements of continuity: the idea of a link between the growth of population and increased food supply is not new, nor is the idea that the abundance or scarcity of the latter may influence changes in the population by affecting the death rate.

Yet before Malthus it seemed clear to economists studying population size (Cantillon and Steuart, among others) that except in a primitive society based on 'hunting and gathering' or on production for self-consumption, the availability of food for the working classes depends not only on resources (area and fertility of land) and

---

18. Malthus's proposition that the Poor Laws do not cause an increase in the means of subsistence available for the working classes is criticized by Ricardo (see below).

technical skills, but above all: 1) on opportunities for employment, which in turn depend on the development of productive activities, and 2) on the wage level. They held that where a division of labour exists it is the workers' ability to pay that activates agricultural production and enables the working classes to consume. In their view, agricultural production obeys the same laws that regulate the production of any other commodity: it adjusts to the 'effectual demand', which in the case of food depends mainly on the purchasing power of the working classes. Thus a persistent increase in that power, following an increase in employment or wages, could lead to an increase in the supply of food for the workers. Natural limits on the expansion of agricultural production seemed nonexistent or, at least, irrelevant to the present situation.

In addition, the pre-Malthusian economists saw the relation between food supply and population as being regulated by the habits of consumption prevailing at different social levels. Even among the working classes, decisions about marriage and the number of children were regarded as dependent on the ability to maintain one's family at the appropriate levels, which may change in the course of time.[19]

With regard to the food supply, the difference between Malthus's view and that of the earlier theorists emerges explicitly when he criticizes Smith for having erroneously identified 'every increase of the revenue or stock of a society as an increase in these funds [for the maintenance of labour]' (ibid., p. 108). According to Smith, the increase in wealth of a nation causes an increase in the demand for labour, and thus leads to an improvement in the living conditions of the workers. According to Malthus, such an improvement is possible only if the increase in wealth follows an increase in agricultural production, and thus in the quantity of food available for the maintenance of the workers. An increase in manufacturing production and employment would bring no benefit, and any rise in wages would in this case be only nominal since the food supply would remain unchanged: 'It is a self evident proposition that any general rise in the price of labour, the stock of provisions remaining the same, can only be a nominal rise, as must very shortly be

---

19. This last difference from the preceding tradition was attenuated in later editions of the *Essay* (see below, pp.112–4)

followed by a proportional rise in the price of provisions' (ibid., p. 109).

This might seem a pointless remark, as obviously the workers' consumption cannot rise unless there is a corresponding rise in production of the agricultural goods they consume. But it actually reveals Malthus's particular view, whereby the supply of food, unlike that of other products, adjusts to changes in demand only slowly and with difficulty, if at all. It follows that for Malthus, unlike Smith, the increase in employment and wages (and hence in workers' purchasing power), determined by the growth of national wealth, does not in itself ensure a corresponding increase in the food supply.[20]

Malthus's criticism of Smith is evidently open to the same objection one might make to his argument about the ineffectiveness of a transfer of money income to the working classes. His answer to the objection is also the same:

> it may be said, perhaps, that such an instance as I have supposed could not occur because the rise in the price of provisions would immediately turn some additional capital into the channel of agriculture. But this is an event which may take place very slowly. (Ibid., p. 109)

The points at which the *Essay* departs from the previous economic theory can now be summarized:

1. Malthus tends to consider the supply of food for the working classes as a given quantity, whose production can be increased only slowly and with difficulty; whereas the earlier economists (and, as we shall see, Ricardo) saw the supply of food for the working classes as dependent on their purchasing power, and hence on the level of employment and the normal wage rate; these writers never gave much weight to natural limits on resources.

2. For Malthus, the hard living conditions of the working classes were unalterable, because even if the production of food increases the benefit is nullified by the increase in population. Before Malthus's essay (and after it by Ricardo) it was generally

---

20. In this connection see Ricardo's illuminating criticism of Malthus precisely on the question of whether the increase in agricultural production must precede the increase in wages and population (Malthus's position) or follow it (Ricardo's view). See Chapter 5, pp. 132–3.

held that the conditions of the working classes could undergo lasting change through economic development, political and institutional changes, or changes in the habits of consumption of the working classes.

3. Earlier writers saw the laws governing population growth in a much more open and flexible way than Malthus did in the first edition of the *Essay*. In particular, they gave a central role to the working-class habits of consumption in regulating marriage and fertility, whereas Malthus believed in an irresistible natural impulse to procreate.

4. In all these differences the common thread is Malthus's tendency to stress the importance of natural phenomena (available resources, the reproductive instinct) in explaining the poverty of the working classes, rather than the complex of economic, institutional and social factors which in the classical view determined the natural wage and the level of employment.

That Malthus diverged from his predecessors and contemporaries on the points listed above is shown by the criticisms he received during the controversy that followed the publication of the *Essay*.[21] From the start the critics' arguments revolved around: 1) the fact that population growth was not necessarily limited only by poverty, but could be limited in general by 'prudence'. Individuals would tend to marry and have children only in so far as they could support their families at the prevailing standards of living (Godwin, 1801; Hall, 1805; cf. Smith, 1978, pp. 38–40, 53); 2) the importance of social causes, such as the existing distribution of income and private property, in producing the poverty of the working classes (Hall, 1805, cf. Smith, 1978, pp. 53–5); 3) the fact that food production is not fixed but depends on demand, as natural limits to an increase in agricultural production are absent or remote in time (Hall, 1805; Jarrold, 1806; Hazlitt, 1807; cf. Smith, 1978, pp. 53, 58–9).[22]

With regard to the theory of wages, Malthus's tendency to take the supply of food for the working classes as a datum anticipates a notion that later characterized the wage fund theory. In common

---

21. This controversy is illustrated and commented on in the interesting monograph by K. Smith, 1978.

22. Later the point was again raised by Weyland (1816) to whom Malthus replied in the *Appendix* to the 1817 edition of the *Essay* (III, pp. 616–7), and by Ricardo, both in his *Principles* and in his correspondence (see below, Chapter 5, pp. 132–3)

with that theory, he also states that any increase in income for one section of the working class must be at the expense of another part of it. The other feature of the wage fund theory – the inverse relation between wages and employment – does not appear in the first edition but is introduced later, beginning with the 1817 edition.[23] This does not mean that Malthus was a consistent and systematic exponent of the wage fund theory, whose full statement came later. In the *Essay* there are statements that contradict that theory, for example the passages (also added in the 1817 edition) where Malthus argues that there is wide unemployment in England and attributes it not to high wages but to the disappearance of the 'extraordinary stimulus to production' caused by the war, which in the preceding years had favoured the accumulation of capital and the growth of the population (III, pp. 510–13).

Evolution of Malthus's thinking on population
Since Malthus's economic writings cover a fairly long period of time, we may ask if, and in what manner, his analysis evolved after the first edition of the *Essay*.

Considerable changes were made between the first and second edition (1803), which transformed it from a pamphlet into a treatise. The second edition contains a wide-ranging discussion of how the principle of population operates in different countries and historical periods, using information gathered by Malthus himself during a European tour. In later editions the alterations were much less extensive although some of them are analytically important, such as the passages added in 1817 which were mentioned above.

According to what Malthus himself wrote, the new analytical element in the second edition is the consideration of a preventive constraint on population growth which does not fall into the category of vice: that is to say, the prudent abstention from marriage (and from immoral sexual behaviour) until one has enough resources to maintain a family (preface to the second edition, II,

---

23. These passages are quoted and discussed in Chapter 5, p. 134, together with the critical reaction of Ricardo. Marx, in his discussion of the wages fund, includes Malthus among the exponents of that theory: 'The dogma [to conceive social capital as a fixed magnitude], was used by Bentham [...] Malthus, James Mill, MacCulloch, etc., for an apologetic purpose, and especially to represent one part of capital, namely, variable capital, or that part convertible into labour-power, as a fixed magnitude' (Marx, 1887, p. 571).

p. iii).

The introduction of this 'preventive check' tends at least in principle to soften the pessimism of the first edition. Better education, for example, might prevent excessive population growth and improve the standards of living of the workers.

Scholars disagree, however, as to how radically the pessimism of the *Essay*'s conclusions is modified by the introduction of a preventive restraint on population growth. If in theory the 'principle of population' becomes more open in its possible consequences, in practice Malthus re-proposes all the conclusions already present in the first edition. There are therefore some grounds for the view of R. Meek and K. Smith that not only is there no essential change in the basic lines of Malthus's analysis, but there is no real attenuation of his pessimism (Meek, 1954; Smith, 1978). In their view he saw little possibility of redeeming the condition of the poor through widespread prudence with regard to marriage and fertility; his main point seems to be to blame the poor for their own condition.[24]

However, apart from the question of Malthus's pessimism, the essence of his analysis of the causes of poverty remains unchanged; that is, the argument is based on the different progressions (arithmetical and geometrical) operating in the growth of food production and of population, and the resulting continuous pressure of population on scarce resources. These central features of the analysis are present in all the editions of the *Essay*, and are restated

---

24. As to the possibility that the effect of the different rates of progression of population and food production will be modified through prudent behaviour, Meek comments: 'Malthus himself seems to have placed very little reliance on this remedy. [...] One is led to suspect that Malthus's main reason for introducing "moral restraint" was to preserve the good name of the Deity from the imputations which some evilly-disposed people might maintain that the principle of population cast upon it' (Meek, 1954, p. 181). In support of this view Meek cites the following passage of Malthus: 'As it appears therefore, that it is in the power of each individual to avoid all the evil consequences to himself and society resulting from the principle of population, by the practice of a virtue clearly dictated to him by the light of nature, [...] we can have no reason to impeach the justice of the Deity, because his general laws make this virtue necessary, and punish our offences against it by the evils attendant upon vice, and the pains that accompany the various forms of premature death'(Malthus, 1826, quoted in Meek, 1954, n. 26). In effect, the assignment to the poor of the blame for their own state (through not abstaining from marriage and procreation), which emerges in this and other passages of Malthus, is an important and recurrent theme of his analysis – so much so that Bendix considers it the main ideological innovation of the *Essay*, as against the former paternalism of the aristocratic classes in relation to the lower social ranks, with its associated idea of a duty to relieve their distress (Bendix, 1956, pp. 81–6).

in the appendix that Malthus added to the *Essay* from 1817 on, to summarize and sharpen his position and answer the criticisms against it. The same ideas appear again in the *Summary View on the Principle of Population* published in 1830.

In Malthus's works on population one can undoubtedly also find statements that contrast with the aspects I have emphasized. For example, in one passage of his *Principles* he summarizes his point of view on population in the following way:

> I all along said, that population might be redundant, and greatly redundant, compared with the demand for it and the actual means of supporting it, although it might most properly be considered as deficient, and greatly deficient, compared with the extent of territory, and the powers of such territory to produce additional means of subsistence. (Malthus, 1820, VI, pp. 263–4)

Here Malthus explains the limits to population growth as Steuart had done, in terms not of the 'physical' impossibility of increasing agricultural production, but of the existing demand for labour: it is the insufficiency of that demand that leads to an 'excess' of population. This position, however, is inconsistent with his argument that the living conditions of the working population cannot be ameliorated because agricultural production cannot increase (fast enough) in response to an increase in wages or in population.

Despite the existence of elements belonging to the earlier tradition, which conflict with the idea of the 'constantly operating' check on population due to scarcity of resources, it is the latter view which undoubtedly forms the hub of the Malthusian theory of population, and it is that view which was regarded with approbation or hostility by his contemporaries. James Mill, for example, sums up Malthus's contribution as follows:

> Though no part of the doctrine of Mr. Malthus has been left uncontested, it is now, among thinking men, pretty generally allowed that, excepting certain favourable situations, as in new countries, where there is unoccupied land of sufficient productiveness, which may be placed under cultivation as fast as men are multiplied, a greater number of human beings is produced than there is food to support. This, it is understood, is the habitual condition of human nature. (J. Mill, quoted by St Clair, 1965, p. 111)[25]

25. Unlike Spengler (1945), I do not believe it is possible to harmonize Malthus's different propositions, and combine the analyses contained in the *Essay* and the *Principles*, by attributing to him the idea that population growth depends on the

The chapter on wages in Malthus's *Principles of political economy* include elements of different origin. Some seem derived from the Smithian tradition, and others are closer to the *Essay*.

Like Smith, in the *Principles* Malthus sees population changes as regulated by the relation between the income of the working classes (given by wage and employment levels) and the minimum level of 'subsistence', seen as historically determined and modifiable only with difficulty and very slowly over time (Malthus, 1820, V, pp. 183, 187–8). He also takes up the theme, already introduced by earlier writers, of the influence of forms of government on the living conditions and habits of the working classes (ibid., p. 184). Thus the social and institutional elements which had characterized Smith's theory of wages are given attention in the *Principles*. But Malthus stresses the effect of these elements on the fertility of the working classes rather than directly on their relative power in wage bargaining.

He also explicitly criticizes Smith's assertion that in stationary economies wages do not fall below the minimum level compatible with common humanity. For Malthus that sentiment has nothing to do with determining wages:

> [...] it is not common humanity which interferes to prevent the price of labour from falling still lower [...] common humanity cannot alter the funds for the maintenance of labour. While these are stationary, and the habits of the lower classes prompt them to supply a stationary population cheaply, the wages of labour will be scanty, but still they cannot fall below what is necessary, under the actual habits of the people, to keep up a stationary population; [...] the principle of demand and supply would always interfere to prevent such wages as would either occasion an increase or diminution of people. (Ibid., p. 181)

Malthus therefore excludes the role of custom and social norms in sustaining the minimum level of wages even when there is unemployment. According to him, what determines the wage rate in a stationary, declining or growing economy is simply the cost of supporting the required stationary, declining or growing population.

increase of employment, which in turn depends on the 'effective demand' for the products. Even in the appendix to the 1826 edition of the *Essay*, and in the *Summary View on the Principle of Population* of 1830 (that is, after the publication of his *Principles*), Malthus restates the argument about geometrical and arithmetical progressions, i.e. the idea that it is the scarcity of subsistence goods that restrains population growth. The idea that the positions taken in the *Essay* and in the *Principles* are contradictory and irreconcilable is also expressed by Stigler (1952, p. 148).

Consumption habits play a role only in so far as they determine that cost by regulating reproduction. This goes together with his insistence, in opposition to Smith, on the role of the 'principle of supply and demand' in determining both the average level of wages and the relative wages for different occupations (ibid., pp. 178–181).

RICARDO, THE MALTHUSIAN THEORY OF POPULATION AND THE 'IRON LAW OF WAGES'

Factors determining the amount of food available for the working classes

Ricardo[26] is generally said to have concurred with Malthus's theory of population, which is considered to play an important role in his theory of wages. In the next chapter I shall discuss Ricardo's wage theory in depth and consider the role of population adjustments in that context; here we shall examine his attitude towards Malthus's population theory.

The idea of an affinity between Ricardo and Malthus with regard to population theory is supported by their agreement on the necessity of abolishing the Poor Laws and by the reasons they gave to justify this position. Both believed those laws would encourage population growth, and that the growth of population tends to keep wages at

---

26. David Ricardo (1772–1823) came from a rich Jewish family. As a young man he began a career as a stockbroker. The considerable economic success of this activity enabled him to devote himself to his studies from the age of 25. His first publications on economics, dealing with monetary questions, made him one of the main protagonists of the 'bullion controversy' of that time. In 1815 he published his *Essay on the Influence of a Low Price of Corn on the Profits of Stock*, in which he argued against the restriction of corn imports (this was nevertheless imposed by law in the same year). In 1817 he published the first edition of his *Principles*, followed by a second, with small modifications, in 1819, and finally a third, with more extensive and important changes, in 1821 (for an analysis of the problems underlying the successive transformations of the *Principles* see Sraffa, 1951). In 1819 Ricardo became a Member of Parliament; he did not belong to any party, and on many points sided with the opposition, but on monetary questions he supported the Conservative government. After the publication of the *Principles*, though he published other essays on monetary and fiscal matters, Ricardo concentrated on problems connected with the theory of value, and worked on the essay *Absolute Value, Exchangeable Value*. This work, which J. Mill considered too provisional in form to be publishable, lay forgotten until it was rediscovered and published by Sraffa in the *Works and Correspondence* of Ricardo.

their lowest levels.[27]

But there are important analytical differences between Malthus and Ricardo even with regard to the theory of population and its consequences.[28]

Ricardo certainly shared the view that there is a relation between the amount of food available for consumption by the working classes and population growth. This idea, as we have seen, is not peculiar to Malthus but characterizes all the eighteenth-century theories of population (although after the publication of the *Essay* it was generally associated with Malthus's name). The real distinguishing feature of his analysis is the idea that what causes the scarcity of food for the working classes is the difficulty of increasing its production in response to increases in demand. On this point Ricardo differed from Malthus. For example, he did not share Malthus's idea that an increase in the food supply is a precondition for increases in wages or employment:

> Mr. Malthus appears to me to be too much inclined to think that population is only increased by the previous provision of food [...] instead of considering that the general progress of population is affected by the increase of capital, the consequent demand for labour, and the rise of wages; and that the production of food is but the effect of that demand. [...] This demand then is the effect of an increase of capital and population, but not the cause – it is only because the expenditure of the people takes this direction, that the market price of necessaries exceeds the natural price, and that the quantity of food required is produced. (Ricardo, 1821, I, pp. 406–7)[29]

Thus Ricardo held that the supply (production) of food depended on the size and purchasing power of the working population, not vice

27. Consider the following passages from Ricardo's *Principles*: 'The pernicious tendency of these laws [poor laws] is no longer a mystery, since it has been fully developed by the able hand of Mr. Malthus; [...] It is a truth that admits not a doubt, that the comforts and well being of the poor cannot be permanently secured without some regard on their part, or some effort on the part of the legislature, to regulate the increase of their numbers, and to render less frequent among them early and improvident marriages' (Ricardo, 1821, I, pp. 106–7); 'From the effect of the principle of population on the increase of mankind, wages of the lowest kind never continue much above that rate which nature and habit demand for the support of the labourers' (ibid., I, p. 159).
28. This view is shared by Cannan, who mentions Ricardo's criticisms of Malthus on some aspects of population theory (1893, p. 239)
29. On this subject, again in a polemic with Malthus, see also *Notes on Malthus*, II, pp. 135–6 and the letter to Malthus, Jan. 1816, VII, pp. 2–3; see also the letters to Trower, 15 and 26 Sept. and 3 Oct. 1820, VIII, pp. 236–7, 255–8, 273.

versa as Malthus said. Consequently, in one respect Ricardo had a different opinion on the effects of the Poor Laws, and criticized Malthus for not recognizing that these laws actually increase the quantity of food available to the working classes:

> You do not always appear to me to admit that the tendency of the poor laws is to increase the quantity of food to be divided, but assume in some places that the same quantity is to be divided among a larger number. (Letter to Malthus, 21 Oct. 1817, VII, p. 202, see also letter to Malthus, 2 Jan. 1816, VII, p. 3)

The difference in the analytical premises of the two writers is also shown by the fact that Ricardo did not believe even a rapid increase in population would necessarily lead to a scarcity of food for the working classes. The following is his comment on an essay by Place on population:

> in the latter part of the first chapter it is I think *inferred that under a system of equality population would press with more force against the means of subsistence than it now does*. This I do not think is true. I believe, that under such system, mankind would increase much faster than it now does, but so would food also. A larger proportion of the whole capital of the country would be employed in the production of food-necessaries, and a less proportion in the production of luxuries, and thus we might go on, with an increase of capital, without any increase in difficulty [...] It should always be remembered that we are not forcing the production of food to the extent of our power. (Letter to Place, 9 Sept. 1821, IX, pp. 49–50)[30]

This passage is of particular interest as it shows that, as has been argued, accepting one aspect of the 'Malthusian' population theory (i.e, that population increases when workers' living conditions improve) does not necessarily lead to the same conclusions as those drawn by Malthus. Ricardo also holds that following a change in the distribution of income and wealth in favour of the working classes, the population will tend to increase. But this does not imply impoverishment (as Malthus believes); it simply leads to a change in the composition of production in favour of goods consumed by these social classes. In principle, therefore, the redistribution of income under an egalitarian system may bring lasting improvements in the living conditions of the working classes.

---

30. The work by Place on which Ricardo is commenting is *Illustrations of the Principle of Population: Including an Examination of the Proposed Remedies of Mr. Malthus, and a Reply to the Objections of Mr. Godwin and Others*, London, Longman, 1822.

Wages and population growth

Thus Ricardo's different view of the forces determining the amount of food available for the working classes leads him to dissent from Malthus even while accepting his position on the causes of change in the population. Let us now examine this latter aspect of the Malthusian theory, in which one might expect more agreement between the two writers.

Ricardo often states, especially in his *Principles*, that there is a positive relation between wages and population growth. But he often appears cautious in treating the 'principle of population' as a general 'law', and he seems more open than Malthus to the possibility of variations in that relation. In a letter to McCulloch commenting on an article by the latter in the *Edinburgh Review*, Ricardo argues that it can change in different circumstances, and may actually go in the opposite direction to what is usually assumed:

> Wages may be regulated, and may continue for a series of years, on a scale which shall allow the population regularly to increase from year to year in such a proportion as shall double it in 25 years. Under other circumstances this power of doubling may not be possible in less than 50, 100, or 200 years – or population may be so little stimulated by ample wages as to increase at the slowest rate – or it may even go in a retrograde direction. (Letter to McCulloch, 29 March 1820, VIII, p. 169)

Ricardo takes a similar position in the *Notes on Malthus*, suggesting that in his opinion there is not necessarily a close connection between population and food supply. In response to Malthus's assertion that the wages of the lowest paid workers can be considered constant over time, Ricardo writes:

> Why is this? Because population is found to increase invariably with the means of providing for it, and therefore its value in corn does not rise – but population and necessaries are not necessarily linked together so intimately – it is not difficult to conceive that with better education and improved habits, a day's labour may become much more valuable estimated even in what are now called the necessaries of the labourer (II, p. 115)

Also in the *Principles*, Ricardo states that '[t]he increase of population, and the increase of food will generally be the effect, but not the necessary effect of high wages' (I, pp. 406–7).

In substance, while Ricardo uses the 'Malthusian theory of population', taken as a positive relation between working-class income and population growth, he does not see that relation as a necessary one. He uses it with some caution, and reacts strongly (as in the letter to McCulloch and the comment on Malthus) when it is applied too mechanically.

Causes of poverty and the 'Iron Law of Wages'

On the whole, Ricardo seems closer to the ideas of Malthus's predecessors, such as Steuart and Cantillon, than to those of Malthus himself. He sees the relation between population and working-class income as something historically and socially given, which may change over time and in different social conditions, and which in any case depends on the consumption habits of the working classes. Furthermore, in his view the food supply depends on the demand for food, and thus mainly on the size of the working population and its purchasing power – which in turn depend on the levels of employment and wages. Thus Ricardo's view of the causes of poverty differs from that of Malthus.

Ricardo saw the causes of poverty in a growth of population more rapid than the accumulation of capital, and hence more rapid than the increase in *employment:*

> The real question at issue is not whether under favourable circumstances population will double in 25 or 50 years, but whether it has or not a tendency to increase faster than the capital which is to employ it, and if so what measures of legislation should be pursued. (Letter to Trower, 21 Apr. 1821, VIII, p. 368)[31]

The difference in the rates of growth of population and capital causes poverty as it results in unemployment and low wages.[32]

It follows that diminishing returns in agriculture may be a cause of poverty in Ricardo for different reasons than in Malthus. For Ricardo, it is not the case that diminishing returns make the adjustment of the food supply impossible or 'slow' in response to increased demand; rather, as the costs of production of wage goods increase, they cause a fall in the net income (surplus) available for investment. This leads to a slower rate of accumulation and to the

31. In this letter Ricardo comments on Malthus's *Essay* and Godwin's criticisms of it. Passages in which the poverty of the workers is attributed to a faster rate of population growth rather than of accumulation are also frequent in the *Principles* (see for example I, pp. 101, 165–6)
32. This point will be taken up again in Chapter 5, pp. 132–9.

emergence or widening of an excess supply of labour.[33]

Though the diminishing returns of agriculture play a central part in Ricardo's analysis, in contrast with Malthus he considers the attainment of a 'stationary state', in which accumulation cannot proceed because it is physically impossible to increase food production, to be an extremely remote event:

> The richest country in Europe is yet far distant from that degree of improvement, but if any had arrived at it, by the aid of foreign commerce, even such a country could go on for an indefinite time increasing in wealth and population, for the only obstacle to this increase would be the scarcity, and consequent high value, of food and other raw produce. Let these be supplied from abroad in exchange of manufactured goods, and it is difficult to say where the limit is at which you would cease to accumulate wealth and to derive profit from its employment. (*Funding System*, 1820, IV, p. 179; see also I, p. 109)[34].

Interpreters have tended to attribute to Ricardo and his predecessors a theory of population similar to that of Malthus. Accordingly, the tendency of wages to coincide with subsistence is usually seen as the consequence of population growth, i.e. as a statement of the 'iron law of wages'. I have argued that some important distinctions are necessary in this connection.

Malthus identifies the factors that lead to food scarcity as natural phenomena, in particular the limits to the increase of agricultural production. This leads Malthus, unlike the earlier economists and Ricardo, to treat the poverty of the working classes as impossible to modify. Or at least – and this is the main point here – as modifiable not through changes in income distribution,[35] but only through a drop in birth rate and hence population. That is why Marx described Malthus as the inventor of what Lassalle called the 'iron law of wages'.[36]

---

33. Cf. Ricardo. I, p. 98; again, for further discussion of this point, see Chapter 5 pp. 132–9

34. Note that in the quoted passage, in making further accumulation more or less possible, Ricardo stresses not the possibility (or otherwise) of further increasing agricultural production, but the possibility of deriving sufficient profit for investment. The conditions of agricultural production are important because, through their effects on the natural wage, they determine the rate of profit.

35. For example through the action of 'coalitions' of workers; cf. Malthus's assertion and Ricardo's criticism cited in Chapter 5, p. 134

36. This was criticized by Marx: '[i]t is well known that nothing of the "iron law of wages" belongs to Lassalle except the word "iron" [...] what is [his basis for it]? [...] it is the malthusian theory of population [...] But if this theory is correct, then again I

For the predecessors of Malthus (and, as we shall see, for Ricardo) the tendency for wages to coincide with the minimum subsistence level rests on considerations different from those that characterize the Malthusian 'iron law'. They saw this tendency as neither immutable nor necessary; they imputed it to specific and economic conditions such as unemployment, or the political and institutional features of the society under observation.[37]

SUMMARY

The aim of this chapter has been to examine the relation between the theory of population and the analysis of the labour market in the classical economists.

Until Smith, the population trends and the situation of the labour market were not usually seen as related through changes in wage levels. The prevailing idea was that of a direct link between the size (and growth) of employment and that of the population. This idea apparently developed in response to the question of how the growth (or decline) of productive activities is generally accompanied by an increase (or reduction) of the labouring population available for employment in those activities. This rise (or fall) of the labouring population was explained by migratory flows as well as by variations in the rates of death, marriage and birth which are directly induced by persistent changes in opportunities for employment. As persistent unemployment is regarded as a normal feature of the economy,

cannot abolish the law even if I abolish wage labour a hundred times over, because the law then governs not only the system of wage labour but every social system. Basing themselves directly on this, the economists have proved for fifty years and more that socialism cannot abolish poverty, which has its basis in nature, but can only generalize it, distribute it simultaneously over the whole surface of society!' (Marx, *Critique of the Gotha Programme* (1875), quoted in Meek, 1953, p. 118). See also Engels's comment on the subject: 'the Lassallean "iron law of wages" [...] is based on a quite antiquated economic view, namely, that the worker only receives on the average the minimum of the labour wage, because, according to Malthus's theory of population, there are always too many workers (this was Lassalle's argument). Now Marx has proved in detail in *Capital* that the laws regulating wages are very complicated, that sometimes one predominates and sometimes another, according to circumstances, that therefore they are in no sense iron but on the contrary very elastic [...] The malthusian basis for the law which Lassalle copied from Malthus and Ricardo (*with a falsification of the latter*) [...] has been refuted in detail by Marx in the section on *The process of capital accumulation*.' (Engels, letter to Bebel 18–28 March 1875, quoted by Meek, 1954, p. 117, italics added).

37. Chapter 3, pp. 35–58, above.

changes in the level of employment (at given wage levels) modify the total income received by the working classes.

This aspect of the role of population theory in the analysis of the labour market is still present in the work of Smith, who also meant to explain how 'the demand for men [...] regulates the production of men' (Smith, 1776, I.viii.40). But in Smith the increase of population is more closely linked with wage variations. On the basis of this, some interpreters take the view that Smith's theory of wages presupposes a precise mechanism for the adjustment of population to rising or falling wages, so that the natural wage is determined as the wage level at which the population growth rate matches that of employment.

This interpretation has been criticized on the grounds that such a definition of the natural wage conflicts with other important aspects of Smith's analysis – particularly with the role of 'constant scarcity of employment' or 'scarcity of hands' in determining the natural wage level. Hence I have suggested an interpretation whereby the influence of wages on population leads to a *tendency* for the latter to vary in the same direction as the demand for labour. Yet the natural wage is not determined as a 'dynamic equilibrium' price, and wage variations do not ensure equality between those two magnitudes or their rates of growth. Smith does not see the link between wages and population growth as a precise quantitative relation which is valid in all circumstances. In any case it depends on the habits of consumption of the working classes, which may change as a consequence of a rise in the wage level.

In Malthus the 'principle of population' is used to explain the poor living conditions of the working classes, and also to argue that those conditions cannot be permanently improved. These conclusions, however, depend on the presence in Malthusian theory of a new element, the idea that the means of subsistence cannot be increased in response to changes in demand. The food available for the working classes is taken as a fixed quantity that can be augmented only through an increase in agricultural production, which is too slow to keep up with population growth.

This notion, rather than the idea that population growth follows a wage increase, lies behind Malthus's conclusions as to the impossibility of permanently improving workers' living conditions through a change in income distribution. This emerges clearly from the comparison with Ricardo who, while accepting that a redistribution of wealth and income in favour of the working classes would lead to a faster population growth, did not share the opinion that this would cancel out the initial improvement of workers' living conditions. This difference arises from the fact that in Ricardo's theoretical framework, unlike that of Malthus, natural impediments to the increase of food production play no part. For Ricardo, diminishing returns in agriculture do not imply a difficulty in the adjustment of food supply to a change in demand (induced, for example, by a wage increase). What occurs is that diminishing returns lead to a slower pace of accumulation by reducing the surplus available for investment, and this will negatively affect the working classes by reducing the rate of growth of employment.[38] Poverty therefore is caused by the difference between the rates of growth of population and employment, not by pressure on fixed resources.

Another point of distinction between Malthus on the one hand and Ricardo and the previous tradition on the other is that the latter shows more caution with regard to the nature of the relation between changes in income and in population. Ricardo often remarks that this relation is not necessary, that population response may vary according to circumstances, and that it depends on the habits of life of the working classes, which are by no means immutable.

Thus we may conclude that the 'iron law of wages' cannot be attributed to the whole classical tradition: as Marx indicated, it arose from the Malthusian theory of population.

Until Smith the theory of population seems to have served mainly to provide an explanation – which *a posteriori* may appear inadequate[39] – of the tendency for the labour supply (i.e. the

---

38. Indeed, after the publication of the chapter 'On machinery' in the third edition of the *Principles*, and the consequent admission that capital accumulation may not be accompanied by increases in employment, or may actually generate unemployment, Ricardo's theoretical system already potentially contains elements of what would later be Marx's explanation of the existence of 'overpopulation' in the capitalist system (see note below).

39. In *Capital* Marx criticizes the theory of population as an explanation of a persistent excess supply of labour in the course of accumulation. He contrasts it with his own notion of the continuous formation of an 'industrial reserve army' generated by accumulation itself through the expulsion of labour power from pre-capitalist sectors and technical innovation: 'it is capitalistic accumulation itself that constantly

working population) to move in step with employment in the course of accumulation or decline. In this respect Ricardo's theory seems closer to that of Smith and his predecessors than to that of Malthus.

Probably as a result of the historical events they witnessed, Malthus and Ricardo expressed a more pessimistic view than that of their predecessors with regard to the consequences of population growth for the conditions of the working classes. There is evidence that in England around the middle of the eighteenth century the population began to grow faster than in the past, accelerating further from about 1780 to reach very high growth rates – never afterwards repeated – in the first two decades of the nineteenth century. While it seems sufficiently proven that the workers' standard of living improved between the end of the seventeenth century and about the middle of the eighteenth century, the same thing does not seem to have happened in the century that followed; in fact there are many indications that the workers' living conditions deteriorated in the second half of the eighteenth and the first decades of the nineteenth century.[40] Perhaps it was because of this experience that Ricardo wrote, '[t]he tendency of the population to increase is, in our state of society, more than equal to that of the capital to increase' (letter to Malthus, 5 Oct. 1816, VII, p. 72).

produces, and produces in the direct ratio of its own energy and extent, a relatively redundant population of labourers, i.e. a population of greater extent than suffices for the average needs of the self-expansion of capital, and therefore a surplus–population. [...] The labouring population therefore produces, along with the accumulation of capital produced by it, the means by which itself is made relatively superfluous, is turned into a relative surplus-population [...] This is a law of population peculiar to the capitalistic mode of production; and in fact every specific mode of production has its own special laws of population, historically valid within its limits alone. An abstract law of population exists for plants and animals only, and only in so far as man has not interfered with them' (Marx, 1887, I, pp. 590–2).

40. Cf. Deane, 1965. The demographic data are estimated by historians until the end of the eighteenth century; afterwards they come from census figures.

5. The Theory of Wages in Ricardo

INTRODUCTION

There is an ongoing controversy over the interpretation of Ricardo's wage theory, which is crucial for the evaluation of his work as a whole. The problem is whether Ricardo's theory and classical theory in general, was different from and alternative to the marginalist approach (as suggested by Sraffa and his followers),[1] or whether it contains elements that foreshadow today's prevalent theory, though without reaching a full formulation of it.[2]

The controversy has been fuelled by certain weaknesses and ambiguities in Ricardo's wage theory. I shall try to pinpoint these and trace their possible analytical origins.

After examining the salient propositions of the chapter on wages in Ricardo's *Principles*, I shall indicate the main problems arising from them. The following sections will examine these problems one by one: the role of the supply and demand for labour; why wages adjust following imposition of taxes on wages or wage goods; whether or not the natural wage is associated with a stationary state of the economy. Then we shall examine the differences between Smith's and Ricardo's wage theories, showing how these give rise to inconsistencies in Ricardo, and look into the possible reasons for those distinguishing features of Ricardo's theory. Lastly, in the light of the resulting interpretation, I shall discuss some representative contributions to the current debate on Ricardo's wage theory.

---

1. Actually, many neoclassical authorities have also denied any continuity between the neoclassical and classical theories of distribution, but have seen this lack of continuity as a proof of the shortcomings of the latter. See for example Hutchison, 1952.
2. This interpretation of Ricardo can be traced back to Marshall (1920, p. 671). Recent restatements of it are in Samuelson (1978, p. 1415) and Hollander (1979, pp. 3–4).

THE DEFINITIONS IN THE CHAPTER ON WAGES

Natural price of labour

In the *Principles* Ricardo opens his chapter on wages by stating that labour is a commodity like any other, in that labour is producible and is bought and sold on the market. This implies a distinction, analogous to that applied to the prices of goods, between the natural wage and the market wage. The former is defined as follows:

> The natural price of labour is that price which is necessary to enable the labourers, one with another, to subsist and to perpetuate their race, without either increase or diminution. (Ricardo, 1821, I, p. 93)

The level of this natural wage, Ricardo continues, depends on the commodities ('food, necessaries and conveniences') which have become 'essential from habit' for the worker and his family. Hence when the price of those goods changes the natural wage has to change so as to remain unaltered in real terms.[3]

As the natural wage is linked to the habits of consumption of the working classes, it is not constant over time:

> It is not to be understood that the natural price of labour, estimated even in food and necessaries, is absolutely fixed and constant. It varies at different times in the same country, and very materially differs in different countries. It essentially depends on the habits and customs of the people. (Ibid. p. 96–7)

Along the same lines are his remarks on the changes in workers' consumption habits which had occurred in England: 'many of the conveniences now enjoyed in an English cottage, would have been thought luxuries at an earlier period of our history' (ibid., p. 97).[4]
Yet many interpreters of Ricardo, even when they disagree on other

---

3. Ricardo defines the 'real value' of wages as 'the quantity of labour and capital employed in producing them', whereas their nominal value is defined as that measured 'either in coats, hats, money or corn' (Ricardo, 1821, 1, p. 50). To indicate what today we call real wages (i.e. the purchasing power of a given money wage), Ricardo generally refers to the goods which that wage can 'command'. In the following discussion, for the sake of simplicity, I shall use the current terminology rather than that suggested by Ricardo. Thus the term real wages will have its usual meaning, while I shall speak explicitly of changes in production costs or prices of wage goods when these cause changes in the natural wage. The latter term, as usual, refers to the money wage corresponding to a given level of consumption on the part of the workers.

4. On the importance of 'habits and customs' and their variations in determining the natural wage, see also *Notes on Malthus*, II, p. 115, quoted above, Chapter 4, p. 119

aspects, tend to treat the natural wage as constant in the course of economic development.[5]

Ricardo's belief that the natural wage may vary significantly during development is fully compatible with his treatment of the natural wage as a datum known at the moment of determination of relative prices and of incomes other than wages. The point is clearly explained by Torrens, to whose discussion of wages Ricardo explicitly refers (ibid., p. 96–7):

> [Alterations in the the natural price of labour] can be effected only by those circumstances of prosperity and decay, and by those moral causes of instruction and civilization, which are ever gradual in their operation. The natural price of labour, therefore, though it varies under different climates, and with the different stages of national improvement, may, in any given time and place, be regarded as very nearly stationary. (Torrens, 1815, pp. 64–5)

Market price of labour

After defining the natural wage as we have seen, Ricardo defines the market wage:

> The market price of labour is the price which is really paid for it, from the natural operation of the proportion of the supply to the demand; labour is dear when it is scarce, and cheap when it is plentiful. However much the market price of labour may deviate from its natural price, it has, like commodities, a tendency to conform to it. (Ricardo, 1821, I, p. 94)

Unlike Smith and the other authors heretofore examined, Ricardo then attributes the gravitation of the market wage around the natural wage to mechanisms of population adjustment induced by wage variations:

> It is when the market price of labour exceeds its natural price, that the condition of the labourer is flourishing and happy, that he has it in his power to command a greater proportion of the necessaries and enjoyments of life, and therefore to rear a healthy and numerous family. When however by the encouragement that high wages give to the increase of population, the number of labourers is increased, wages again fall to their natural price, and indeed from a reaction sometimes fall below it.
>
> When the market price is below its natural price, the condition of the labourer is most wretched: then poverty deprives them of those comforts which customs

---

5. What varies in the so-called 'variable-wage interpretations' is the market wage, while the natural wage remains unchanged through economic growth. The same is true in the interpretations of Kaldor (1955-56) and Pasinetti (1959-60) – though the latter states explicitly that the idea of wages as constant in time is just a simplifying assumption, not necessary to Ricardo's theory (cf. id. 1982, p. 240).

renders absolute necessaries. It is only after their privations have reduced their numbers, or the demand for labour has increased, that the market price of labour will rise to its natural price, and that the labourer will have the moderate comforts which the natural rate of wages will afford. (Ibid.).[6]

PROBLEMS OF INTERPRETATION

Ricardo's definitions, in view of other aspects of his economic theory, pose certain interpretative problems which I shall summarize briefly before discussing them in greater detail.

First, in defining the natural wage Ricardo draws a close analogy between it and the natural price of a commodity. In this he differs from Smith, who did not mention the adjustment of the supply of labour (i.e. the working population) to the level of demand as a condition for the establishment of the natural price of labour in the market. Rather, Smith saw the natural wage as influenced by labour market conditions, so that with a large excess supply of labour, other things being equal, the natural wage will tend to be lower than when there is a 'scarcity of hands'.

This innovation by Ricardo is associated with the fact that unlike Smith he introduces mechanisms of population change to correct deviations of the market from the natural wage due to imbalances between supply and demand for labour. This leads to a difficulty. Ricardo himself several times mentions the slowness of the adjustment process, owing to the time required for changes in the population to be felt on the labour market:

> labour is a commodity which cannot be increased and diminished at pleasure. If there are too few hats in the market for the demand the price will rise, but only for a short time; [...] but it is not so with men; you cannot increase their number in one or two years when there is an increase of capital, nor can you rapidly diminish their number when capital is in a retrograde state. (Ibid., p. 165; see also p. 220)

In addition, Ricardo sometimes treats as uncertain the mechanism whereby the market wage gravitates around the natural wage, that is

---

6. The gravitation of wages around the natural wage, when deviations are induced by changes in the proportion between employment and population, is attributed to the adjustment of population also by Torrens (1815, pp. 64–5).

the response of population to wage changes (Chapter 4, pp. 119–20). But such slowness and uncertainty conflict with the central role he assigns to the natural wage as opposed to the market wage:

> Having fully acknowledged the temporary effects which, in particular employments of capital, may be produced on the prices of commodities, as well as on the wages of labour, and the profits of stock, by accidental causes, without influencing the general price of commodities, wages, or profits, since these effects are equally operative in all stages of society, we will leave them entirely out of our consideration, whilst we are treating of the laws which regulate natural prices, natural wages and natural profits, effects totally independent of these accidental causes. (Ibid., pp. 91–2)

Second, Ricardo's definition of the natural wage as corresponding to a situation where the population reproduces itself 'without either increase or diminution' (ibid.) has suggested that the natural wage is associated with the stationary state. This raises two problems of interpretation. One is that such an association belies the centrality of the natural wage in Ricardo's analysis, as he regarded the stationary state as a very remote possibility (Chapter 4, p.121). The other is that in other parts of the *Principles* Ricardo uses a different definition of the natural wage.

Third, the gravitation of wages around the natural wage is attributed to population changes only when deviations arise from imbalances between the supply and demand for labour. According to Ricardo, however, this is not the mechanism whereby the natural (money) wage adjusts to changes in prices of necessary goods consumed by workers, or to taxes on such goods and on wages, so as to leave the purchasing power of the net wage unchanged. Why wages adjust in this case is a question which has often perplexed interpreters of Ricardo.

Lastly, an aspect of Ricardo's theory which must be clarified is what role the relation between population and the demand for labour plays in altering wages. This question has generally been dealt with in terms of the wage fund theory, whereby the wage equals the ratio between the 'demand for labour' (i.e. the given 'fund') and the fully employed working population. But this interpretation of Ricardo's theory conflicts with other aspects of his analysis, such as the conclusions of his chapter on machinery where he admits the possibility of unemployment. Thus we shall have to reassess the view that Ricardo's wage theory is based on the doctrine of the wages fund.

Let us consider the above questions in reverse order, beginning with the last.

THE 'PROPORTION OF SUPPLY TO DEMAND'

Absence of wage fund notions

As we have seen, Ricardo considers the 'proportion of supply to demand' for labour as one of the causes of variation in the market wage. In the chapter on wages he writes that: 'as we have considered money to be uniformly of the same value, it appears then that wages are subject to a rise or fall from two causes: 1st. The supply and demand of labourers. 2dly. The price of the commodities on which the wages of labour are expended' (ibid. p. 97).[7] Let us try to see what Ricardo had in mind when referring to this 'proportion'. According to the commonest interpretation, what he meant was the ratio between a given wage fund (in real or monetary terms) and the whole labouring population: this ratio determines the market wage, which is thus a full-employment equilibrium wage. Real wage flexibility ensures that the whole labour supply will be employed – on the assumption that there is a 'fund' which is always entirely expended in wages.

Though Ricardo uses expressions like 'the funds for the maintenance of labour', there are many indications that in his analytical framework this fund plays a very different role from that which it plays in the wages fund theory: it is not the independent but the dependent variable.

As we saw in the last chapter, in the *Principles* Ricardo openly criticized Malthus's view of the food supply as given prior to and independently of the demand for food. Ricardo makes it clear that an increase in capital, and hence in employment and wages, leads to population growth; and that it is the resulting increased demand for food that leads to increased food production. He returns to this question in a letter to Trower, where he objects to the latter's idea

7. See also *Notes on Malthus*, II, p. 265, where Ricardo states: 'I contend that I have also recognized the other cause, the relative amount of population to capital, which is another of the great regulator of wages'

that an increased quantity of 'corn' must be available before an increase in employment can take place:

> Does the supply of corn precede the demand for it, or does it follow such demand? You are of the former - I of the latter opinion. (Letter to Trower, 26 Sept. 1820, VIII, p. 255)

According to Ricardo, the amount of food produced in the economic system is determined, as for any other commodity, by the 'effectual demand'. Hence it depends on the purchasing power of the workers, which in turn depends on the distribution of income. Thus the supply of food cannot be taken as a given quantity known before the determination of wages, as the wages fund theory assumes. In another letter to Trower, part of the same discussion, Ricardo argues:

> If in the division of gross produce, the labourers commanded a great proportion the demand would be for one set of commodities – if the masters had more than a usual share, the demand would be for another set [..] In every state of society there will be a demand for some commodities, and it is these which it will be the interest of capitalists to produce. (Letter to Trower, 3 Oct. 1820, VIII, pp. 272-3)[8]

Thus one cannot reasonably attribute to Ricardo the notion of a 'wages fund' in real terms, i.e. in terms of subsistence goods, given independently of income distribution. On the other hand the idea of a wages fund predetermined in monetary terms would conflict with Ricardo's idea that an increase in the price of corn induces an immediate proportional increase in the natural wage in money terms – an idea which is of central importance in his analysis.

Absence of the inverse relation between wages and employment
Ricardo's analysis also lacks the other main element of the wages fund theory – the concept of an inverse relation between wages and

---

8. A similar idea appears in the following passage, where the increase in food production is seen as the consequence of a previous increase in wages: 'The aggregate capitals will be increased! If labour cannot be procured no more work will be done with the additional capital, but wages will rise, and the distribution of the produce will be favourable to the workmen. In this case no more food will be produced if the workmen were well fed before, their demand will be for conveniences and luxuries. But the number of labourers are increased, or the children of labourers! Then indeed the demand for food will increase, and food will be produced in consequence of such demand'(letter to Trower, 26 Sept. 1820, VIII, p. 258).

employment, which follows directly from the idea that such a fund is fixed before distribution and independently of it. This comes out clearly in certain very interesting passages from his correspondence, which until now have been neglected by interpreters.

Commenting on some passages that Malthus added to the fifth edition of the *Essay on the principle of population*, Ricardo discusses the following assertion by Malthus:

> Dr. Smith has clearly shown that the natural tendency of a year of scarcity is either to throw a number of labourers out of employment, or to oblige them to work for less than they did before, from the inability of the masters to employ the same numbers at the same price. (Letter to Malthus, 21 Oct. 1817, VII, pp. 202–3)[9]

Ricardo's dry rejoinder is 'I can neither agree with Adam Smith nor with you' (ibid.) – in other words he did not believe that unemployment and wage cuts were alternatives even in a single 'year' when food is scarce because of a bad harvest.

Again, also with reference to Malthus's additions to the fifth edition of the *Essay*, Ricardo strongly rejects the idea that a wage rise brought about by 'combinations of artificers and manufacturers' would lead to a proportional rise in unemployment. In his opinion the only effect of a wage increase won by workers' organizations would be to increase the purchasing power of the working class as a whole:

> A combination among the workmen would increase the amount of money to be divided among the labouring class. (Ibid.).[10]

---

9. Malthus attributes this statement to Smith without indicating its exact location; nor is this discussed by the editors of the recent edition of Malthus's *Works*. He may well have been referring to a certain passage where Smith discusses what happens on the labour market in 'a year of scarcity'; but what Smith is actually saying is that in a year of sudden and extraordinary scarcity many workers may be unemployed, and that competition among them 'sometimes lowers both the real and the money price of labour' (Smith, 1776, I.viii.55). In this passage Smith does not suggest the possibility that such a reduction in wages may lead to an increase in employment, or, consequently, the idea of an alternative between wage cuts and unemployment. He refers simply to a temporary reduction in wages as a possible consequence of increased unemployment in a year of bad harvests.

10. Since Ricardo treated money as a commodity exchanged for others according to the labour necessary for its production, an increase in money income meant an immediate increase in real income (see note 3 above). Hollander (1979, pp. 232–3) cites this passage and others of those cited above, as textual evidence against attributing to Ricardo the notion of a given wage fund. But the passage just quoted also contradicts

This passage is very important. In the first place, it shows that Ricardo definitely did not see the wages fund as given before distribution, in either real or monetary terms. In the second place, like the preceding passage it shows that he did not think there was an inverse relation between wage and employment levels.[11] Finally, it shows that contrary to what is often thought, Ricardo's theory of wages is fully compatible with the statement that 'combinations' of workers may effectively change the distribution of income in their own favour. This is consistent with what he says in the correspondence with Place regarding the effects of a 'system of equality', where, as we saw in the last chapter, he recognized the possibility in principle of such a redistribution.

The 'proportion of supply to demand' as an indicator of unemployment size

What, then, is this 'proportion' between supply and demand or between capital and population, which regulates wages? Ricardo defines the demand for labour in his chapter on wages. After defining capital as that part of the wealth of a nation which is employed in production, consisting of 'food, clothing tools, raw materials, machinery, etc., necessary to give effect to labour', he states:

Hollander's own interpretation of Ricardo, which implies a decreasing relation between wage level and labour demand.

11. Blaug, while recognizing that Ricardo saw the possibility of structural and technological unemployment, claims that he 'could and did recommend wage cuts as an effective device for clearing the labour market' (Blaug, 1973, p. 76). In support of this assertion (which clearly contradicts the passages I have quoted) Blaug cites a letter Ricardo wrote to Malthus in 1821, in which he says: '[...] if wages were previously high, I can see no reason whatever why they should not fall before many labourers are thrown out of work [...] I must say that a sudden and diminished demand for labour *in this case* must mean a diminished reward to the labourer, and not a diminished employment of him' (letter to Malthus, 21 July 1821, IX, p. 25, italics added). This passage is taken out of context; Ricardo was referring to the particular case under discussion between him and Malthus – a situation where the current demand for labour is already larger than the labouring population, and therefore any further increase in capital tends to be translated solely into increased wages (and a reduced rate of profit), while it is impossible to increase employment and hence production. In these very particular circumstances, according to Ricardo, a drop in investment (and hence in the demand for labour) leads not to less employment but only to lower wages. The more general context of this argument is Ricardo's criticism of Malthus's statement that an excess of investments may cause unemployment and at the same time a reduced rate of profit (ibid., pp. 18–27).

'in proportion to the increase of capital will be the demand for labour; in proportion to the work to be done will be the demand for those who are to do it' (1821, I, p. 95).[12]

Thus the 'demand for labour', i.e. the level of employment, depends on the existing capital and on its growth; here the term 'capital' should be understood as 'productive capacity' including fixed and circulating capital. The full utilization of this productive capacity (with given technology and composition of output) will correspond to a certain level of employment ('in proportion to the work to be done will be the demand'). Employment times the wage rate is 'the fund for the maintenance of labour', which is therefore determined after wages and the employment level are known. So when Ricardo speaks of the proportion between supply and demand or between capital and population as regulating wages, he is talking about the ratio of the demand for waged labour to the working-class population. Since that ratio provides a way of quantifying explicit and disguised unemployment, its variations serve as an indicator of labour market conditions – in other words of the ease or difficulty of finding work.

This interpretation is directly confirmed in Ricardo's parliamentary speech in December 1819 *On Mr. Owen's Plan*, where he discusses the problem of pauperism in the working classes and Owen's proposals for dealing with it. Ricardo argues: '[w]hat [does] the country want at the present moment? A demand for labour', and maintains that the current distressed condition of the working classes are due to the 'insufficiency of capital, and the consequent disproportion between wages and population' (Ricardo, V, pp. 31–2) This insufficiency of capital, in turn, may be the result of exporting capital abroad, which has the effect of causing unemployment:

12. The difference between Ricardo, who links the increase of employment with the increase of capital, and Smith, who associates it more generally with the increase in national wealth, arises from the fact that while Smith refers to dependent workers in general including 'menial servants', Ricardo refers here exclusively to 'productive' workers. Like Smith, he tends to take techniques and the composition of output as given when referring to the effects of accumulation on employment; the effects on employment of new techniques and changes in composition of output in the course of accumulation, are separately analysed. This explains why here Ricardo states that the demand for labour is proportional to the increase of capital, whereas elsewhere he recognizes that there can be accumulation without a proportional increase in employment (ibid., p. 278 and the chapter 'On machinery').

The capitalist would be induced to remove his property from Great Britain to a situation where his profits would be more considerable: [...] the effect of it was to produce a deficiency of *employment* and consequent distress. (Ibid., italics added)

Thus it is this situation of lack of employment which earlier in the speech had been described as a 'disproportion between wages and population', i.e. between available employment (determined by 'capital', the existing productive capacity) and the supply of labour.

It is interesting that later in the speech Ricardo envisaged overcoming the situation through the recovery of accumulation which he maintained would follow the abolition of the corn laws.[13] This is similar to the view expressed later in the chapter on machinery added to the third edition of the *Principles*, where he suggests that unemployment caused by introduction of machines can be overcome through faster accumulation. Here again, his reasoning clearly did not follow the lines of the wage fund theory, whereby an increase in employment would be brought about without any further accumulation of capital by the downward flexibility of real wages.[14]

The parliamentary speech *On Mr. Owen 's Plan* was made before Ricardo changed his views on the possible negative effects of new machines on employment; indeed, in that same speech he expressed an opinion contrary to what he later argued in the chapter on

13. In a private letter Ricardo appears less optimistic about the positive effects of the abolition of the corn laws on the condition of the working classes, and also shows awareness of the negative, if short-term, effects of liberalizing trade. In response to a letter from Brown, who called for urgent measures to alleviate the distress of the working classes (and its dangerous political consequences), and who saw unemployment as the cause of that plight ('the people want employment and nothing else'), Ricardo writes: 'We all have to lament the present distressed situation of the labouring classes in this country, but the remedy is not very apparent to me. The correcting of our errors in legislation with regard to trade would ultimately be of considerable service to all classes of the community, but it would afford no immediate relief: On the contrary I should expect that it would plunge us into additional difficulties' (letter to Brown, 13 Oct. 1819, VIII, p. 103).

14. Schumpeter, following a well established tradition (see above, Introduction), says that Ricardo's conclusion that the introduction of machines might 'make population redundant' cannot be taken as referring to the permanent effects of machines 'for we are not told what happens to the workmen who have lost their jobs, yet they cannot remain unemployed, unless we are prepared to violate the assumption that perfect competition and unlimited flexibility of wages prevail' (Schumpeter, 1954, p. 683). However, in contradiction with this statement, the only 'correction' of the negative effects of machines on employment which Schumpeter can find in Ricardo's text has nothing to do with the 'flexibility of wages'. Instead, this correction may arise from the increase in the rate of profit (due to technological progress with unchanged real wages), which may lead to an increased rate of accumulation.

machinery (Sraffa, 1951, pp. lvii–lx). It must be remembered, however, that Ricardo's change of opinion concerned the possibility that an *investment* in new machines might *reduce* employment. This is a different question from the possibility that the existing productive capacity and the techniques in use will be such as not to employ the whole available work force, or that the rate of growth of capital and employment will be lower than that of the labouring population. This possibility is admitted by Ricardo (as it was by his predecessors) independently of his conclusions about the effects of machines.[15]

The 'proportion' (i.e. the ratio) between population and the demand for labour, I have argued, influences wages because it is an indicator of unemployment. It is to the growth of unemployment that Ricardo attributes the worsening of workers' conditions when capital (and hence employment) grows more slowly than the population[16] – that is, when there is an 'excess in the supply of labour' (1821, I, p. 165). Conversely, full employment, or a scarcity of labour, tends to favour the workers and enable them to obtain better wages: 'In new settlements, [...] it is probable that capital has a tendency to increase faster than mankind: and if the deficiency of labourers were not supplied by more populous countries, this tendency would very much raise the price of labour' (ibid., p. 98). And again: '[a]n accumulation of capital naturally produces an increased competition among the employers of labour, and a consequent rise in its price [...] But when the supply [of labour] is obtained, wages will again fall to their former price' (ibid., p. 163).[17] In his *Notes on Malthus*, Ricardo writes, referring to the circumstances that make real wage increases possible: 'I fully agree [...] that an increase in the wages of labour implies full employment to all the labouring classes' (II, p. 412). In the essay

15. It is often said that Ricardo's support of 'Say's law' is incompatible with the admission of unemployment (see for example Morishima, 1989, pp. 168–88). But that would be true only if Ricardo accepted not only Say's law but also the wages fund doctrine; and the latter, as I have argued, is not part of his theory. This question will be examined in the next chapter.

16. Ricardo, 1821, I, p. 101; 1815, IV, p. 23 (quoted below, p. 154); letter to Trower, 21 Apr. 1821, VIII, p. 368 (quoted in Chapter. 4, p. 120).

17. Note here the similarity with Smith's assertion that in growing economies competition between employers makes wages rise above the minimum subsistence level.

Absolute Value and Exchangeable Value we also find comments on the influence of labour market conditions on the division of the product between wages and profits: 'it depends also on the state of the market for labour [...], for if labour be scarce the workmen will be able to demand and obtain a great quantity of necessaries' (IV, pp. 365–6).

For Ricardo, then, as for Smith, persistent unemployment is possible and may be corrected only gradually by changes in population or in the rate of accumulation. The amount of unemployment, or its absence, or a scarcity of labour, determines wage variations which Ricardo, unlike Smith, considers as deviations of the market wage from the natural wage.[18]

FORCES ENSURING THE ADJUSTMENT OF THE NATURAL WAGE TO PRICE VARIATIONS AND TAXATION

In discussing the forces that keep the market wage close to the natural wage, and the role of population adjustment mechanisms, Ricardo distinguishes between two different cases: one in which deviations in the market wage are caused by imbalances between population and the demand for labour; and the other in which these deviations are caused by changes in food prices, or by direct taxation on wages or indirect taxation on the goods habitually consumed by workers. In this second case, the natural wage (in money) must rapidly adjust to keep the workers' purchasing power unchanged:

> It is very easy to perceive why, when the capital of a country diminishes, wages should fall [...] the reason is, because labour is a commodity which cannot be increased and diminished at pleasure. [...] the number of hands increasing or diminishing slowly, whilst the funds for the maintenance of labour increase or diminish rapidly, there must be a considerable interval before the price of labour is exactly regulated by the price of corn and necessaries; but in the case of a fall in the value of money, or a tax on corn, there is not necessarily any excess in the supply of labour, nor any abatement of demand, and therefore there can be no reason why the labourer should sustain a real diminution of wages. (1821, I, pp. 165–6; part of the passage has already been cited above, p. 130)

In the first case the change in wages is linked with a change in the

18. I shall give fuller attention to this point below.

workers' bargaining position, and it will last until that position is again modified by changes in population and employment during the accumulation process. But in the second case, Ricardo concludes:

> it appears to me that no interval which could bear oppressively on the labourer, would elapse between the rise in the price of raw produce, and the rise in the wages of the labourer. (Ibid., p. 166)[19]

Ricardo's conviction that the adjustment of wages does not work through variations in population is expressed very clearly also in his correspondence with McCulloch, in the context of a discussion of the effects of taxes on necessary goods. According to McCulloch real wages will return to the pre-tax level only after hunger and poverty have first reduced the population, and then very high wages have stimulated its growth to the required level. Ricardo replies:

> In truth however, I think that wages will neither be very low or very high, but that they will undergo such a moderate increase as will compensate the labourer for the tax laid on his necessaries. It is in the interest of all parties that they should so rise. [...] the question between us comes to this. Will the population be in the first instance very much depressed and then afterwards violently stimulated, or will it continue in that course which the circumstances of the capital and the demand for labour originally required it to be? The value of things I believe to be influenced not by immediate supply and demand only, but also by contingent supply and demand. (Letter to McCulloch, 13 June 1820, VIII, p. 196)[20]

This view is difficult to explain if one follows the traditional interpretation of the classical and Ricardian theory of wages as based on the wages fund theory.[21] In the first place, Ricardo's position implies that following a tax on wages, the 'wages fund' paid by capitalists to workers must increase in both real and monetary terms to maintain the workers' real wage (net of taxes) unaltered. Hence it is the latter which (for a given employment level) determines the amount of the 'fund', not vice versa.

In the second place, one may ask why capitalists should pay

---

19. See also ibid., p. 161 ff, where Ricardo criticizes the idea that wages adjust only slowly to changes in prices or taxes.
20. Note the similarity between Ricardo's assertion that it is in the interest of all parties for wages to increase, and the statement made by Turgot in the same context (see Chapter 3, p.76–7).
21. See, for example, Shoup, 1960, p. 73; St Clair, 1965, pp. 129–31; Hollander, 1979, pp. 393–5.

higher (money and real) wages when the conditions of the labour market are unchanged? Ricardo's reply to McCulloch raises the question of why employers should worry about the effects of current real wages on population – effects that will be felt on the labour market only in a rather distant future. One may also wonder whether a decision on the part of employers to raise wages in proportion to the tax is compatible with competition in the labour market. Yet such competition is certainly important in Ricardo's theory: for example it causes the tendency towards uniformity of wages received by equally qualified workers.[22]

Here Ricardo shares the conclusions of Smith and most of his predecessors and contemporaries. They also had regarded the adjustment of money wages following changes in prices or taxes as independent of population changes.

Thus Ricardo seems to have followed (perhaps not entirely consciously, as his explanations do not seem to be relevant to the problem)[23] a view of the forces determining wages, that characterized the most important economists before him – especially Smith, who was considered the main authority in the field of political economy. Indeed, in the *Principles* Ricardo explicitly refers to and defends Smith's conclusions about the effects of taxing wages, against the criticisms directed at Smith by Buchanan in his *Observations* (Ricardo, 1821, I, pp. 216–20, 382).[24] In that tradition, the forces that tend to keep wages unchanged in real terms were identified in the habits and conventions, and in the bargaining position of the parties in a particular historical and economic context, which underlie the determination of the natural wage (see Chapter 3, pp. 70–83).

22. See in particular Hollander, 1979, p. 395. The problem here is similar to the one which many scholars (including Cannan, Knight, Hollander) have noted in relation to Smith's assertion that wages never fall below the minimum level 'consistent with common humanity' even when there is unemployment (on this point see Garegnani, 1990, p. 119).

23. Ricardo's explanation to McCulloch in the quoted passage does not seem pertinent, and elsewhere Ricardo uses ad hoc arguments to explain the adjustment of wages.

24. Buchanan was the author of an edition of Smith's *Wealth of Nations* with commentary, and of a companion volume of *Observations* on that work. Buchanan's criticism of Smith – restated by Ricardo – is based on the assertion that changes in food prices, or taxes on wages, cannot induce changes in wage levels because (in Buchanan's view) wages are determined exclusively by the relation between supply and demand, which is unchanged.

THE NATURAL WAGE AND POPULATION

Differing definitions of the natural wage

At the beginning of the chapter on wages the natural wage is defined as the wage that maintains the labouring population unchanged. On the other hand, in the discussion of taxation the natural wage, towards which the actual wage adjusts after changes in taxation, is the wage 'regulated' by the 'circumstances of the country', namely the growth of the demand for labour:

> Suppose the circumstances of the country to be such, that the lowest labourers are not only called upon to continue their race, but to increase it; their wages would be regulated accordingly. Can they multiply in the degree required, if a tax takes from them a part of their wages, and reduces them to bare necessaries? (Ricardo, 1821, I, p. 220)[25]

In support of his position on the effect of taxation, Ricardo also cites a passage in which Malthus asserts that after a tax is introduced, wages will return to the level that stimulates population growth to the extent required by the rate of accumulation in the economy:

> The price of labour, when left to find its *natural level* [...] taken on the average, independently of accidental circumstances, further expresses, clearly, the wants of the society respecting population [...] according to the state of the real funds for the maintenance of labour, whether stationary, progressive, or retrograde. (Ibid., pp. 218–9; italics added)[26]

In relation to these passages, some scholars have made a distinction between the idea of the natural wage, corresponding to a constant population, and that of a 'dynamic equilibrium wage': higher dynamic equilibrium wages would correspond to higher rates of accumulation and thus assure an equivalent rate of population

---

25. See also the following passage: 'those who maintain that it is the price of necessaries which regulates the price of labour, always allowing for the particular state of progression in which the society may be, seem to have allowed too readily that a rise or fall in the price of necessaries will be very slowly succeded by a rise or fall of wages' (Ricardo, 1821, 1, p. 161) where Ricardo shows that in his view the different conditions of accumulation ('state of progression'), along with the price of food, enter the determination of the natural wage.

26. See also ibid., pp. 215–6 where Ricardo cites a long passage of Smith in which he says: 'the demand for labour, according as it happens to be either increasing, stationary, or declining [...] regulates the subsistence of the labourer, and determines in what degree it shall be either liberal, moderate or scanty [...]'.

growth.[27]

However, in the passages cited above the wage reflecting 'the circumstances of the country' is the natural wage. The passage of Malthus quoted by Ricardo explicitly refers to the natural level of wages, 'taken on the average, independently of accidental circumstances'. Here Ricardo is using a different definition of the natural wage from the one given in the chapter on wages – the definition given by Smith, whose position Ricardo is defending against Buchanan.

Smith's definition implies the possibility that different levels of the natural wage correspond to different rates of accumulation. I have argued that this happens in Smith's analysis because he associates different levels of accumulation with labour-market conditions more or less favourable to the workers. Ricardo too, sees changes in the proportion between employment and population as a factor which regulates wages. He always attributes changes in real wages to changes in the conditions of the labour market arising from differences in the rates of growth of population and capital. From this point of view Smith's definition is consistent with Ricardo's analysis, in that the higher level of wages in growing economies can be explained by the population's tendency to grow less rapidly than capital and employment. In the chapter on wages, however, Ricardo treats wage variations so determined as deviations of the market wage from the natural wage, and not, as in Smith's definition, as changes in the natural wage.[28]

The presence in the *Principles* of a different definition of the natural wage raises a question about the importance of the one in the chapter on wages, and about its interpretation in terms of an association between the natural wage and stationary conditions with no population growth. Ricardo's assertion in the chapter on wages that in a growing economy the market wage may be higher than the natural wage for an indefinite time, has led many to interpret

27. Cf. Hollander, 1979, p. 388. An interpretation of Ricardo based on the idea of the 'dynamic equilibrium wage' is proposed by Casarosa, 1978; similar interpretations appear in Levi, 1976 and Samuelson, 1978; this and other interpretations of Ricardo are discussed below, pp. 157–63.
28. The presence of a 'Smithian' definition of the natural wage in Ricardo's analysis may be at the root of the ambiguities which Tosato finds in Ricardo, concerning which notion of wages (market or natural) is relevant to the analysis of trends in the rate of profit (Tosato, 1985, pp. 203–8).

Ricardo's theory in terms of a process of growth which, because of diminishing returns in agriculture, tends towards the stationary state where wages are at the natural rate.[29] But this conflicts with the role in Ricardo's theory of natural variables as centres of gravitation for actual quantities (pp. 129, 131 above).

Natural wage and stationary population
The problems inherent in Ricardo's definition of the natural wage as that at which the labouring population reproduces itself 'without either increase or diminution' were already noted by Malthus, who in his *Principles* made the following comment:

> Mr. Ricardo has defined the natural price of labour to be 'that price which is necessary to enable the labourers one with another to subsist, and to perpetuate their race, without either increase or diminution' This price I should really be disposed to call a most unnatural price; because in a natural state of things, that is, without great impediments to the progress of wealth and population, such a price could not generally occur for hundreds of years. But if this price be really rare and, in an ordinary state of things, at so great distance in point of time, it must evidently lead to great errors to consider the market prices of labour as only temporary deviations above and below that fixed price to which they will soon return.(Notes on Malthus, II, p. 227–8)

Malthus proposes a different definition of the natural wage, one which would not present the same problems:

> The natural price of labour in any country I should define to be, 'that price which, in the actual circumstances of the society, is necessary to occasion an average supply of labourers, sufficient to meet the average demand. (Ibid.)[30]

Ricardo's reaction to Malthus may help us to understand the reasons for his particular definition. Initially, along with the reasons for his choice, he indicated a readiness to accept the alternative definition

29. The passage of Ricardo, frequently cited, is the following: 'Notwithstanding the tendency of wages to conform to their natural rate, their market rate may, in an improving society, for an indefinite period, be constantly above it; for no sooner may the impulse, which an increased capital gives to a new demand for labour be obeyed, than another increase of capital may produce the same effect; and thus, if the increase of capital be gradual and constant, the demand for labour may give a continued stimulus to an increase of people' (Ricardo, 1821, I, p. 94–5) For the interpretations here referred to, see Hicks and Hollander, 1977; Hollander, 1979; Samuelson, 1978; Casarosa, 1978.
30. Malthus then goes on to make it clear that wages depend partly on the rate of growth of demand and partly on habits, and that therefore different levels of natural wage are compatible with one and the same rate of growth.

proposed by Malthus:

> I have done so that we may have one common language to apply to all cases which are similar. By natural price I do not mean the usual price, but such a price as is necessary to supply constantly a given demand. The natural price of corn is the price at which it can be supplied affording the usual profits. With every demand for an increased quantity it will rise above this price, therefore if capital and population regularly increase the market price may for years exceed its natural price. *I am however very little solicitous to retain my definition of the natural price of labour – Mr. Malthus's will do nearly as well for my purpose.* (Ibid., italics added)

But later Ricardo struck out the last sentence (in italics above), and ended his note as follows:

> With every demand for an increased quantity the market price of corn will rise above this price and probably is never at the natural price but either above or below it – the same may be said of the natural price of labour. (Ibid.)

Some useful inferences can be drawn from Ricardo's answer. As to the association between the natural wage and a stationary state of the economy, Ricardo does not seem worried by Malthus's objection; he refers to the analogy between the price of labour and the price of any other commodity. This suggests that Ricardo's reference to a population that reproduces itself without increase or decrease is not meant to indicate a stationary state, but a normal position of the economy. In other words the definition reflects the view that the market price of labour coincides with its natural price, as happens with any other commodity, in situations where the supply is in the right proportion to the demand and thus the market does not signal a need to increase or decrease production by a market price above or below the natural price.[31] Thus the natural price of labour, like that

31. In the case of goods the market price coincides with the natural price when the quantities supplied and demanded are (approximately) equal. In the case of labour, however, a condition of equality between population and demand for labour would impose severe constraints on the system's capacity for expansion, because the 'production of men' is more difficult to adjust to demand than the production of other commodities. Since neither Ricardo nor other classical authors ever suggest that the scarcity of labour may limit growth – on the contrary they say this can never happen (Ricardo, 1821, I, pp. 289, 292) – I believe the 'correct proportion' between supply and demand in relation to the labour market should be defined as a proportion such that the conditions of the labour market do not cause the market wage to deviate from the natural wage. This could mean conditions in which there is no explicit unemployment but there are sectors of the population which, while not actively present in the labour market, are prepared to enter it whenever production and employment expand; or, if we

of any other commodity, emerges in situations where the supply has had time to adjust to a given 'effectual demand' (i.e. employment level). But as with the natural price of other commodities, this does not imply that the natural wage is associated with a stationary economy. The analysis and determination of normal values is always conducted without regard to the changes induced by accumulation in the quantities produced and demanded (Chapter 1, p. 4). If these changes are taken into account it seems obvious that in a growing economy, while the supply lags behind the increasing demand the market price of a commodity, like that of labour, may be somewhat higher than the natural price. This does not make the natural price any less central from the analytic point of view, provided that the market price tends towards the natural price as the supply of the commodity tends to approach the demand for it.

Thus the analogy between the price of a commodity and the price of labour negates the association between the natural wage and the stationary state of the economy. That association, on the other hand, is clearly absent in the *Principles*, where Ricardo analyses the effects of the process of accumulation on the rate of profit, while treating the wage as given, in real terms, at its natural level.[32]

But the answer to Malthus brings out the problem which arises from this analogy. In it Ricardo neglects the fact (which he himself elsewhere recognizes) that in the case of other commodities the adjustment of supply to demand is more rapid, and works through more reliable mechanisms, than in the case of labour.

Ricardo defends his definition of the natural wage in strict analogy with the definition of the natural price, for the sake of clarity and rigour in the use of economic terms. The first version of his note, as well as the presence of a different, Smithian definition of the natural wage in the *Principles*, suggests that he did not consider the analogy as essential to his analysis; but in the end he decided to

interpret Ricardo's natural wage as a minimum subsistence wage – as seems to be called for – it could mean a situation where there is also explicit unemployment and this drives wages down to their minimum level (as we have seen, this was the attitude of Ricardo's predecessors).

32. Chapters 'On profits' and 'Effects of accumulation on profits and interest'; on this point see also Caravale, 1985. Ricardo (1821, I, p. 98) attributes increased wages in an economy in the early stages of development, not to the requirement of population growth in itself but to the fact that 'the demand for labour would increase still faster than the supply'.

retain it. In the following sections we shall examine the difficulties arising from Ricardo's definition, and its possible analytical reasons.

CONTINUITY AND DIFFERENCES IN THE WAGE THEORIES OF RICARDO AND SMITH

Smith and Ricardo

In its central features, Ricardo's wage theory is in direct continuity with that of Smith. Like Smith he associates the natural wage with the workers' 'habits and customs' – a combination of historical and social elements which may be taken as given for a particular time and place, though they can be modified by social and institutional changes. He also shares the view of Smith and his contemporaries regarding the rapid effects on the natural wage of changes in the price of food, and of taxes on wages or wage goods. Lastly, in some parts of the *Principles* Ricardo adopts the definition of the natural wage as that which reflects the 'circumstances of the country' (see above, pp. 142–3), that is, the economy's rate of accumulation – a definition which appears to be taken from Smith.

On the other hand Ricardo's argument contains new elements not found in Smith, and it is these that lead to problems of interpretation and the weaknesses in his analysis. They are all connected with his treatment of the natural wage as analogous to the natural price of a commodity.

In this connection let us re-examine the different ways in which Smith and Ricardo dealt with the question of how wages are influenced by changes in the proportion between the demand for labour and population.

With regard to the effects on wages of labour market conditions, in Smith we can distinguish two cases. One is the case of temporary fluctuations in the level of activity and employment, induced for example by alternate good and bad harvests in agriculture. These fluctuations can produce oscillations in the market wage, for which Smith does not indicate any corrective mechanisms. Such mechanisms are unnecessary because of the inherently transitory and accidental nature of these fluctuations.[33] The second case is that of

33. 'In a year of sudden and extraordinary plenty, there are funds in the hands of many of the employers of industry, sufficient to maintain and employ a greater number of

persistent changes in the proportion between the demand for labour and the population, which Smith associates with different trends of the economy: whether it is stationary, declining, or growing rapidly. In this case changes in that proportion are linked with structural aspects of the economic system such as its capacity to produce a surplus, the propensity to invest, the existence of an institutional and cultural setup more or less favourable to rapid accumulation. As variations in the proportion between population and the demand for labour induced by these factors have a non-transitory influence on the bargaining position of the workers, they will affect the natural wage. The resulting shifts will be limited by the minimum level of the natural wage (i.e. the workers' subsistence level of consumption) and the minimum profit rate required to compensate for the 'risk and trouble' of investment (Chapter 3, pp. 58–60; Smith, 1776, V.ii.f.2).

In the chapter on wages Ricardo's definition of natural and market wages, unlike that of Smith, implies that changes in the proportion between population and employment, even when arising from such relatively persistent causes as changes in the trend of accumulation unmatched by changes in the population growth rate, lead to deviations of the market wage from the natural wage. The gravitation of the market wage around the natural wage must then be brought about by changes in the population or its rate of growth.

Smith too said that in the course of accumulation the population would tend to grow or shrink in response to changes in wages. But he did not see this tendency as a mechanism whereby the actual wage gravitates around the natural wage; rather, it is treated as a phenomenon that may influence the 'secular' movements of the natural wage itself. Thus population responses to changes in income do not prevent the natural wage from being considered as subject to changes induced by persistent changes in labour market conditions.

Ricardo's position, as I have said, poses problems because of the slowness of population adjustment (1821, I, pp. 165, 220), which

---

industrious people than had been employed the year before; and this extraordinary number cannot always be had. Those masters, therefore, [...] bid against one another [...] which sometimes raises both the real and the money price of labour. The contrary of this happens in a year of sudden and extraordinary scarcity [...] a considerable number of people are thrown out of employment [...] which sometimes lowers both the real and the money price of labour' (Smith, 1776., I.viii.54–55;see also I vii.18–19).

conflicts with the stated analytical centrality of the natural wage compared to the market wage. These problems are aggravated by the fact that Ricardo, though mainly in his unpublished texts, sometimes questions the very existence of reliable mechanisms of population adjustment. This adjustment depends on various factors, in any case including workers' 'habits and customs',[34] which can change when wages change so that the effect on the population is uncertain.[35] As we saw in the last chapter, Ricardo wrote to McCulloch that the effect of wage changes on population may go in either direction depending on circumstances (Chapter 4, p. 119).

The difficulties in Ricardo's theory and a 'Smithian' way out
In conclusion, then, problems arise in Ricardo's definition of the natural wage because, as his theory does not include corrective mechanisms based on demand, imbalances in the labour market (when not caused by transitory fluctuations of the economy) must be corrected by population changes. This means that the gravitation of the market wage around the natural wage depends on those changes. But whereas in the commodity market the adjustment of supply to demand is relatively rapid, and above all based on a reliable mechanism such as the tendency to maximize profits, this is not true in the case of labour. The gravitation of the market wage around the natural wage depends on uncertain forces. In the case of other commodities it seems that divergences between supply and demand, which make market prices deviate from the natural price, can legitimately be seen as accidental and transitory phenomena; but such

---

34. 'The friends of humanity cannot but wish that in all countries the labouring classes should have a taste for comforts and enjoyments [...] There cannot be better security against a superabundant population' (Ricardo, 1821, I, p. 100).
35. Ricardo also considers this possibility in the *Principles*: '[t]he increase of population [...] will generally be the effect, but not the necessary effect of high wages. The amended condition of the labourer [...] does not necessarily oblige him to marry and take upon himself the charge of a family [...] His increased wages then will be attended with no other effect than an increased demand for some of those commodities; and as the race of labourers will not be materially increased, his wages will continue permanently high' (ibid., p. 406). But he continues by asserting that 'in practice it is invariably found that an increase of population follows the amended condition of the labourer' (ibid., p. 407). Significantly, his caution with regard to the 'principle of population' disappears in the discussion of the causes of the tendency for the profit rate to fall, in Chapter XXI: 'no point is better established, than that the supply of labourers will always ultimately be in proportion to the means of supporting them' (ibid., p. 292; see also p. 289).

a view appears less justified in the case of labour when the proportion between employment and labouring population is altered by changes in the (average) rate of accumulation.

Thus the analogy between the price of labour and the price of other commodities, based on the classical idea that labour is produced and exchanged like any other commodity, meets a snag because of the peculiar nature of the 'production of men', identified with the increase of the labouring population.[36]

Once the sources of difficulty in Ricardo's theory are identified, it is fairly clear that his different concepts of wages can be translated into Smith's terminology and the corresponding theoretical framework. And this translation may offer a way out of the problems in Ricardo's argument. Let us attempt this exercise.

In the chapter on wages Ricardo defines the natural wage as the wage that 'nature and habit demand for the support of the labourers', above which wages cannot long remain 'from the effect of the principle of population on the increase of mankind' (Ricardo, 1821, I, p. 159, cited in Chapter 4, n. 27). Thus the natural wage seems to coincide with the (historically determined) subsistence wage in Smith's theory, i.e. the lowest level possible for the natural wage, which is realized on the labour market when there is an excess supply so that the workers compete amongst themselves and bring the natural wage down to its minimum level.

Ricardo then distinguishes two different types of forces that can make the real (disposable) wage diverge from the natural/subsistence level. In the first case these forces are transitory and are corrected independently of changes in the population or in its rate of growth: i. e. variations in food prices and taxes on wages. For Smith, these are deviations of the actual or 'market' wage from the natural wage.

In the second case, the deviation of the real wage from its natural/subsistence level is caused by a changed proportion between population and the demand for labour. As we have seen, this cause of wage variation has a certain persistence because of the slowness and uncertainty of the population adjustment mechanisms which in

36. This problem in Ricardo's theory of wages is noted by Marx, who sets against the classical theory of population his own theory of the 'industrial reserve army' (see p. 125, n. 39 and De Vivo, 1987, p. 191). The problem of adjustment of the market wage towards the natural wage in Ricardo's analysis is also discussed in Rosselli (1985, pp. 247, 249).

this case, unlike the first, must intervene to correct the imbalance between employment and population.

For this reason Smith saw such changes as leading to changes in the natural wage, given its 'subsistence' floor. In the chapter on wages Ricardo considers them as deviations of the market wage; but in the chapters on taxes he regards them as changes in the natural wage. His definition of the market wage in the chapter on wages conflates what for Smith are two different notions: that of the natural wage (when it is above the minimum subsistence level) and that of the actual or market wage reflecting temporary and accidental perturbations of the natural wage. This superposition of two different notions in one term explains many of the difficulties in both Ricardo's argument and its interpretations. We can set out the following equivalents between Smith's definition and those given by Ricardo in the chapter on wages:

Ricardo		**Smith**
Natural wage	=	Subsistence wage
Market wage, type I	=	Actual or market wage
(transitory causes of change)		
Market wage, type II	=	Natural wage greater
(lasting changes in supply/demand ratio)		than subsistence

A key to Ricardo's views

This translation of Ricardo's concepts into Smithian terms may provide a key to Ricardo's ideas on the behaviour of wages during the secular processes of accumulation.

He was more pessimistic than Smith was about the consequences of population growth for the long-term behaviour of wages (Chapter 4, p. 125 and Ricardo, 1821, I, p. 101, cited below, p. 155); and, as we shall see, he wanted to simplify the analysis of the effects of accumulation on the rate of profit. As a result, he argued as if wages, in their secular trends, could never depart far from their historically determined minimum subsistence level. Hence when discussing the tendency of economic variables in the accumulation process he thought it was legitimate to assume that wages were at that level. Variations in real wages owing to changes in labour market conditions were dismissed as 'transitory' and hence negligible phenomena. But at the same time Ricardo was aware that changes in the proportion between population and the demand for labour may raise real wages above the minimum subsistence level, and these changes may be lasting enough to be relevant for the economic analysis. This is true in particular when the analysis refers not to accumulation (i.e. to 'secular' trends in Marshall's sense) but to long-term normal values (again in Marshall's sense); for example, in the discussion of taxation, or of increased food prices. In that context Ricardo uses the same definition of natural wages as the one given by Smith, and thus recognizes the possibility that the natural wage may be influenced by different labour market conditions depending on the growth trends of the economy.[37]

The distinction between the two different concepts that merge in Ricardo's definition of the market wage may also explain his statement that in a growing economy the market wage (evidently 'type II' in the scheme above) may remain for a very long time above its natural (subsistence) level.

---

37. Ricardo's interest in the behaviour of distributive variables in the accumulation process may explain the superposition of two distinct temporal and logical dimensions in the discussion of gravitation around the natural wage (of which there are traces also in Smith: see above, Chapter 3, pp. 81–3). The first temporal dimension (time-frame) is that required for persistent economic forces to carry out their influence in a given state of the economy (i.e. regardless of changes determined by accumulation and technical change) – for example for the natural prices to emerge as gravitation centres of actual or market prices. In other words it applies to the determination of what Marshall called 'long-run normal' variables. The second time-frame applies to the discussion of the 'laws' that govern the economic system in the course of 'secular' (in Marshall's sense) processes – for example the tendency of the profit rate to fall because of diminishing returns in agriculture. The gravitation of market wages towards the natural rate logically belongs to the first time-frame. But the population adjustment which according to Ricardo corrects the 'disproportions' between demand and supply in the labour market, and thus makes the market wage gravitate towards the natural wage, belongs to the second time-frame. Population adjustment is too slow to correct imbalances in the labour market in a given normal position of the economy. But its corrective effects during the process of growth may suggest that the dominant (secular) influence on wages will be increasing food prices. Thus, because imbalances on the labour market are gradually corrected, or because, as argued in the *Essay on Profit*, they alternate (Ricardo, 1815, IV, p. 23, cited below) on the average their effect is cancelled out. This viewpoint also emerges in Ricardo's approving comment on the first two sections of Malthus's chapter on profits (*Notes on Malthus*, II, pp. 264–5).

RICARDO'S THEORY OF WAGES AND THE OBJECTIVES OF HIS THEORETICAL CONTRIBUTION

Ricardo's main objectives

Ricardo's reasons for introducing the close analogy between natural price and natural wage are related to the aims of his contribution to economic theory.

One of the central problems of his analysis was to show the connections between distributive variables, and the way the latter change as development proceeds because of diminishing returns in agriculture.[38] In particular, he proposed to demonstrate that the increased cost of food production would lead to a fall in the profit rate. Wages were conceived in real terms, as a collection of goods (mostly agricultural products), so that the natural (money) wage would rise together with the price of 'corn'[39] in the course of accumulation, and profits would fall.

But if the accumulation process brought about persistent changes in labour market conditions as well as in corn prices, and if these were considered capable of modifying the natural wage in real terms, the relation between the price of corn and the profit rate would be less clear-cut.

In his *Essay on Profits* Ricardo had assumed that 'capital and population advance in the proper proportion, so that the real wages of labour continue uniformly the same' (Ricardo, 1815, IV, p. 12). This assumption is explicitly made in order that 'we may know what peculiar effects are to be ascribed to the growth of capital, the increase of population and the extension of cultivation to the more remote and less fertile land' (ibid.). Thus he makes the simplifying hypothesis that the conditions of the labour market do not change, so that the real wage remains constant through time. His aim is to bring out the effect on the profit rate of diminishing returns in agriculture. The simplifying hypothesis is justified by the

38. 'But in different stages of society, the proportions of the whole produce of the earth which will be allotted to each of these classes, under the names of rent, profit, and wages, will be essentially different [...] To determine the laws which regulate this distribution, is the principal problem in political economy' (Ricardo, 1821, I, p. 5)
39. The word 'corn' was used by the classical economists to cover all agricultural 'subsistence' products – i.e. those widely and habitually consumed in the country, especially by the working classes.

consideration that in the course of accumulation:

> The rise or fall of wages [...] [i]n the advancing state, depends on whether the capital or the population advance, at the more rapid course. In the retrograde state, it depends on whether population or capital decrease with the greater rapidity.
>
> As experience demonstrates that capital and population alternately take the lead, and wages in consequence are liberal or scanty, nothing can be positively laid down, respecting profits, as far as wages are concerned. (Ibid., p. 23)

As in the course of development (or decline) real wages vary unsystematically in response to different labour market conditions, and may alternately increase and decrease, increasing production costs in agriculture are the only systematic force affecting the profit rate.

Between the publication of the *Essay* and that of the *Principles*, Malthus criticized Ricardo's position. In their correspondence Malthus questioned the legitimacy of Ricardo's simplifying hypothesis on the constancy of real wages (letter to Ricardo, 26 Jan. 1817, VII, p. 122), and insisted on the role of supply and demand in determining them (letters to Ricardo, 6 Aug., 8 Sept., 9 and 13 Oct. 1816, VII, pp. 52, 68–70, 77, 80). In particular, Malthus argued that in the course of accumulation the variations in the ratio of labour supply to demand may cause a fall in the real wage, counterbalancing the effects of the increased price of corn on money wages, and thus casting doubt on Ricardo's conclusions.

Ricardo replied by reaffirming his conviction that the effect of changes in corn prices on the natural wage outweighs the effect of variations in the proportion between employment and population on real wages:

> I cannot think it inconsistent to suppose that the money price of labour may rise when it is necessary to cultivate poorer land, whilst the real price may at the same time fall. Two opposite causes are influencing the price of labour, one the enhanced price of some of the things on which wages are expended – the other the fewer enjoyments which the labourer will have the power to command – you think these may balance each other, or rather that the latter will prevail, I on the contrary think the former the most powerful in its effects. I must write a book to convince you (letter to Malthus, 10 Jan. 1816, VII, p. 10)[40]

---

40. See also the letters to Malthus, 9 Aug., and 5, 11 and 14 Oct. 1816, VII, pp. 57, 72, 78 and 81. This debate on the relative importance of supply and demand and the price

As Rosselli has argued (1985, p. 243),[41] this disagreement with Malthus highlights the need for Ricardo to establish a hierarchy between the two causes of wage variation – changes in corn prices and changes in the demand for labour in relation to the population. Both can modify wages but, if Ricardo's conclusions about the effects of diminishing agricultural returns on the profit rate are to be retained unchanged, the second must be unable to counterbalance the effect of the first.

In the chapter on wages in the *Principles* we find an echo of this issue when Ricardo discusses the influence of these two factors in the course of accumulation:

> In the natural advance of the society, the wages of labour will have a tendency to fall, as far as they are regulated by supply and demand; for the supply of labourers will continue to increase at the same rate, whilst the demand for them will increase at a slower rate [...] but we must not forget, that wages are also regulated by the prices of the commodities on which they are expended'. (Ricardo, 1821, I, p. 101)[42]

Ricardo concludes that even if the real wage decreases the second influence will necessarily make the natural wage rise, and profits will tend to fall.

The problem posed by Malthus may explain Ricardo's wish to make the natural wage by definition independent of any influence of

---

of food in determining wages is interwoven with another debate, about the possibility of determining wages and profit independently of each other. While Malthus holds that each of the distribution variables is determined, simultaneously and independently, by supply and demand (letter to Ricardo, 9 Oct. 1816, VII, p. 77), Ricardo replies: 'profits depend on wages, wages, under common circumstances, on the price of food and necessaries, and the price of food and necessaries on the fertility of the last cultivated land' (letter to Malthus, 11 Oct. 1816, VII, p. 78). For a debate on the interpretation of this correspondence between Malthus and Ricardo see Hollander, 1990, pp. 743–6; Peach, 1987, p. 115 and 1990, pp. 752–8.

41. This author's analysis of the role of the natural wage in Ricardo's theory has elements in common with the present one.

42. Notwithstanding this, Malthus in his own *Principles* continues to accuse Ricardo of neglecting the effects of supply and demand on wages (*Notes on Malthus*, II, pp. 255, 264–268). However, in the first section of his chapter 'On profits' Malthus seems to accept Ricardo's conclusions: 'though in the progress of society [...] the real wages of labour gradually fall; yet it is clear that *there is a limit, and probably at no great distance, which cannot be passed.* [...] Consequently, if poorer lands which required more labour were successively taken into cultivation, *it would not be possible for the corn wages of each individual labourer to be diminished in proportion to the diminished produce* [...] and the rate of profits would continue regularly falling till the accumulation of capital had ceased' (ibid. p. 256, italics added). Ricardo comments approvingly on this part of Malthus's work (ibid., p. 258).

labour market conditions and their changes during accumulation. The role he assigns to the mechanisms of population adjustment (with the problems we have seen), and the close analogy in the definition of natural wage and natural price – ruling out the influence on the former of changes in labour market conditions – can thus be explained in the light of the objectives he set himself.[43]

Ricardo's contribution and its relation to Smith's

The fact that Ricardo gives relatively little attention to the weaknesses in his theory of wages may be at least partly explained by the nature of his theoretical contribution in connection with the work of Smith.

Ricardo's explicit aim was to show that Smith was wrong on some specific questions; but he still regarded his overall contribution as the main reference in economics.[44]

For Ricardo's purposes the most important propositions in the theory of wages are 1) the adjustment of the natural wage to changes in food prices, and 2) the existence of a hierarchy between this cause of wage variation and the other cause, i.e. changes in the relative sizes of the demand for labour and the population. In particular, it is important that the declining pace of accumulation, which he indicates as the consequence of diminishing returns in agriculture, cannot induce a fall in real wages such as to compensate for the effect of increased costs in food production. These propositions can also be derived from the theory of wages expounded in the *Wealth of Nations*, as in the works of others among Smith's predecessors and contemporaries. Both Smith and Turgot held that persistent changes in the labour market could produce a shift in the natural rate of

43. A different, but interesting, interpretation of the role of gravitation based on population adjustments in Ricardo's wage theory is given by Picchio del Mercato: 'In Ricardo's analytical scheme the conflict between wages and profit is more explicit. Hence the dynamics of wages must be circumscribed, perhaps by mechanisms of a naturalistic type' (1981, p. 98, author's translation).

44. In the preface to the *Principles* Ricardo writes: [t]he writer, in combating received opinions, has found it necessary to advert more particularly to those passages in the writings of Adam Smith from which he sees reasons to differ; but he hopes it will not, on that account, be suspected that he does not, in common with all those who acknowledge the importance of the science of Political Economy, participate in the admiration which the profound work of this celebrated author so justly excites' (Ricardo, 1821, I, p. 6). Evidence of his feelings of great admiration for the work of Adam Smith, and also of his aim of criticizing those of Smith's conclusions which he considered erroneous, is in his correspondence (Ricardo, VII, pp. 2, 88, 100, 246).

wages. However – and this is most important for the problem Ricardo was dealing with – reductions in the natural wage due (for example) to a decline of the rate of accumulation would soon meet their limit in workers' minimum 'subsistence' consumption.[45]

While Ricardo introduced some elements not found in Smith, to give greater clarity and force to his own conclusions about the effects of diminishing returns on the profit rate, he was not necessarily trying to reformulate Smith's wage theory. In other words he may not have been fully conscious of introducing new ideas about wages that would conflict with the *Wealth of Nations* on the same subject. This would explain Ricardo's lack of thoroughness in dealing with the question, the presence of two different definitions of the natural wage, and the scant concern about problems in the adjustment mechanism described in the chapter on wages – though he did seem aware of these problems.

THE DEBATE ON THE INTERPRETATION OF RICARDO'S WAGE THEORY

The 'New View'

In the following discussion I shall examine some representative positions in the ongoing controversy on Ricardo's wage theory in the light of the interpretation developed in the foregoing pages. At the end of this section I shall try to give a more general evaluation of the terms in which the debate has been conducted.

Let us begin with the 'new view' or 'variable wage' (Hollander, 1983) interpretation advanced by Levi (1976), Samuelson (1978), Casarosa (1978), Hicks and Hollander (1977). According to this interpretation, Ricardo does not consider wages as constant in the course of development; this conflicts with other interpretations which, they maintain, attribute to Ricardo the idea of a constant real wage at subsistence level.[46]

Following the 'variable wage' interpretation, Ricardo's natural

45. See Chapter 3, pp. 36, 48–9, 58 above. This argument is also used by Malthus in the passage cited above, note 42, and approved by Ricardo.
46. According to the authors mentioned, the interpretations based on the notion of a constant or 'fixed' wage are those of Stigler (1952) and of the 'Cambridge School', by which is presumably meant Pasinetti (1959-60) and Kaldor (1955-56).

wage is the minimum subsistence wage which is realized when the population and the economy are stationary. Along the growth path of the economy wages are at their 'market' level. This is determined either according to the wage fund theory (Casarosa), or by a 'neoclassical' demand function coinciding with the decreasing marginal product of labour (Hicks and Hollander).

The population growth rate is an increasing function of the difference between the market wage and subsistence, while the rate of accumulation is an increasing function of the difference between the current profit rate and the minimum rate at which there is no motivation to invest. Given the inverse relation between wages and profit, the rate of accumulation may also be represented as a decreasing function of the difference between market wage and subsistence.

On these premises a model is constructed showing the convergence of the system towards the stationary state where wage and profit rates are both at their minimum level. As accumulation proceeds, given diminishing returns, the market wage moves within the ever-narrowing space between subsistence and the maximum wage corresponding to the minimum rate of profit.[47] Within this space the market wage decreases if the population grows faster than capital, and vice versa; whereas if population and capital grow at the same rate it remains constant at a level above that of subsistence. Here we find a difference of emphasis between the argument of Casarosa, Levi and Samuelson and that of Hicks and Hollander. In the former, the wage relevant to the analysis of the economic system outside the stationary state is not so much the market wage in general as the particular market wage that equalizes the rates of growth of population and capital, which Casarosa calls the 'dynamic equilibrium wage'.

Let us attempt to evaluate this interpretation in the light of the foregoing discussion.

With regard to the natural wage, as defined in the chapter on

---

47. Hicks and Hollander's model meets some problems, which I here disregard, in the definition of the 'roof' that is the maximum possible level of wages corresponding to each level of capital accumulation (given the existence of diminishing returns). One of these problems, mentioned but not dealt with in their article, is that when you go from a model based on grain alone to a more general one, there is no reason to expect that, other things constant, an increase in capital must lower the profit rate (Hicks and Hollander, 1977, p. 360).

wages, I agree that it corresponds to subsistence. But like the natural price of any other commodity, it is not associated with the stationary state. It is simply associated with a certain proportion between supply and demand for labour, such as not to induce changes in the real wage (see note 31 above).

The determination of the market wage according to either the wage fund or 'neoclassical' theory is inconsistent with Ricardo's views concerning the possibility of persistent unemployment, the absence of an inverse relation between wages and employment, and the possibility of a redistribution of income in favour of the working classes – not to mention his conclusions about the incidence of taxation. With regard to the correspondence between the market wage as defined in these interpretations and Ricardo's two different concepts, we must distinguish between the ideas of Hicks and Hollander and those of the other economists under discussion.

For Hicks and Hollander the market wage is a 'long run normal' price (erroneously regarded as determined by a neoclassical demand function). In this sense it corresponds to Smith's natural wage (and to Ricardo's as defined in the chapter on taxation). Hicks and Hollander's argument completely excludes the concept of what we have called the 'type I' market wage, whose variations, for example following a tax on wage goods, are only temporary and are corrected independently of changes in the population or its growth. The forces ensuring the immediate adjustment of wages in such cases, i.e. the bargaining position of the parties and social conventions, are also left out of consideration.

In the other contributions we are discussing, the central importance of the 'dynamic equilibrium wage' might be regarded as a reflection of the 'vacuum' which Hicks and Hollander leave when they omit one of the two concepts combined in Ricardo's definition of the market wage. When the growth rates of population and capital do not coincide, the market wage is not regarded as a 'normal' variable but gravitates towards the 'dynamic equilibrium wage'. In this respect it might then correspond to the 'type I' market wage in Ricardo. But it is still determined according to the wage fund theory, and hence can adjust towards the 'equilibrium' wage only through changes in the growth rate of population or capital: the rapid adjustment of wages that according to Ricardo follows changes in prices or taxation remains unexplained.

The 'dynamic equilibrium' wage, on the other hand, might correspond to Smith's idea of the natural wage as reflecting the country's pace of economic growth.[48] But in all the works under discussion, a higher 'dynamic equilibrium' wage corresponds to higher growth rates – equal to each other – of population and capital. In contrast, I have argued above that the definition of the natural wage derived from Smith, and adopted in Ricardo's chapter 'Taxes on wages', does not imply equality between the growth rates of population and capital. Instead, it refers to the tendency for population to lag behind accumulation in rapidly growing economies and to outstrip it in declining ones, thus persistently modifying the relation between supply and demand for labour. This interpretation is consistent with Ricardo's idea that together with food prices, the other 'great regulator' of wages is the 'proportion' between supply and demand. Supposing the growth rates of the population and the demand for labour were constantly equal, that proportion would remain unchanged; why then should higher growth rates be associated with higher levels of wages?

The answer to this question implicit in most interpretations is that higher wage levels are necessary to ensure higher growth rates of the population, and that hence wages cannot possibly remain constant for different population growth rates (and vice versa).

Yet it must be remembered, in the first place, that the classical economists had a much more flexible idea of the relation between wages and population than many modern interpreters think (see below). Hence at different moments in the course of development, according to circumstances, different population growth rates may correspond to the same wage.

In the second place, even supposing that higher wages are needed to raise the population growth rate, and disregarding other (institutional, cultural) factors that may affect wage levels, it is not hard to imagine a process of growth of population and capital which is compatible with the idea that changes in the ratio between employment and population are what induce changes in the real

48. Ricardo follows Smith in the chapter on taxation where the term 'natural level' of wages is used (cf. passage cited above, p. 142). Therefore it seems redundant to introduce a new term, foreign to the classical tradition.

wage. For example such a process might begin with wages at subsistence level; an increased rate of accumulation will induce a rise in real wages that will stimulate the growth of the population. When the effects of this growth are felt on the labour market, restoring the initial proportion between the (adult) labouring population and the demand for labour, wages will return to their initial level. If this reduces the rate of population growth below the rate of accumulation, when this impinges on the labour market wages will rise again, and so on. In the course of development the (average and ordinary) wage will tend to be higher than the original level for fairly long periods because of the population's tendency to lag behind.

In support of their interpretation, and against what they call 'fix wage' interpretations, 'new view' exponents cite the passages where Ricardo says that in a growing economy wages can remain above the natural wage for an indefinite time; that wages tend to rise in real terms during the early stages of a country's development, and to fall later when the effect of diminishing returns is felt and accumulation slows down (Ricardo, 1821, I, pp. 94–5, 98, 101; cited above: n. 29 and pp. 138, 155).

These propositions are fully compatible with the picture of Ricardo's approach outlined here. They do not imply any problem for Ricardo's analysis, if one accepts the proposed translation into the terms of Smith's theory. Otherwise problems arise from the coincidence of the natural wage with subsistence, because persistent changes in the conditions of the labour market may cause the (average) wage to diverge from the subsistence level for fairly long periods.

Like other statements by Ricardo (see Chapter 4), some of the passages cited in support of the interpretation under discussion conflict with the idea of a functional relationship between wages and the population growth rate. In them Ricardo says that when accumulation slows down wages tend to fall, because the population keeps growing at the former rate – i.e. faster than capital (ibid., p. 101). Thus Ricardo describes situations where the population growth rate remains unchanged – at least for some time – notwithstanding the fall in real wages.

Similar problems arise when a precise and stable quantitative relation between the profit rate and accumulation is attributed to Ricardo. This idea is based on a passage where he says that any reduction in the profit rate will reduce the motivation to invest. But Hollander himself (despite his adherence to the interpretation under discussion) cites numerous passages from Ricardo showing what he calls 'the extreme vagueness of the relationship supposed to exist between "profits" and savings' (Hollander, 1979, p. 319, n. 39), including the following, from the *Notes on Malthus* '[high profits] might, or might not lead to further productions, accordingly as the masters accumulated, or spent their increased incomes' (ibid.).

Hollander also points out that Ricardo's discussion on the effects of taxation does not support a necessary influence of the rate of profit on accumulation: taxes, insofar as they fall on profits, reduce the income potentially available for accumulation. But according to Ricardo taxes may lead capitalists to reduce their consumption rather than cut back their savings and investments. Indeed Ricardo argues that a reduction in consumption on the part of capitalists, rather than a reduction of accumulation, is the most probable effect of a fall in profit income due to taxation (Ricardo, 1821, I, pp. 152–3).

Ricardo actually explains at length that the profit rate is not the only factor to influence the rate of accumulation. In particular, he argues that the propensity to invest may increase thanks to the fall in the cost of the goods consumed by capitalists as a result of technical progress (ibid., p. 131).

In the light of these considerations it is impossible to define a precise quantitative (functional) relation between the rates of profit and accumulation, or to consider such a relation sufficiently stable over time to be significant: on the one hand because changes in income distribution may themselves lead to changes in profit earners' propensity to save/invest, and on the other because accumulation is constantly accompanied by technical change. Hence in principle any act of investment, like any variation in the profit rate, could modify the relation between the rates of profit and accumulation.

All this calls into question the legitimacy of taking wages as determined by the simultaneous operation of 'supply and demand curves' representing the relations, respectively increasing and decreasing, between wages and rates of increase of population and capital.

'Natural wage' interpretations

In opposition to the interpretations relegating the natural wage to the stationary state are those that see the natural variables as central in Ricardo's economic analysis. Some of these interpretations have simply assumed, as Ricardo does at times, that the natural/subsistence wage is given at a level that remains constant in time, ignoring the fluctuations of market wages (in both the senses in which Ricardo uses that term) in order to bring out certain characteristics of the development process (Pasinetti, 1959-60, 1982). Others have dealt more directly with the problem of interpreting Ricardo's wage theory. Caravale argues for the centrality of the natural rather than market variables in Ricardo's theory (Caravale, 1985, 1988). Accordingly, he suggests using the definition taken from Ricardo's *Essay on Profits*, whereby wages remain constant (at the natural rate) if the growth rates of population and capital remain equal in the course of development (Ricardo, 1815, p. 12; cited above, p. 153). This he regards as more consistent with the role of natural variables in Ricardo's theory than the definition provided in the chapter on wages.[49] Unlike the 'dynamic equilibrium wage' in Casarosa, Samuelson and Levi, the natural wage as defined by Caravale is independent of population and capital growth rates, and hence does not change when the rate of accumulation falls because of diminishing returns in agriculture.

In this way, under the assumption that the growth rates of population and capital are constantly equal, wages remain at their

49. On the basis of the interpretation suggested above (pp. 144–6), Ricardo's definition of the natural wage in the chapter 'On wages' is fully compatible with the view proposed by Caravale (and by Ricardo in the *Essay on Profits*) whereby, beginning with a situation where wages are at their natural level, hypothetically they will remain fixed at that level (in real terms) if the growth rates of population and capital (and hence employment) remain equal to each other. I have argued that the definition provided in the *Principles*, whereby the population neither increases nor decreases when wages are at the natural level, refers to a given normal position of the economy (as with the natural prices of commodities), and does not imply a stationary state. If one then turns from the examination of a single normal position to consider the process of accumulation, Ricardo's definition of the natural (subsistence) wage in the chapter 'On wages' implies that wages will remain at their natural (subsistence) level if the conditions of the labour market do not change; and this is precisely the case implied by the hypothesis that accumulation and the growth of the labouring population proceed at the same rate.

natural level, and they can be treated as an 'exogenous' quantity, in the sense that they are independent of the economy's rate of accumulation. This, according to Caravale, makes it possible to analyse the development process in terms of natural values as Ricardo did.

But it must be admitted that the assumption of constant equality between the growth rates of population and capital is far from realistic, and that Ricardo's theory offers no mechanisms capable of ensuring such equality. Indisputably, as Ricardo himself recognized, in the course of development there may well be persistent divergences between the two growth rates. On the other hand his aim was not to construct abstract models on arbitrary assumptions but to understand and explain the real tendencies of the economic system. The natural variables were conceived as 'centres of gravitation' of actual quantities. Thus Caravale's definition of the natural wage does not solve the problems posed by Ricardo's wage theory. Rather, its merit lies in bringing them out more clearly by showing that only under very particular conditions – equal growth rates of population and capital – can one rule out persistent changes in real wages due to changed conditions in the labour market (whether caused by different average growth rates of population and capital or simply by the time lag before a change in population size or growth rate affects the labour market).

Our 'translation' into Smithian terms of the two concepts that meet in Ricardo's definition of the market wage may help in the assessment of Caravale's position. As Caravale rightly argues, Ricardo's first concept – referring to transitory fluctuations of the real wage – must be considered irrelevant to the analysis of distribution, both in a given 'long-run normal' position and for a series of such positions studied to determine the 'secular' trends of the system.

The second concept refers to variations in real wages due to changes in labour market conditions which tend to be more lasting (because of the slowness and uncertainty of population adjustment). For reasons mentioned earlier, Ricardo often tends to argue as if this second type of wage variation could legitimately be disregarded and relegated to the sphere of transitory phenomena. It is to preserve this aspect of Ricardo's theory that Caravale suggests the assumption of instantaneous adjustment of population growth to variations in the rate of accumulation, so that the two growth rates remain constantly equal. But it is precisely this aspect of Ricardo's theory which causes the problems and inconsistencies that we have noted, and it is not essential to his conclusions. These remain valid even if one recognizes (as did Smith and in some places even Ricardo) that lasting changes in the labour market may cause the natural (normal) wage to deviate from the historically determined minimum subsistence level, which is its lower limit.

Some other interpretations, in which the concept of natural wage is central, emphasize the importance in classical analysis of habits, institutions and power relationships in determining its level (Garegnani, 1984, 1990; Picchio del Mercato, 1981). Clearly my interpretation has many points in common with these earlier ones. However, I have also sought to highlight those inconsistencies in Ricardo's thought which make its interpretation more difficult, and to trace their analytical origins.

The role of 'demand' in determining wages

Hollander presents the debate on Ricardo's wage theory in terms of 'fix wage' interpretations vs 'variable wage' interpretations (Hollander, 1983). Caravale sees it as a conflict over whether the natural wage or the market wage should be placed at the centre of Ricardo's analysis (Caravale, 1985). Actually, the debate has revolved around whether Ricardo considered wages to be determined 'exogenously' or, as Hollander, Samuelson, Casarosa and others suggest, by 'market forces' (i.e. by 'supply and demand'), in a manner not unlike that proposed by contemporary theory. This opposition between the ideas of wages as 'exogenously given' on the one hand, or as subject to the influence of 'supply and demand' on the other, has been generally accepted as the main ground for argument. But in my view the opposition is ill-conceived and may be misleading. The real issue is the interpretation of the meaning and role of labour 'demand' in determining wages.

In the classical tradition the natural wage is taken as exogenously given when determining relative prices and incomes other than wages. But this in no way rules out the influence of economic factors on the natural wage.[50] In particular, from the theoretical point of view there is no problem in recognizing the influence on wages (even the natural wage, as in Smith and Turgot) of the 'proportion between supply and demand', provided this is correctly interpreted as a ratio between the level of employment (in the capitalist or market sector of the economy) and the given labour supply. In any given period this proportion results on the one hand from the preceding history of accumulation, and hence from existing productive capacity and techniques in use, and on the other hand from demographic phenomena that determine the size and age structure of the population. Persistent changes in the ratio between employment and population are generally associated with variations in the average rate of accumulation. Such variations can also be taken as known data at the moment of determining relative prices and net product.

Hence the influence on wages of the 'proportion of supply to demand', thus interpreted, does not conflict with taking the wage rate as a datum when determining relative prices and net product. The role of 'supply' and 'demand' in determining wages in classical theory differs profoundly from what it is in contemporary neoclassical theory. In the latter, supply and demand schedules determine the wage rate as a full-employment equilibrium price, an indicator of the scarcity of the resource labour relative to other, similarly fully employed resources. In the classical theory variations in the ratio between the quantity of wage labour demanded and the given supply influence the normal wage because the bargaining position of the parties is modified by persistent changes in (explicit and disguised) unemployment expressed by that ratio.

Ricardian models
In the debate on the interpretation of Ricardo, the tendency to construct growth models seems to have a negative effect. Such models may serve to bring out specific aspects and conclusions of his analysis, but they involve very restrictive simplifying assumptions

50. An analogy may make this clearer: for commodities, the classical economists considered the quantities produced (the effectual demand) as given at the moment of determination of relative prices and the net product. But this obviously does not mean excluding the influence of economic circumstances, in particular accumulation, on those quantities.

that can be justified only by the need to isolate particular aspects. These simplifications should not be taken, as they sometimes are, as features of Ricardo's economic theory which are necessary to give it consistency. In other words, the 'Ricardian' growth models cannot correctly be seen as representing Ricardo's general economic theory and his view of economic development. They only focus on his point of view on a particular question: how profits are affected by diminishing returns in agriculture, under a series of simplifying assumptions.

In discussing this question it is undoubtedly useful, for example, to assume that wages are constant at a given subsistence level – a simplification adopted by Ricardo himself. But this simplification cannot be taken as Ricardo's theory of wages. That theory must and does have a more general character, taking account of possible changes in subsistence levels over time, and the possibility that wages may remain, even for fairly long periods, at a level other than subsistence. On the other hand the above simplifying assumption must and can be justified in the light of the more general theory of wages. As I argued earlier, the classical idea of a minimum subsistence level as the historically determined lower limit of the natural wage means that even if real wages vary in the course of accumulation, such variations cannot counterbalance (and thus put in doubt) the long-term or 'secular' tendency for profits to fall when food production costs increase. The assumption of a constant wage thus simplifies the analysis, but does not lead to erroneous conclusions in the light of the general theory of wages. Other frequently employed simplifications involve ignoring the effects of technical progress on both manufacturing and agriculture, the possibility of changes in the propensity to invest due to variations in distribution, the possibility of changes in the subsistence wage, or the effects of cultural changes on demographic trends. While all these elements (and others) are sometimes disregarded (by Ricardo and by his interpreters) in order to simplify the analysis by isolating a particular economic relation or tendency, these simplifications cannot legitimately be used to characterize Ricardo's general economic theory.

SUMMARY

The aim of this chapter has not been to present Ricardo's theory of wages as fully consistent, but rather to understand the sources of some of its difficulties.

The Smithian background is the nucleus of Ricardo's wage theory and the origin of many aspects of his argument. Characteristic of this background are:

1. The central role of customary, historical and institutional factors in determining the natural wage and its adjustment to changes in prices of necessary goods and to taxes on such goods or on wages.
2. The possibility of unemployment, whose variations (measured by variations in the ratio between demand for labour and population) affect wage levels by influencing the bargaining power of the workers; this point follows from the absence of the wage fund theory, which belongs to later developments in economic thought.
3. The Smithian definition of the natural wage, adopted at some points in the *Principles*, as the wage that reflects the particular 'circumstances of the country': the natural wage is higher in rapidly growing economies for the same reasons given by Smith – i.e. because the conditions of the labour market are such as to improve the bargaining position of the workers.

Along with these ideas Ricardo introduces novel elements which all arise from his definition of the natural wage in close analogy with the natural price of any commodity; these elements cause the difficulties involved in his theory.

Because of this analogy, in the chapter on wages, changes in wages induced by variations in the ratio between employment and population (even those arising from relatively persistent phenomena such as divergences between the rates of accumulation and population growth) are defined as deviations of the market wage from the natural wage, not as shifts in the natural wage as in Smith. This definition (provided by Ricardo) is inconsistent with his general framework of analysis, whereby market (actual) price deviations from natural prices are due to (continuously occurring) temporary and accidental disturbances rather than to the persistent and systematic forces which determine natural variables and which are the main object of economic enquiry.

In defence of his analogy between the natural price of labour and any other commodity, Ricardo characteristically argues for clarity and terminological consistency: ('I have done so that we may have one common language to apply to all cases which are similar'). But the correspondence between Ricardo and Malthus before the publication of the first edition of the *Principles* suggests another possible reason for Ricardo's choice of a definition that makes the natural wage independent of labour market conditions: to sharpen his conclusions on the effects on profits of diminishing returns in agriculture.

On the other hand the many elements of continuity between the wage theories of Ricardo and Smith, and the latter's compatibility with Ricardo's conclusions, may suggest that Ricardo did not fully realize that his own formulation contained innovations that might prove contradictory to Smith's theory.

6. Wages and the Labour Market in Classical Political Economy

INTRODUCTION

In the light of the foregoing discussion, it can be affirmed that the classical economists agreed as to the basic forces determining wages, despite some differences in emphasis. Thus we may attempt a synthesis of the ideas they largely shared.

Their perspective will be compared with that of the two wage theories that developed afterwards. The first of these – now obsolete – was the wage fund theory, which is commonly (and, I shall argue, wrongly) ascribed to the classical economists. The second, the marginalist or neo-classical theory, explains wages as the equilibrium price between the supply of and demand for labour – both understood as functions of wages. This is the dominant view today, though it has met some very serious difficulties both at the purely theoretical level and in attempting to explain observed phenomena. Most economists still use the apparatus of supply and demand curves in analysing the labour market and distribution.

Comparing these positions will help to clarify the analytical foundations of the classical theory of wages. The main distinctive feature of classical theory is that it does not entail the inverse relation between wages and employment which characterizes both the wage fund and marginalist theories (though on different theoretical grounds).

Accordingly, although Say's law was often adhered to by classical economists, they did not see the economic system as tending towards full employment of labour. This in turn may explain their ideas on the effects of competition in the labour market.These ideas differ in some respects from those of today, and are based on a picture of human behaviour quite unlike the narrowly individualistic view that currently pervades economic theory.

FACTORS DETERMINING WAGES IN THE CLASSICAL APPROACH

Role of subsistence consumption
In the works of the classical economists the definition of the natural (or normal) rate of wages is closely associated with that of subsistence consumption. This is the level of consumption which 'habits and customs' have rendered indispensable for the working classes of a particular country and historical period. The relation between the natural wage and the workers' necessary or subsistence consumption is more complex than is commonly suggested. Subsistence consumption corresponds to a historically determined minimum below which wages cannot long remain; whereas the natural rate of wages is the central or average value around which the wage actually observed on the labour market gravitates. Depending on circumstances, the natural wage may be at or above subsistence, but cannot be below it.

It is true that the classical economists often used the two terms interchangeably. But even the early eighteenth-century writers, as well as Turgot, Smith and Necker, argued that the natural wage tends to approach the minimum subsistence level not because they believed the two would necessarily coincide, but because certain observed historical conditions (political–institutional features, unemployment, poverty) weakened the workers' bargaining position. Changes in these conditions could lead to a lasting improvement in the workers' bargaining power and raise the natural wage above the subsistence level defined by habits and customs (Chapter 2, pp. 19–24; Chapter 3, pp. 35–8).

In turn, as the subsistence level is defined by historical and social factors, changes in the natural wage may affect it because they may lead to changes in consumption habits, and raise the minimum threshold of consumption considered indispensable by the working classes (Chapter 3, pp. 65–70).

Factors determining the natural wage
The natural wage can be seen as determined by two sets of

conditions. One set comprises all the elements of custom prevalent in a given historical period, which reflect the history of bargaining relationships between social classes as sedimented in widely accepted social conventions and/or institutions. These elements determine the minimum wage which is the starting point for wage bargaining. The other main factor is the relative bargaining power of employers and workers. This depends, for example, on the relative amounts of employment and population; on political and institutional changes; and on successful collective action to increase wages (or to reduce them, when employers join forces). These circumstances determine the normal rate of wages in relation to the minimum subsistence level (Chapter 2, pp. 19–24; Chapter 3, pp. 35–58).

The main factors and relationships which together determine the normal wage are shown schematically in *Figure 1*.

Figure 1

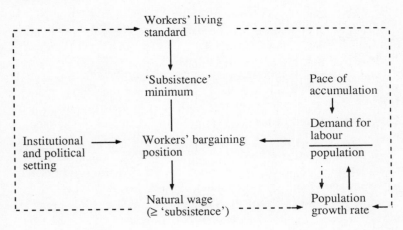

The workers' historically determined standards of living determine the minimum wage, which the classical economists called the 'subsistence' wage. Power relationships between workers and capitalists affect the determination of the normal wage rate, making it coincide with subsistence if conditions are unfavourable to the workers, or raising it above that level if they are favourable.

The main factors indicated by the classical economists as

determining the relative bargaining power of the parties can be reduced to two elements. The first is the political and institutional setting, understood in a broad sense: it includes the essential feature of the capitalist system – the fact that waged workers can live only by selling their labour – as well as the institutional structure at any historical moment: the 'form of government' (i.e. the existing political system), laws regulating the labour market, and the existence of workers' or employers' organizations.

The second element is the conditions of the labour market, that is the opportunities for employment available to members of the working classes. This is indicated in *Figure 1* by the ratio of the demand for labour to the population. Labour demand is not a 'demand curve' but a single quantity, which varies in accord with the processes of accumulation.[1]

The classical economists saw changes in this ratio as indicators of changing levels of overt and latent unemployment, and hence of the ease or difficulty of finding work. Thus it is an important index of the relative bargaining power of the workers. The ratio of employed workers to population also determines the average per capita income of the working classes for a given wage level. Therefore changes in this ratio may have a direct effect on population growth, as indicated in the figure. This effect will in turn influence the labour market (i.e. the ratio of employment to population) in later periods, when the grown children of the workers present themselves on the labour market.[2]

It must be emphasized that only persistent changes in the employment–population ratio can influence the determination of the natural wage. Transitory oscillations in employment – caused for example by seasonal fluctuations in agricultural production – may at most produce temporary deviations in the market wage around the natural wage. The latter is affected only by labour-market conditions linked with persistent features of an economy – for example an increased average rate of accumulation which causes a relative

1. The forms of employment included in this 'demand' appear to differ somewhat between writers. While for Ricardo it usually comprised only wage labour in the capitalist sector, Smith would generally include also menial servants hired at a wage, and sometimes also artisans selling their services or products on the market.
2. The positive effect of improved living standards on population, it will be recalled, was seen as the result of lower infant mortality and increased marriages and hence births.

'scarcity of hands' because employment grows faster than the working population, or vice versa a situation where 'the hands multiply beyond their employment', with resulting chronic problems of unemployment or underemployment (Chapter 3, pp. 53–7).

The gap between the natural wage and subsistence may in turn affect both the rate of population growth and the workers' habits of consumption and hence the subsistence minimum.

These effects – shown by a broken line in the figure – take a fairly long time to manifest themselves. Moreover, the result is not certain: for example if workers' consumption patterns are modified by a normal wage above 'subsistence' level, it is possible that the higher income may not stimulate the formation of new families or an increased birth rate, and that the population may not increase.

The relation between employment and population (or between the labour 'demand' and supply' as conceived by the classical economists) obviously cannot determine wages. It can only influence them, taking account of the levels prevailing in a particular historical context. In the classical view two countries with the same proportion between employment and population would have different normal wage rates if they had different political–institutional arrangements, or different historical experiences of bargaining between workers and employers.

Trade union organization, and political and institutional changes favouring the workers, can in principle act independently of labour market conditions to modify the natural wage by raising it above subsistence level without setting in motion reactions in the economic system tending to restore the previous wage level. Of course a rise in wages may lead to an increase in population; but even if this happens and eventually undermines the workers' bargaining power, it will not necessarily bring the natural wage down to the level preceding the political or institutional change.

Changes in population

Contrary to what is often asserted, according to the classical economists population changes are not what guarantee that actual (market) wages will move towards the natural rate. Such adjustments (for example in response to changes in the prices of subsistence goods), which are relatively rapid, depend not on population but on the same forces that determine the natural wage itself: elements of custom which fix the subsistence minimum, and the relative bargaining power of workers and employers.

Changes in population or its rate of growth may influence the 'secular' trends of the natural wage in the course of economic development. In this context the classical economists express varying degrees of pessimism within the same theoretical approach. Their differences probably reflect the different historical circumstances they observed. Thus Smith held that while the population would tend to grow in response to increased employment opportunities and wages, in growing economies employment would generally increase faster than the labour supply, so the natural wage would remain above subsistence level. Ricardo, on the other hand, seems inclined to the view that even in growing economies the population would increase faster than opportunities for employment, and hence wages would tend to remain around the minimum level which 'nature and habit demand for the support of the labourer' (Chapter 4, n. 27 and p. 125).

Whether or not they drew pessimistic conclusions about the prospect of improving workers' living conditions, Turgot, Smith, Ricardo, Steuart and Cantillon differed significantly from Malthus on the subject of population. The Malthusian theory, which may be seen as the basis for the so-called 'iron law of wages', claims that population exerts a constant pressure on agricultural subsistence goods. Malthus viewed the excess of population over food production as the cause of the working classes' low standards of living. This conflicts with the analysis of the other classical economists, who saw food production as determined by the 'effectual demand' for food, and hence by the income of the working classes (Chapter 4, pp. 103–12). According to Smith and Ricardo population growth may lead to poverty not because it exceeds food production, but because it outstrips the opportunities for employment created by economic development and this leads to unemployment and low wages.

Natural prices of commodities and labour
The absence of an inverse relation between wage and employment levels in the classical approach obviously means that imbalances

between the 'supply of labour' (i.e. the labouring population) and the 'demand for labour' (the level of employment in the market sector of the economy) cannot be corrected through variations in wages. Hence it rules out a tendency towards full employment even in a competitive economy.

On the other hand adjustments from the supply side are much slower and more uncertain for labour than for other commodities: such adjustments, according to the classical economists, depend on changes in the labouring population. This means unemployment is possible in normal positions of the economy, and its presence and extent play a part in determining the normal rate of wages.

Consequently, the definition of the natural price of labour cannot be the same as for other commodities. Unlike other prices, the normal price of labour can be influenced by persistent imbalances between supply and demand, and cannot therefore be defined as the price that would be established in the market when the quantity supplied equals the quantity normally demanded.

At times the difference between the natural price of labour and that of other commodities causes problems and ambiguities in the writings of the classical authors. This is especially true of Ricardo, who in his chapter on wages stretches the definition of the natural wage and the mechanisms of gravitation around it in order to maintain a rigorous analogy between the natural price of labour and the natural price of any other commodity. This leads him into certain inconsistencies, ultimately due to the fact that variations in the proportion between population and the demand for labour may be of a persistent nature (Chapter 5, pp. 130–1, 147–51).

THE WAGE FUND THEORY, THE INVERSE RELATION BETWEEN WAGES AND EMPLOYMENT, AND CLASSICAL THEORY

Main features of the wage fund theory

The wage fund theory was not fully formulated until after Ricardo's death, by post-Ricardian economists such as McCulloch, Senior and J.S. Mill.[3]

---

3. Interpretations indicating a difference between Ricardo's wage theory and that of the wages fund are proposed in Baradhwaj, 1983 and Picchio Del Mercato, 1992.

The works of the classical economists (except for Malthus, discussed above in Chapter 4) contain none of the features of the wage fund theory. A superficial continuity of terminology may help to explain why the contrary idea has taken hold among historians of economic thought. Smith and Ricardo often used expressions like 'the fund for the maintenance of the labourers', which might have suggested a continuity of analysis between their wage theories (and those of their predecessors and contemporaries) and the later formulations. In other words the earlier writers are interpreted in the light of the theory formulated by later ones. This is all the more natural since modern economists have difficulty in interpreting the classical wage theory because of the profound difference between it and the modern marginalist approach.

The wage fund theory appeared in somewhat different formulations, but its essential characteristics are well summarized in the following passage by J.S. Mill:

> The theory rests on what may be called the doctrine of the wages fund. There is supposed to be, at any given instant, a sum of wealth, which is unconditionally devoted to the payment of wages of labour. This sum is not regarded as unalterable, for it is augmented by saving, and increases with the progress of wealth; but it is reasoned upon as at any given moment a predetermined amount. More than that amount is assumed that the wage-receiving class cannot possibly divide among them; that amount, and no less, they cannot but obtain. So that, the sum to be divided being fixed, the wages of each depend solely on the divisor, the number of participants. In this doctrine it is by implication affirmed, that the demand for labour not only increases with the cheapness, but increases in exact proportion to it, the same aggregate sum being paid for labour whatever its price may be. (J.S. Mill, 1869, p. 515)

Thus the salient principles of the wage fund theory are:

1. The real wage is flexible and is equal to the wage fund divided by the active working population ('the number of participants').
2. The wage fund, generally (though not necessarily) specified in real terms, is predetermined independently of the real wage rate – with any reduction of wages the number of workers employed will increase proportionately and this, along with the flexibility of real wages in response to unemployment or excess demand, ensures the tendency to full employment of labour (this is implicit anyway in the determination of wages as equal to the ratio

between wage fund and active population).

3. If wages are fixed (for example by workers' combinations) at a higher level than that corresponding to this ratio, some workers will be unemployed.[4]

Changes in the role of 'market wages'

In the wage fund theory there is a shift in the meaning and analytical role of the market wage and the natural wage. The former, which for Smith and Ricardo was simply the actual observed rate, becomes a normal theoretical variable. The natural wage, which they saw as resulting from the action of persistent and systematic forces in the economic system (and thus approximated by the actual average wage level), is now regarded as a minimum threshhold which is hardly ever approached by the wage actually paid.[5]

Unlike the proponents of the wage fund theory, the classical economists did not see the normal wage as fully flexible; and wages are never indicated as equal to the ratio between the wage fund and the labour supply, or as determined exclusively by 'supply and demand'.[6] Such an idea is in direct contradiction with the importance attributed by economists like Smith, Necker, Hume and Ricardo to

4. The quoted passage by J. S. Mill was chosen for its clarity. However, the three propositions listed are implicit every time wages are said to be determined *exclusively* by the ratio between circulating capital and the number of workers, as was already done in earlier writings, for example by McCulloch and by J. S. Mill himself (see Mill, 1965, II, pp. 337-8; McCulloch 1826, p. 5 and 1830, p. 378; Taussig, 1896, pp. 192, 222, 234; according to this latter author, however, Ricardo also held a definite wage fund theory: ibid., pp. 168 ff). Concerning the third of the propositions listed, see Mill, 1865, II, p. 365 and III, pp. 929-930; Bharadwaj (1983), p. 67 and McCulloch's passages quoted there. It is true that Mill and other wage fund theorists (McCulloch for example) were not adverse to trade unions and favoured the repeal of the 'combination law' that prohibited them. However, the role they envisaged for the unions was that of substituting competition among employers - which might fail to operate rapidly and efficiently in the short run - when the wage is below equilibrium level. Thus, unions could help bringing the wage up to its equilibrium rate, but any attempt on their part to raise it above this rate would eventually fail because of market forces (i.e. because of the emergence of unemployment and competition among workers) (Mill, 1865, III, p. 392; see also the discussion of this point in Blith, 1987, p. 835-36; O'Brien, 1970, pp. 366-370; Maffeo, 1987, pp. 76-81).
5. On this last point, see also Schumpeter, 1954, p. 666.
6. In fact Ricardo objected vigorously to the assertion, then beginning to appear in part of the economic literature, that prices or wages could be so determined: '[t]he opinion that the price of commodities depends solely on the proportion of supply to demand, or demand to supply, has become almost an axiom in political economy, and it has been the source of much error in that science. It is this opinion which has made Mr. Buchanan maintain that wages are not influenced by a rise or fall in the price of provisions, but solely by the demand and supply of labour'(Ricardo, 1821. I, p. 382).

institutional factors in determining and modifying normal wages.

Advanced wages do not imply a given wage fund

The notion of a wage fund determined *before* wages is usually ascribed to the classical authors on the basis of their conception of wages as circulating capital that must be advanced by employers to workers at the beginning of a period or 'year' of production.[7]

This idea of wages as 'advances' is certainly present in the works of Smith and Ricardo, and in those of their predecessors such as Cantillon, Turgot and the Physiocrats. But for these economists it does not imply a predetermined fund independent of the wage rate. Such a notion is incompatible with an idea shared by all the classical economists: the immediate adjustment (not mediated by population changes) of the natural wage to variations in food prices or direct taxation of wages, so that the workers' real disposable income remains constant (Chapter 3, pp. 70–83; Chapter 5, pp. 139–42). This conflicts with the idea of a wage fund advanced by employers to workers, which is fixed in either real or monetary terms. The 'fund' advanced by the employers must increase (either in monetary terms, or in both monetary and real terms) as the natural wage rises following taxation or changes in the price of corn.

Ricardo's differences with the wage fund theory emerged explicitly as he had to confront some elements of that theory that were already emerging, for example in Malthus. As we have seen, in his *Principles* and his correspondence with Malthus, Trower and Place, Ricardo criticizes the tendency to consider the available quantity of subsistence goods as determined independently of the demand for those goods – a demand which depends on the income of the working classes. According to Ricardo the amount of food produced in the economic system is determined, as for any other commodity, by effectual demand. Therefore it cannot be known before the determination of wages and cannot be independent of wages, as in the wage fund theory (Chapter 4, pp. 117–8; Chapter 5, pp. 132–3).

The analytic reason why the idea of 'advances' does not imply a

7. For example Schumpeter writes that '[t]he basis of the wage-fund doctrine is the proposition that (industrial) wages are "advanced" from capital [...] He who accepts it cannot oppose the wage-fund doctrine' (Schumpeter, 1954, p. 667); the same position appears, among others, in Blith, 1987, p. 836 and O'Brien, 1975, p. 111.

fixed wage fund independent of distribution is that the normal or natural wage rate in the theory of Ricardo and his predecessors results from the operation of persistent forces, acting over a longer period than that of a single production period or 'year'. The normal wage rate and the level of employment together determine, on the average, the amount of subsistence goods produced in each year which can be advanced to the workers for the following one. This is because a rise in the natural wage increases the effectual demand for food and this leads to a rise in the market price of subsistence goods. Production will increase in response to the new level of wages and demand, and when that happens prices will return to their natural level.

It is true that the production of food, more than of any other commodity, used to be subject to fluctuations due to unpredictable climatic conditions. A year of bad harvests will reduce the total amount of food available until the next harvest, and market prices of food will increase. In this case either money wages must rise or the workers must cut their consumption. But these are obviously temporary fluctuations of real wages around their natural level, caused by accidental factors. Scant or abundant harvests, compared to the effective demand for food, are clearly seen by Ricardo and the other classical economists as inducing oscillations in actual wages around their natural rate – never as possible causes of change in that rate.[8]

Moreover, even in a year of bad harvests the amount of food available for the workers should not be taken as 'fixed' and predetermined. Food is also consumed by other social classes, and in a situation of exceptional scarcity the share of the total production that goes to the workers may be more or less than normal, depending on circumstances. The market wage varies in real terms with fluctuations in agricultural production – not because it is equal to the ratio between a fixed 'wage fund' and population size, but because the market prices of food change, while the workers' bargaining power is affected by fluctuations in employment (due to changes in output levels). Thus the recognition of 'discontinuities' in agricultural production and the idea of wages as capital 'advanced' to

---

8.   With regard to Ricardo, cf. Ricardo, 1821, I, p. 162; for the other authors see Chapter 3, pp. 71, 73, 81.

workers do not necessarily imply the notion of a predetermined 'wage fund', as is sometimes claimed.

Apart from accidental fluctuations in agricultural production, changes in the natural wage will modify production so as to adjust the quantity of wage goods to the altered income distribution. On the other hand, as Ricardo stresses, the production of these goods absolutely cannot be activated without clear signals from the market – in other words before there is a demand for them.

The inverse relation between wages and employment

Ricardo explicitly criticizes not only the idea of a 'wage fund' determined independently of income distribution, but also the idea of an inverse relation between wages and employment – which in the wage fund theory follows precisely from the notion of a fixed fund. In some illuminating passages in his correspondence he takes issue with Malthus's assertion that in a year of bad harvests there must be a fall in either real wages or employment. He also vigorously objects to Malthus's claim that a wage increase determined by 'combinations of artificers and manufacturers' would cause unemployment. According to Ricardo the only effect of such a rise in wages would be to increase the money income and purchasing power of the working class as a whole (Chapter 5, p. 134). Thus Ricardo saw no theoretical objections to the possibility of redistributing the total income in favour of the working classes.

One element in Ricardo's argument which has perplexed interpreters is his admission that the introduction of machines may lead to unemployment. Since Wicksell, many commentators have seen this as contradicting Ricardo's theory and his method of long period analysis, since it supposedly fails to take account of all the consequences of introducing machines. But in fact Ricardo's view is perfectly consistent, and it does apply to the long period. Unlike the later wage fund theorists, he and the other classical economists did not see the real wage as fully flexible, and, most importantly, in their view its reduction would not necessarily lead to an increase in the level of employment.[9]

---

9.   On this point see Montani, 1985, which brings out the consequences of the different theoretical approaches of Ricardo and Wicksell for analysis of the possibility of unemployment owing to technical progress.

Although for historical reasons Ricardo's opposition to wage fund notions was more explicit, there is a substantial continuity in this respect, as in his wage theory in general, between his analysis and that of Smith and other eighteenth–century English and French economists.[10]

That whole tradition – unlike the wage fund theory – presupposed that in normal states of the economy unemployment can (and usually does) exist, and may be widespread. The explicit or latent level of unemployment is one of the factors that determine the normal or natural rate of wages (Chapter 2, pp. 21–4; Chapter 3, pp. 39–42, 53–7; Chapter 5, pp. 135–9). Here we see a continuity between the classical economists and the earlier mercantilist tradition, which always recognized the possibility of widespread unemployment. In the late mercantilist period the creation of employment was a central economic issue: Furniss has argued that the mercantilists' preoccupation with a positive balance of payments was essentially due to the view that this would favour the creation of additional employment in the country (Chapter 2, pp. 23–4).

The classical economists and their forerunners did not link unemployment with 'excessively high' wages or with their downward rigidity. Nowhere in Smith, or his contemporaries or predecessors, is there any reference to a systematic inverse relation between wages and employment.

On the contrary, in a few places we find statements pointing in the opposite direction – associating a fall in real wages with a drop in production, and hence in employment, due to a decrease in the demand for goods on the part of the workers. Considerations of this kind play a fairly prominent part in Turgot's analysis. In his view an initial reduction in workers' real wages, due to taxation on subsistence goods, leads to a fall in consumption and hence in the prices of those goods. This phenomenon, if prolonged, must ultimately induce a reduction in agricultural production (Chapter 3, p. 76). Two important points follow from Turgot's idea that reduced purchasing power for the workers would lead to reduced income and employment.

First, this view clearly conflicts with that of the 'wage fund' as a

10. On the relation between the theories of Ricardo and Smith, see above, Chapter. 5, p. 168.

predetermined quantity of subsistence goods independent of income distribution. On the contrary, the level of real wages determines the production of goods consumed by the workers. While Ricardo was aware of the implications of the assumption that all income is always spent (Say's law), and hence believed that changes in distribution would modify only the composition of the social product, Turgot also related the level of production, and hence employment, to the purchasing power of the workers.[11]

Second, when a price increase caused by new taxes on subsistence goods is met by an increase in money wages, according to the wage fund theory this must lead to a reduction in employment in the private sector. Turgot, on the contrary, saw such a wage increase as favouring the maintenance of production and employment levels.

Clearly, then, in the classical tradition up to Ricardo the 'funds destined for the maintenance of labour' were not conceived as a sum fixed before the determination of wages. Rather, they are simply equal to the wage rate times the number of employed workers: changes in one or the other of these will induce a corresponding change in that 'fund'. So when the classical economists state that the accumulation of 'capital' will raise wages they do not refer to increases of a predetermined wage fund, but to the favourable influence on wages of changes in employment due to the creation of productive capacity (Chapter 3, pp. 55-6; Chapter 5, pp. 135-9). The demand for labour – the level of employment – depends on accumulation and on the techniques in use (Ricardo says: 'in proportion to the work to be done will be the demand [for labour]').

SAY'S LAW AND THE LABOUR MARKET

Does Say's law imply a given wage fund?

Like many other classical economists Ricardo supported Say's law, and it is sometimes suggested that this implied a wage-fund theory. The question is whether Say's law, that is, the idea that the entire

11. Some well-known passages in Turgot and Smith show that they too believed that all income is always spent, in the sense that savings coincide with investments. But they were not always aware of the full consequences of this, and this left room for the opinion (also shared by mercantilist writers) that paying higher wages, at the expense of savings or non-productive consumption by the capitalists, favoured economic growth.

income is always spent, need imply the idea of a given amount of 'investible income', determined by savings, which will give employment to more or less labour according to the wage level. This view might seem to be suggested for example by Schumpeter's statement that '[f]unds are, in the classic theory, "destined" for the maintenance of productive labour by the decision of the saver and thus are determined if annual savings are' (1982, p. 667, n. 51). In other words, it might be inferred that, given that under Say's law the accumulation of capital requires an act of saving, and as wages are treated as capital advanced to the workers, it must follow that the wage fund can *only* be increased by a previous decision to save on the part of the capitalists. This, I shall argue, would be a false conclusion. A very simple numerical example will show that an increase in the wage fund can take place independently of a previous decision of the saver. For simplicity the example will be in terms of a single good economy,[12] assuming that both capitalists and workers consume in the current period the income produced in the previous 'year'.

Suppose a stationary economy producing 1000 units of corn per year by means of 200 units of corn used as seed and 100 units of labour paid a yearly wage of 4 units of corn. Six hundred units of corn are therefore the capital advanced each year by the capitalists, while the remaining 400 units are their profits, entirely consumed. Suppose now that in this economy, at the beginning of the period, a successful combination of the workers manages to impose a higher wage rate, 6 units of corn. The same amount of seed and number of workers must still be used in order to produce 1000 units of corn, and profits will be reduced to 200. On the other hand an attempt on the part of the capitalists to keep their consumption unaltered by reducing employment and output would be in vain, and only postpone the income reduction to the next period.

The increase of the 'wage fund' in this case is simply the other face of the reduction in profit income and does not require a previous decision on the part of capitalists to increase their

---

12. Should two (or more) goods be produced, one consumed by the capitalists and the other by the workers, the substance of the argument would not change, but a time lag would be required to allow production to adjust to the changed distribution of income (see above, pp. 180–2).

savings.[13]

Therefore, while it is rightly maintained that Ricardo usually regarded saving, and the accumulation of capital (machinery, tools, raw materials) as conditions for the expansion of employment (and consequently, with a given wage rate, of the 'funds for the maintainance of labour'), this should not lead to the false conclusion that a rise in the wage rate also necessarily requires it.

Now consider an economy with a positive net investment. If the capitalists' propensity to save/invest is constant, and other factors such as production techniques are unchanged, a rise in real wages will reduce overall profits and hence investments, resulting in a lower rate of increase of employment. However, if the capitalists' aim is not to obtain a certain consumption growth, but rather to increase their capital (productive capacity) at a given rate, then, as in the former case, the effect of a wage increase will be a greater propensity to invest at the expense of the capitalists' propensity to consume. Of course there may be any number of intermediate combinations for the capitalists between fully maintaining the rate of accumulation and fully maintaining their consumption growth. But in any case the possibility of changes in the propensity to invest implies that wage increases do not necessarily cause a fall in the rate of growth of employment.

Say's law and full employment

For the classical economists Say's law did not necessarily imply a tendency to full employment of labour, but only the full utilization of existing productive capacity. Say's law implies full employment only if supported by two additional propositions shared by the wage fund and marginalist theories: 1) wages tend to decrease in the presence of unemployment; 2) a fall in wages leads to a rise in employment. If these conditions obtain, Say's law ensures that the increased employment and production following a fall in wages will not be hindered by a shortage of aggregate demand. As we have seen, however, neither of these propositions can be found in the theories of Ricardo or the other classical economists.

Say's law thus implies only that the productive capacity realized

13. See Garegnani, 1960, pp. 165–75, for discussion of a similar point in the context of the criticism of Wicksell's notion of 'subsistence fund'.

through investment will be fully utilized, and that its expansion will meet no constraints from the aggregate demand side – in other words accumulation depends only on the amount of net income and the propensity of those who receive that income to invest. But there is no reason why the productive capacity and techniques in use should necessarily be such as to allow full employment of the available labour force.

All this explains how, in the same speech (*On Mr. Owen's Plan*) where he asserts that unemployment exists and can be overcome only through a recovery of accumulation (Chapter 5, p. 137), Ricardo could use arguments based on Say's law against the proposal to sustain employment through public works. He claims that the money used by the government to finance public works, raised by taxes on profits, would otherwise be spent by the capitalists and would create an equal amount of employment. Barton's well known pamphlet on the effects of introducing machines was aimed against just such arguments. He demonstrated that a given amount of income spent by the government to maintain unemployed workers can support more workers than the same sum invested by the capitalists, who may use it to buy machines, increasing employment little or not at all, or even diminishing it. In the chapter on machinery in the third edition of his *Principles* Ricardo accepts this argument and implicitly admits, in principle, its consequences with regard to public intervention to support employment and the income of the unemployed.

The above argument also explains how (contrary to what is sometimes maintained), in Ricardo's analytical framework the admission that introducing machinery may create unemployment is consistent with Say's law.[14]

14. Blaug seems to concur with this argument. With regard to the compatibility, in Ricardo's thought, of Say's law with unemployment (including technological unemployment), he writes: 'For Ricardo full employment meant nothing more than full-capacity use of the existing stock of capital', and: 'In an era when the number of individuals on public relief hovered steadily around one million [...] the existence of a hard core of surplus labour must have been taken for granted' (Blaug, 1973, p. 75). But Blaug does not note that Ricardo's view depends on the absence of theoretical relations assuring a tendency to full employment even with complete flexibility of wages. On the contrary, as we have seen (Chapter 5, p. 135, n. 11), he holds that according to Ricardo wage cuts may induce an increase in employment until full employment is reached. As a consequence of this, and in contrast with the remarks quoted above, Blaug sees Ricardo's statement that machines may create unemployment

CLASSICAL THEORY AND SUBSTITUTION BETWEEN 'FACTORS OF PRODUCTION'

Substitution in contemporary theory

The idea of an inverse relation between wages and employment is central to the marginalist or neoclassical wage theory. In that context it depends on the possibility of substitution between production factors (direct substitution) and consumer goods (indirect substitution) following changes in distribution. It is argued that when, for example, the labour supply increases, the fall in wages due to competition among workers will make it advantageous for employers to use more labour-intensive production techniques, and this, other things being equal, will bring an increase in employment (and vice versa if wages rise).[15] In addition, it is argued that (in the same situation) a drop in wages will reduce the prices of those goods whose production requires relatively more labour. On the basis of the marginalist theory of consumer behaviour this will lead to an increase in demand for such goods compared to those whose production is less labour-intensive. This will result in increased employment in the economy as a whole.[16]

as inconsistent; he agrees with Wicksell that on this question Ricardo failed to follow his own method of investigating 'permanent effects' rather than transitory ones (ibid., p. 67). Morishima has recently argued that Ricardo's conclusions in the chapter on machinery are inconsistent with his acceptance of Say's law. But the model he constructs to demonstrate this includes not only Say's law but also the wage fund theory, and hence propositions 1) and 2) given in the text (Morishima, 1989, pp. 168-86). It is the combination of these with Say's law, not the law alone, which is incompatible with unemployment.

15. Recently economists have tended to construct 'short-period' demand curves for labour, which assume given equipment, rather than the type of substitution described in the text - based on change in production methods and in the type of machinery used - which takes a longer time to carry out. This way of dealing with the demand for labour, however, meets the following problems, described by Hicks: 'one of the cooperating factors - capital - is, at any particular moment, largely incorporated in goods of a certain degree of durability [...] the change in conduct which follows from the change in relative profitability cannot immediately be realised. [...] In the short period therefore it is reasonable to expect that the demand for labour will be very inelastic, since the possibility of adjusting the organization of industry to a changed level of wages is relatively small [...] Since the whole conception of marginal productivity depends upon the variability of industrial methods, little advantage seems to be gained from the attempt which is sometimes made to define a 'short period marginal product' the additional product due to a small increase in the quantity of labour, when not only the quantity, but also the form, of the cooperating capital is supposed unchanged. It is very doubtful if this conception can be given any precise meaning which is capable of useful application' (Hicks, 1932, pp. 19-21).

16. Both these substitution mechanisms are subject to serious difficulties and criticisms,

If these arguments are accompanied by the idea that competition means unlimited downward flexibility of wages when there is unemployment, we have a tendency for the labour market to adjust automatically towards full employment.[17]

Presently I shall discuss the view according to which mechanisms similar to those just described were also envisaged by the classical economists. In this respect, it ought to be clear from the start that the issue is not whether the classical economists conceived the production coefficients or the composition of output as absolutely fixed and unchangeable; or whether or not they would admit that changes in income distribution or relative prices might affect them. Much more specifically, the issue is whether they envisaged the relationships of a systematic and general nature between those variables which are the necessary logical foundation of the decreasing demand schedule for labour in neoclassical theory. In other words the question is whether we can say that the classical economists thought that a rise in the wage rate would always set in motion a change in production methods and/or in consumption patterns such as to lead (other things being equal) to a reduction in the employment level (and vice versa).

Substitutability in production
Concerning direct subsitution between labour and other inputs, it is fairly widely recognized that such a mechanism was not envisaged by the classical economists, for techniques tended to be regarded as given in any normal position of the economy, and as gradually changing with the accumulation process because of innovations and returns to scale.[18]

> which I shall not go into here; suffice it to mention that both direct and indirect mechanisms fail because, as was shown by Sraffa and then during the 1960s in the debate on capital theory, relative prices do not necessarily change in the direction predicted by marginalist theory following variations in distribution: if wages fall the prices of more labour-intensive products may actually go up rather than down, and the more labour-intensive techniques may become *less* advantageous. The marginalist theory of demand also meets serious problems in demonstrating that changes in relative prices really do lead to substitution in consumption favouring goods whose relative price has fallen; on the latter point see Kirman, 1989.

17. Of course, downward sloping labour demand curves and wage flexibility ensure a tendency to the full employment of labour only if there are no obstacles to the adjustment of investments to full employment savings, such as persistent rigidities in the interest rate.

18. In this connection Blaug argues 'the real question is whether [the classical economists]

Ricardo (and before him Barton, 1817) discussed the possibility of substitution of machinery for labour in his famous chapter *On Machinery*. Although he was clearly concerned with technical innovation ('the discovery and use of machinery': Ricardo, 1821, I, pp. 390, 391, 392), rather than with choice among already known alternatives, as is the case with marginalist economic theory, he maintained that the introduction of machinery could be stimulated by changes in the wage rate (ibid., p. 395), a view that might seem suggestive of later neoclassical developments. His analysis however appears to be lacking some of the essential features of the latter. He argues that a fall in the employment level following the introduction of machinery (perhaps stimulated by a higher wage rate) is possible in principle. In practice, however, according to Ricardo, funds for machinery would often be acquired not by 'diverting' existing capital from its previous employments, but by investing net savings in its acquisition (ibid.). Thus its introduction would often reduce the rate of growth of employment, but not its level, as would instead be required for the construction of a decreasing demand schedule for labour. The latter also requires reversibility of change, and this is not contemplated in Ricardo's (nor in Barton's) treatment. He did not envisage the possibility that unemployment following the introduction of machinery would induce a reduction of the wage rate and, consequently, a rise of the employment level until full employment was reached again. This, by the way, is precisely the aspect of Ricardo's discussion that has puzzled many contemporary economists, leading them to attribute peculiar errors and inconsistencies to his treatment of machinery (Wicksell, 1934, I, p. 137; Schumpeter, 1954, p. 683; Blaug, 1985, p. 185, among others).

Indeed, the conclusions of Ricardo and Barton on the effects of introducing new machinery are very far from those later reached on the basis of the supply and demand curves: they held that machines could cause persistent unemployment, and concluded, in contrast with Smith's more optimistc views, that the accumulation of capital

conceived of this state of techniques *à la* Sraffa as ruling out factor substitution. On balance [...] the answer to this question must be yes' (Blaug, 1987, p. 441). Schumpeter too argues that classical economists conceived of technical change as resulting only from innovations or scale economies, not from subsititution (1954, p. 679, n. 94).

and wealth could be accompanied by persistent poverty, low wages and unemployment among the working classes.

Market prices and changes in consumption

Downward sloping demand schedules for goods are often attributed to the classical economists on the basis of their discussion of market prices. The main argument advanced in support of this view is that classical economists maintained that a rise in the market price of a commodity would induce a reduction in its consumption, and vice versa (Hollander, 1987, pp. 29, 66–7).

But market prices in Smith and Ricardo are not equilibrium prices. For example, they do not necessarily equalize supply and demand: in cases of excess supply there are indications that both Smith and Ricardo thought the commodity would not necessarily be entirely sold (Smith, 1776, I.vii.10; Ricardo, I, pp. 297–98). In cases of excess demand on the other hand, the diminished consumption is the unavoidable consequence of the (temporary) scarcity of the commodity and not the result of consumers' substitution in their consumption baskets as relative prices change. The classical economists thought that in such circumstances working class people would not be able to compete with the upper classes to obtain the scarce commodities whose prices would become too high relative to their incomes. As Steuart explains 'food must then become more scarce, demand for it rises; the rich are always the strongest in the market; they consume the food, and the poor are forced to starve' (Steuart, 1766a, p. 184–5). Malthus's argument is similar: 'When an article is scarce, and cannot be distributed to all, he that can shew the most valid patent, that is, he that offers more money, becomes the possessor' (Malthus, 1798, I, p. 31), and so is that of Ricardo: 'A bad harvest will produce a high price of provisions [...] the price would at last be so high, that the least rich would be obliged to forego the use of a part of the quantity which they usually consumed' (Ricardo, 1821, I, p. 162).

Market prices in the classical approach are not theoretical variables (as are the equilibrium prices in neoclassical theory) but simply the actual, observed prices which may continually deviate from natural prices because of accidental mismatching between quantities supplied and demanded (or because of any other accidental event interfering with the operation of the 'long run' forces in the economic system). Accordingly, the classical economists were not concerned with determining the exact value that market prices would assume in different circumstances, or with constructing demand curves to establish an exact correspondence between the deviation of the market price from the natural price of a commodity and the demand for it. They believed that no general quantitative relation could be established between a change in market price and the size of the excess production over 'effectual demand' causing it, or the change in consumption resulting from it. On the first of these points Ricardo is quite explicit:

> Some indeed have attempted to estimate the fall of price which would take place, under the supposition of the surplus bearing different proportions to the average quantity. Such calculations, however, must be very deceptious, as no general rule can be laid down for the variations in proportion to quantity. (Ricardo, *Protection to Agriculture*, 1822, IV, p. 220; see also Roncaglia, 1982a, p. 355)

Steuart makes the second point in the context of his description of the effects of a price fall caused by overproduction:

> But it may be asked whether, by this fall of prices, demand will not be increased? That is to say, will not the whole of the goods be sold off? I answer, that this may or may not be the effect of the fall, according to circumstances: it is a contingent consequence [...] not the certain effect. (Steuart, 1766a, p. 192)

In conclusion, then, the classical economists saw the fluctuations of market (i.e. actual) prices and the (possibly) resulting oscillations in demand as transitory phenomena, caused by accidental divergences between production and normal demand (or other accidental events). Market prices oscillate around the normal or natural prices of goods; these are regarded as known, and so are the 'effectual demands' of each commodity (Smith, 1776, I.vii.7–8). But if natural prices and 'effectual demands' are known, the natural rates of payment and hence the natural wage must also be known. This rules out any possible influence on the natural (normal) wage of the fluctuations in demand due to changes in market prices.

Natural prices and changes in consumption
We may now ask whether a systematic decreasing relation was envisaged between the *natural* price of any commodity and the

demand for it. Any such relation is denied by several passages in Ricardo's writings (1821, I, pp. 237, n., 325–6, 385). Besides, it has been argued that the instances in which changes in the natural price influence the quantity demanded can be more consistently analysed (and were in fact analysed) within the classical framework by other means than demand schedules (Garegnani, 1987, pp. 564–5).

In their occasional references to the effects of changes in natural price on a commodity's consumption, classical and pre-classical economists do not appear to have been in search of 'laws' of general validity.[19] Rather, they followed a 'case by case' type of analysis in which, for example, the effects of changes in the natural price of a commodity depend on the needs it is meant to satisfy (i.e. whether it is a 'luxury' or 'necessary', and which social groups consume it).

Locke, for example, held that the consumption of certain luxury goods by the upper classes might be positively related to their price, while on the other hand price changes would not affect the consumption of necessary goods.[20] The idea that a rise in the natural

19. Their lack of interest in identifying general relations between changes in relative prices and in demand for goods has been connected with the more general difference between their approach and that of the marginalist theory. In the latter, the demand curves for goods aim not so much to determine the level of demand for each commodity – indicated (in the usual graph) by the position of the curve in the plane (which in turn depends on an exogenous factor: the tastes of consumers) – as to determine the marginal variations of that demand following changes in distribution and prices. That is, their role is to enable the simultaneous determination of the price system, distribution, and the quantities produced. The demand curves could not play that role in the classical approach, where wages are treated as given at the moment when relative prices are determined, and thus changes in demand for finished goods (under the assumption of constant returns to scale generally made in neoclassical theory) have no effect on the price system (Pasinetti, 1981, pp. 214-5; Garegnani, 1983, pp. 309-14, 1987, p. 563 ff). In other words, in the classical theory not only do changes in relative prices have no necessary effect on the demand for consumer goods (and therefore on the demand for labour), but neither do autonomous changes in consumption patterns (for example due to changes in tastes) have any effect on the relative prices of consumer goods (apart from those possibly due to returns to scale, which may go in either direction). The classical economists examine case by case the relation between price changes and the 'effectual demand' of individual commodities, in a stage of analysis separate from the determination of the price system. This can be said to reflect their way of proceeding 'by short chains of arguments ' (Garegnani, 1987, p. 563). These economists themselves appear to have been aware of this choice: see for example Turgot's ironic comment on the abstractness of the 'creators of systems' (Faure, 1961, n. 3), or Steuart's methodological warning, 'nothing is more essential in political reasonings than [...] to proceed by the shortest steps when we draw a conclusion from a general proposition, and still to keep experience and matter of fact before our eyes' (Steuart, 1766b, II, p. 121; see also the section on method in Skinner, 1966).

20. '[A]ny tax laid on foreign commodities raises its price, and makes the importer get

price of necessary goods could not reduce their consumption by workers was generally shared by the classical economists; as we have seen, they held that such a rise must lead to a proportional increase in money wages.[21] Ricardo says that a fall in the natural price of a particular subsistence commodity cannot induce a significant increase in the amount consumed:

> If the natural price of bread should fall 50 per cent. from some great discovery in the science of agriculture, the demand would not greatly increase, for no man would desire more than would satisfy his wants. (Ricardo, 1821, I, p. 385)[22]

Competition and decreasing demand schedules
Sometimes decreasing demand curves for goods are attributed to the classical economists on the basis of passages describing the competitive process whereby quantities produced adjust to changes in demand, due for example to changed tastes or fashions.[23] Yet these passages contain no reference either to changes in relative prices as causes of changes in demand, or to effects of changes in tastes, and hence of demand and quantities produced, on the system

more for his commodity [...] For things of necessity must still be had, and things of fashion will be had, as long as men have money, or credit, whatever rates they cost, and rather because they are dear. For, it being vanity, not use, that makes the expensive fashion of your people, the emulation is, who shall have the finest, that is the dearest things, not the most convenient or useful' (John Locke, 1692, V, p. 50).
21. In this connection see the discussion of the effects of indirect taxes on subsistence goods: Chapter 2, pp. 15–9; Chapter 3, pp. 70–83; Chapter 5, pp. 139–42.
22. Consider also the following: 'M. Say says, that "[...] Every increase in the price of a commodity, necessarily reduces the number of those who are able to purchase it, or at least the quantity they will consume of it." This by no means is a necessary consequence. I do not believe that if bread were taxed, the consumption of bread would be diminished, more than if cloth, wine, or soap were taxed' (Ricardo, 1821, I, p. 237).
23. See, for example, Hollander, 1987, pp. 28, 67; Blaug, 1985, p. 43. Hollander quotes the following passage from Cantillon: '[w]hen a landowner has dismissed a great number of domestic servants, and increased the number of his horses, there will be too much corn for the needs of the inhabitants, and so the corn will be cheap and the hay dear. In consequence the farmers will increase their grass land and diminish their corn to proportion it to the demand. In this way the fancies or fashions of landowners determine the use of the land and bring about the variations of demand which cause the variations of market prices. If all the landowners of a State cultivated their own estates they would use them to produce what they want; and as the variations of demand are chiefly caused by their mode of living the prices which they offer in the market decide the farmers to all the changes which they make in the employment and use of the land' (Cantillon, 1755, p. 65). Hollander comments: 'Cantillon does not explicitly define a demand schedule, but his adjustment process makes little sense unless one attributes to him an implicit appreciation of the law of demand' (Hollander, 1987, p. 28.). But, as argued in the text, Cantillon's statement is perfectly intelligible without recourse to the notion of a demand curve.

of natural prices.

In the classical theory, the adjustment of production to a change in normal demand for a commodity requires only that the difference between supply and demand cause the market price to rise temporarily above the natural price if demand exceeds supply, or to fall below it in the opposite case. Competition and profit-seeking behaviour by the capitalist entrepreneurs will then tend to draw capital into industries with a higher profit rate and increase their production (and vice versa) until parity is re-established between the quantities produced and demanded, and the price returns to its natural level (Smith, 1776, I.vii.12–15; Bowley, 1976, p. 124–6). Downward sloping demand curves are not required to explain this adjustment (Roncaglia, 1982a, pp. 354–5).

Clearly economists formed in the neoclassical tradition tend to associate the adjustment of supply to demand with the notion of 'demand curves', because they tend to identify the very existence of competition with the determination of prices, distribution and quantities produced by means of supply and demand functions. But in this way the conclusion that was to be demonstrated is actually presupposed.

However, despite the recent revival of interpretations following the original example of Marshall, which tend to emphasize the similarity of the classical and neoclassical theories (Hollander, 1973; 1979; 1987; Samuelson, 1978; Rankin, 1980), many scholars have denied the existence of those notions in the body of classical economic theory.[24] Indeed, even those who emphasize similarity often admit that substitution mechanisms were not really formulated by classical economists, but maintain that their theory would benefit from being integrated and 'rationalized' by introducing such mechanisms (Hollander, 1982, p. 370; 1979, p. 276; Barkai, 1967, p. 75; 1986, pp. 609, 611–12).

24. See for example Cannan, 1893, pp. 200–206 and 382; Knight, 1956, p. 75. Hutchison denies that Ricardo provided any contribution to neoclassical economics, and lists a large number of neoclassical authorities who 'explicitly rejected the Ricardian theory of value and distribution in the bluntest terms' (1952, p. 76). He also includes Smith in this negative appreciation of the classical contribution to subsequent developments (p. 78). On Smith's distribution theory see also Schumpeter, 1954, pp. 268, 557–61, 566–7. The interpretation of classical economics advanced by Hollander has been criticized in Roncaglia, 1982a and b; Peach, 1988b and 1993, pp. 277–86.

COMPETITION AND CONVENTIONS

The classical analysis of the labour market does not include automatic mechanisms leading the economic system towards the full employment of labour. Hence the amount of persistent explicit or latent unemployment may influence the natural wage.

The role of imbalances between employment and population in determining the natural wage explains why the classical economists typically refer to competition between workers or, alternatively, between employers, as a factor in the relative bargaining power of the parties in a given normal economic situation. Competition among workers (associated with lack of employment opportunities) is generally mentioned as a cause of bargaining weakness for them, and hence of the tendency of wages to coincide with the subsistence minimum; competition among employers (in a tight labour market) is said to strengthen the workers' bargaining power and hence to establish wages at a rate above the minimum.

All this brings out a conception peculiar to the classical wage theory, which contrasts with the later idea of how competition works. For the classical economists, competition among workers when there is unemployment (or among employers if labour is scarce) does not lead to an indefinite fall (or rise) in wages: its effect is to bring wages to the minimum historically determined level (or to a particular higher level; see above, Chapter 3, pp. 48–9, 53–4).

For both the classical economists and their successors, competition in the labour market is seen as an impersonal process, which tends to establish uniform rates of wages for labour units with the same characteristics. But in the classical analysis, unlike the later theories, competition does not imply an unlimited decrease or increase in wages continuing as long as there are imbalances on the labour market.

This means, for example, that when there is unemployment workers will not try to outbid each other by offering to work for a wage below the 'subsistence' minimum. It also means that employers will not exert strong pressure on the workers to make them accept a wage below that minimum. Similarly, when labour is scarce the employers, while competing, will not offer increasingly high wages to obtain it.

What is the origin of this view of competition? The arguments of the classical economists suggest that the very norms and conventions that define the 'subsistence' level of consumption – i.e., to use Smith's formulation, 'whatever the custom of the country renders it indecent for creditable people, even of the lowest order, to be without' – also work to keep wages from falling below that level. These generally accepted norms and conventions do not eliminate and replace competition but they do fix the limits within which it can operate. This is especially clear in Smith, where the minimum wage level, below which the normal wage does not fall even when there is widespread unemployment, is repeatedly defined as the minimum 'consistent with common humanity' (Chapter 3 pp. 58–60). The role of norms and conventions in maintaining wage levels is also indicated by Tucker and Steuart, who say that to reduce wages it is necessary to bring in foreign workers prepared to accept lower pay than that customarily received by local workers (Chapter 2, p. 20; Chapter 3, p. 72).

The gravitation of actual or market wages around the natural wage, often attributed to population change, seems rather to be related to habits and customs – to the same forces, as Turgot says, that determine the natural wage itself (Chapter 3, pp. 73–7). Turgot says it is not in the employers' interest – though it may increase the rate of profit – to cut wages below the habitual level. This is because the employers know that if all of them impose such a reduction, this will lead to a fall in food consumption and hence in the total income of the employers and landowners. Like Smith's idea of common humanity, Turgot's reasoning shows a conception of economic behaviour different from the narrowly individualistic and atomistic view of today's theory. The pursuit of individual interest and competitive economic behaviour are constrained by social norms and conventions, and in particular by those shared in the social group one belongs to. These norms in turn may arise from the perception of a conflict between the pursuit of immediate individual gain and social or group interest.

Smith, in his *Theory of Moral Sentiments*, presents an anti-utilitarian view of human behaviour as determined by a plurality of motivations not reducible to mere self-interest, and an interaction with the social environment, which determine the standards of behaviour to which individuals must always conform.

This view accords well with the role of social norms and conventions in limiting competition and in maintaining the minimum wage even when there is unemployment (Chapter 3, pp. 60–1).

A similar view of human behaviour is shared by the other classical economists; this emerges not only in connection with income distribution, but also very clearly in the discussion of how habits of consumption are formed. The argument – which in Steuart is especially interesting and well developed – is conducted in terms of the individual's adoption of models and norms proper to his own social class, and the desire for social improvement which leads him to imitate the consumption patterns of higher social classes (Chapter 3, pp. 66–8). Here again, behaviour is seen as determined by interaction with the social environment and by adherence to its norms.

It should not be surprising that widely accepted habits and norms play an important role in the classical theory of distribution. In that theory there are no reliable mechanisms of adjustment for imbalances between quantities in the normal functioning of the labour market: from the demand side because there is no downward sloping 'demand curve', and from the supply side because variations in the labour supply depend on changes in population, which responds slowly and unevenly to changes in wages or availability of employment.

In this context a relative stability of distributive variables inevitably depends on social standards and conventions, or institutions, which do not prevent or replace competitive behaviour but which do impose limits on it. At the same time the classical theory, because it contains no automatic necessary relations between wages on the one hand, and labour supply and demand on the other, entails the possibility that changes in institutions or cultural context play an important and independent role in determining the level of the natural wage, and its changes over time. Thus in the classical approach, unlike in neoclassical economic theory, institutions or customs do not appear as 'rigidities' in an otherwise self-regulating economic system. Rather, they play an important role in ensuring its viability.

Bibliography

PRIMARY SOURCES

Anonymous (1738), *An enquiry into the Causes of the Increase and Miseries of the Poor*, A. Bettesworth & C. Hitch, London.

Barbon, Nicholas (1690), *A Discourse of Trade*, T. Milbourne, London.

Barton, John (1817), *Observations on the Circumstances which Influence the Conditions of the Labouring Classes of Society*, W. Mason, London.

Berkeley, George (1735), *The Querist*, G. Faulkner, Dublin, 1750.

Braddon, Lawrence (1717), *The Miseries of the Poor are a National Sin, Shame and Charge*, T. Warner, London.

Cantillon, Richard (1755), *Essai sur la Nature du Commerce en Général*, edited by H. Higgs, A. M. Kelley, New York, 1964.

Cary, John (1695), *An Essay on the State of England*, W. Bonny, Bristol.

Child, Sir Josiah (1693), *New Discourse on Trade*, J. Everingham, London.

Davenant, Charles (1696), *A Memoriall Concerning Creditt*, in Evans, G. H. Jr (ed.) *A Reprint of Economic Tracts*, Baltimore, 1942.

Davenant, Charles (1699), *An Essay on the Probable Methods of Making a People Gainers in the Balance of Trade*, J. Knapton, London.

Defoe, Daniel (1704), *Giving Alms No Charity*, in McCulloch, J. R. (ed.) *A Select Collection of Scarce and Valuable Tracts*, Harrison & Sons, London, 1859.

Defoe, Daniel (1728), *A Plan of the English Commerce*, C. Rivington, London.

Fauquier, Francis (1756), *An Essay on Ways and Means for Raising Money*, Cooper, London.

Fortrey, Samuel (1673), *England's Interest and Improvement*, N. Brook, London.

Godwin, William (1801), *Thoughts Occasioned by Dr. Parr's Spital Sermon*, London.

Hall, Charles (1805), *The Effects of Civilization on the People in European States*, reprint Phoenix Library, 1850.

Harris, Sir Walter (1691), *Remarks on the Affaires and Trade of England and Ireland*, T. Parkhurst, London.

Haynes, John (1715), *Great Britain's Glory*, J. Marshall, London.

Hazlitt, William (1807), *A Reply to the Essay on Population, by the Rev. T. R. Malthus*, Longman Hurst, Rees and Orme, London.

Hume, David (1750), *Of the Populousness of Ancient Nations*, in *Writings on Economics*, edited by E. Rotwein, Nelson, Edinburgh, 1955.

Hume, David, (1752), *Of Commerce*, in *Writings on Economics*, edited by E. Rotwein, Nelson, Edinburgh, 1955.

Law, John (1705), *Money and Trade Considered*, R.& A. Foulis, Edinburgh, 1750.

Jarrold, Thomas (1806), *Dissertations on Man, Philosophical, Physiological and Political; in answer to Mr. Malthus's 'Essay on the Principle of Population'*, London.

Locke, John (1692), *Some Considerations of the Consequences of the Lowering of Interest and Raising the Value of Money*, in *The Works of John Locke*, vol. V, Tegg & Sharpe, London, 1823.

Malthus, Thomas Robert (1798), *An Essay on the Principle of Population*, in *Works*, edited by E. A.Wrigley ane D. Souden, vol. I, Pickering & Chatto Publisher, London, 1986.

Malthus, Thomas Robert (1826), *An Essay on the Principle of Population*, 6th edition, in *Works*, edited by E. A. Wrigley and D. Souden, vols II and III, Pickering & Chatto Publisher, London, 1986.

Malthus, Thomas Robert (1820), *The Principles of Political Economy, Considered with a View to their Practical Application*, (second edition, 1836) in *Works*, edited by E. A. Wrigley and D. Souden, vols IV and V, Pickering & Chatto Publisher, London, 1986.

Manley, Thomas (1677), *Discourse Showing that the Exportation of Wool is Destructive to This Kingdom*, S. Coruch, London.

Manley, Thomas (1699), *Usury at 6 per cent Examined*, Ratcliffe & Daniel, London.

McCulloch, John Ramsay (1826), *A Treatise on the Circumstances which Determine the Rate of Wages and the Condition of the Labouring Classes*, (second edition, 1854), reprint A. M. Kelley, New York, 1963.

McCulloch, John Ramsay (1830), *Principles of Political Economy, with a Sketch on the Rise and Progress of the Science*, second edition, Longman, Rees, Orme, Brown and Green, London.

Mill, John Stuart (1865), *Principles of Political Economy, with Some of Their Applications to Social Philosophy*, 6th edition, in J. M. Robson (ed.) *Collected Works of J. S. Mill*, Toronto University Press, Toronto.

Mill, John Stuart (1869), 'Thornton on Labour and its Claims', part one, *The Fortnightly Review*, May.

Mun, Thomas (1664), *English Treasure by Foreign Trade*, T. Clark, London.

Necker, Jacques (1775), *Sur la législation et le commerce des grains*, in Id. *Oevres Complètes*, edited by M. le Baron de Staël, vol. I, Paris, Treuttel and Wurtz (1820–1821).

Necker, Jaques (1785), *De l'administation des finances de la France*, in Id. *Oevres Complètes*, edited by M. le Baron de Staël, vol. V, Paris, Treuttel and Wurtz (1820–1821).

Petty, William (1676), *Political Arithmetick*, in Hull, C. (ed.) *Economic Writings*, A. M. Kelley, New York, 1899.

Petyt, William (1680) *Britannia Lauguens, or a Discourse of Trade*, Dring & Crouch, London.

Postlethwayt, Malachy (1757), *Great Britain's True System*, A. Millar, London.

Ricardo, David (1815), *An Essay on the Influence of a low Price of Corn on the Profits of Stock* in Sraffa, P. (ed., with the collaboration of M. Dobb) *The Works and Correspondence of David Ricardo*, vol. IV., Cambridge University Press for the Royal Economic Society, Cambridge, 1951.

Ricardo, David (1821), *The Principles of Political Economy and Taxation,* in Sraffa, P. (ed., with the collaboration of M. Dobb) *The Works and Correspondence of David Ricardo,* vol. I., Cambridge University Press for the Royal Economic Society, Cambridge, 1951.

Smith, Adam (1766) *Lectures on Jurisprudence,* edited by R. L. Meek, D. D. Raphael and P. G. Stein, *The Glasgow Edition of the Works and Correspondence of Adam Smith,* Oxford University Press, Oxford, 1976.

Smith, Adam (1776), *An Inquiry into the Nature and Causes of the Wealth of Nations,* edited by R. N. Campbell, A. S. Skinner and W. B. Todd, *The Glasgow Edition of the Works and Correspondence of Adam Smith,* Oxford University Press, Oxford, 1976.

Smith, Adam (1790), *The Theory of Moral Sentiments,* (first edition 1759), edited by A.L. Macfie and D. D. Raphael, *The Glasgow Edition of the Works and Correspondence of Adam Smith,* Oxford University Press, Oxford, 1976.

Steuart, Sir James (1766a), *An Inquiry into the Principles of Political Oeconomy,* abridged edition, Skinner, A. S. (ed.) Edinburgh & London, Oliver & Boyd for the Scottish Economic Society, 1966.

Steuart, Sir James (1766b), *An Inquiry into the Principles of Political Oeconomy,* in *The Works, Political, Metaphysical and Chronological of the Late Sir James Steuart* collected by Sir J. Steuart Bart, his son, London, 1805.

Temple, William (1758), *Vindication of Commerce and Arts,* London.

Temple, William (1765), *Considerations on Taxes,* W. Nicoll, London.

Torrens, Robert (1815), *An Essay on the External Corn Trade,* J. Nourse, London.

Townsend, Rev. Joseph (1786), *A Dissertation on the Poor Laws,* University of California Press, Berkeley, 1971.

Tucker, Sir Josiah (1750), *A Brief Essay on Trade,* T. Trye, London.

Turgot, Anne-Robert-Jaques (1766), *Reflections on the Formation and Distribution of Wealth,* in R. L. Meek (ed.) *Turgot on Progress, Sociology and Economics.,* Cambridge University Press, Cambridge, 1973.

Turgot, Anne-Robert-Jaques (1767a). *Lettre à Hume*, in G. Schelle (ed.), *Oevres de Turgot et Document le Concernant*, vol. II., Librairie Felix Alcan, Paris, 1913–23.

Turgot, Anne-Robert-Jaques (1767b), *Memoire Graslin*, in G. Schelle (ed.). *Oevres de Turgot et Document le Concernant*, vol. II., Librairie Felix Alcan, Paris, 1913–23.

Turgot, A.R.J. (1767c) *Memoire St. Peravy*, in G. Schelle (ed.), *Oevres de Turgot et Document le Concernant*, vol II., Librairie Felix Alcan, Paris, 1913–23.

Turgot, A.R.J. (1770). *Lettres sur le commerce des grains*, in G. Schelle (ed.), *Oevres de Turgot et Document le Concernant*, vol. III., Librairie Felix Alcan, Paris, 1913–23.

Vanderlint, Jacob (1734), *Money Answers All Things*, T. Cox, London.

Wallace, Robert (1753), *A Dissertation on the Numbers of Mankind in Ancient and Modern Times*, Hamilton & Balfour, Edinburgh.

Wallace, Robert (1761), *Various Prospects of Mankind, Nature and Providence*, A. Millar, London.

Weyland, John (1816), *The Principles of Population and Production, as They are Affected by the Progress of Society*, Baldwin, Cradock and Joy, London.

Young, Arthur (1771), *A Six Months Tour Through the North of England*, Reprints of economic classics, A. M. Kelley, New York, 1967.

SECONDARY SOURCES

Anspach, R. (1972), 'The Implications of the Theory of Moral Sentiments for Adam Smith's Economic Thought', *History of Political Economy*, IV, no. 1, pp. 176–206.

Barkai, H. (1967), 'A Note on Ricardo's Notions of Demand', *Economica*, Feb., pp. 75–79.

Barkai, H. (1986), 'Ricardo's Volte-Face on Machinery', *Journal of Political Economy*, vol. 94, no. 31, pp. 595–613.

Bendix, R. (1956), *Work and Authority in Industry*, University of California Press, Berkeley, 1974.

Benetti, C. (1979), *Smith. La teoria economica della società mercantile*, Etas, Milano.

Bharadwaj, K. (1983), 'Ricardian Theory and Ricardianism', *Contributions to Political Economy*, vol. 2, pp. 49–77.

Bharadwaj, K. (1987), *Subsistence*, in Eatwell, Milgate, Newman (eds), *The New Palgrave*, op. cit.

Blaug, M. (1963), 'The Myth of the Old Poor Law and the Making of the New', *Journal of Economic History*, XXIII, no. 2, pp. 151–84.

Blaug, M. (1973), *Ricardian Economics: a Historical Study*, (first edition 1958), Greenwood Press, Westport.

Blaug, M. (1985), *Economic Theory in Retrospect*, Cambridge University Press, Cambridge.

Blaug, M. (1987), *Classical Economics*, in Eatwell, Milgate, Newman (eds), *The New Palgrave*, op. cit.

Blith, C.A. (1987), *Wage Fund Doctrine*, in Eatwell, Milgate, Newman (eds), *The New Palgrave*, op. cit.

Bonar, J. (1931), *Theories of Population from Raleigh to A. Young*, London.

Bordes, C. and Morange, J., (eds, 1982), *Turgot, Economiste et Administrateur*, Actes d'un séminaire organisé par la Faculté de droit et des sciences économiques de Limoges pour le bicentenaire de la mort de Turgot, Presses Universitaires de France, Paris.

Bowley, M. (1976), *Studies in the History of Economic Theory Before 1870*, London, Macmillan.

Campbell, R. A. and Skinner, A. S. (1976), 'General Introduction' to A Smith, *Wealth of Nations*, op. cit.

Cannan, E. (1893), *A History of the Theories of Production and Distribution in English Political Economy from 1776 to 1848*, Percival & Co, London.

Caravale, G. (1985), 'Diminishing Returns and Accumulation in Ricardo' in *The Legacy of Ricardo*, Basil Blackwell, Oxford.

Caravale, G. (1988), 'The Notion of the Natural Wage and its Rôle in Classical Economics', *Rivista Internazionale di Scienze Economiche e Commerciali*, vol. XXXV , no. 7, pp. 599–624.

Caravale, G. and Tosato D. (1980), *Ricardo and the Theory of Value Distribution and Growth*, Routledge & Kegan Paul, London.

Casarosa, C. (1978), 'A New Formulation of the Ricardian System', *Oxford Economic Papers*, XXX , pp. 38–63.

Casarosa, C. (1982), 'The New View of the Ricardian Theory of Distribution and Economic Growth', in Baranzini, M. (ed.) *Advances in Economic Theory*, Basil Blackwell, Oxford.

Coase, R. H. (1976), 'Adam Smith's View of Man', *Journal of Law and Economics*, vol. XIX , no. 3, pp. 529–46.

Coats, A. W., 'Changing Attitudes to Labour in the Mid-Eighteen Century', *Economic History Review*, XI (1958), no.1, pp.35–51.

Deane P. (1965), *The First Industrial Revolution*, Cambridge University Press, London.

De Vivo, G. (1987), *Ricardo* in Eatwell, Milgate, Newman (eds), *The New Palgrave*, op. cit.

Dobb, M. (1973), *Theories of Value and Distribution since Adam Smith. Ideology and Economic Theory*, Cambridge University Press, Cambridge.

Duesenberry, J. S. (1949), *Income, Saving, and the Theory of Consumer Behaviour*, Harvard University Press, Harvard.

Eatwell, J., Milgate, M., Newman, P. (eds, 1987), *The New Palgrave: A Dictionary of Economics*, Macmillan, London.

Faure, E. (1961), 'Turgot et la théorie du produit net', *Revue d'histoire économique et sociale*, no. 3 and 4.

Furniss, E. S. (1920), *The Position of the Labourer in a System of Nationalism*, The Riverside Press, Boston & New York.

Garegnani, P. (1978), 'Notes on Consumption, Investment, and Effective Demand', *Cambridge Journal of Economics*, vol. 2, reprint in Eatwell, J. and Milgate, M. (eds, 1983) *Keynes's Economics and the Theory of Value and Distribution*, Duckworth, London.

Garegnani, P. (1984), 'Value and Distribution in The Classical Economists and Marx', *Oxford Economic Papers*, vol. XXXVI, pp. 291–325.

Garegnani, P. (1983), 'The Classical Theory of Wages and the Role of Demand Schedule in the Determination of Relative Prices', *American Economic Review, papers and proceedings*, vol. LXXIII, no. 2, pp. 309–14.

Garegnani, P. (1987), *Surplus Approach to Value and Distribution*, in Eatwell, Milgate, Newman (eds), *The New Palgrave*, op. cit.

Garegnani, P. (1990), 'Sraffa: Classical versus Marginalist Analysis' in Bharadwaj, K. and Schefold, B. (eds) *Essays on Piero Sraffa. Critical Perspectives on the Revival of Classical Theory*, Unwin Hyman, London.

Gonner, E. C. K. (1912–13), 'The Population in England in 18th Century', *Journal of Royal Statistical Society*, LXXXVI, Feb. pp. 261–303.

Gregory, T. E. (1921), 'The Economics of Employment in England. 1660–1713', *Economica*, vol. I , no. 1, pp. 37–51.

Groenewegen, P. D. (1969), 'Turgot and Adam Smith', *Scottish Journal of Political Economy*, XVI , pp. 271–87.

Groenewegen, P. D. (1970), 'A Reappraisal of Turgot's Theory of Value, Exchange and Price Determination', *History of Political Economy*, II , no. 1, pp. 177–96.

Groenewegen, P. D. (1977), 'Introduction', in *The Economics of A. R. J. Turgot*, The Hague.

Groenewegen, P.D. (1983), 'Turgot's Place in the History of Economic Thought: a Bicentenary Estimate', *History of Political Economy*, XV, no. 4, pp. 585–616.

Groenewegen, P. D. (1987), 'Marx's Conception of Classical Political Economy: an Evaluation', *Political Economy. Studies in the Surplus Approach*, vol. III no. 1.

Halèvi, E. (1934), *The Growth of Philosophical Radicalism*, Faber & Faber, London.

Hecksher, E. F. (1935), *Mercantilism*, Allen & Unwin, London

Hicks J. (1932), *Theory of Wages*, Macmillan, London, 1973.

Hicks, J. (1972), 'Ricardo's Theory of Distribution', in Corry, B. and Peston, M. (eds), *Essays in Honour of Lord Robbins,* Weidenfeld & Nicolson, London.

Hicks, J. and Hollander, S. (1977), 'Mr Ricardo and the Moderns', *Quarterly Journal of Economics*, vol. XCI , no. 1, pp. 351–69.

Higgs, H. (1931), 'Life and Work of Richard Cantillon' in R. Cantillon, *Essai sur la Nature du Commerce en Général*, op. cit.

Hollander, S. (1973), *The Economics of Adam Smith*, Heineman, London.

Hollander, S. (1977), 'Adam Smith and the Self-Interest Axiom', *Journal of Law and Economics*, XX , April, pp. 133–52, reprint in Wood, J. C. (ed.) *Adam Smith: Critical Assessments*, op. cit.

Hollander, S. (1984), 'The Wage Path in Classical Growth Models: Ricardo, Malthus and Mill', *Oxford Economic Papers*, vol. XXXVI, no. 2, pp. 200–212.

Hollander, S. (1979), *The Economics of David Ricardo*, University Press, Toronto.

Hollander, S. (1983), 'On the Interpretation of Ricardian Economics: the Assumption Regarding Wages', *American Economic Review*, vol. LXXIII, no. 2, pp. 314–8.

Hollander, S. (1987), *Classical Economics*, Basil Blackwell, Oxford.

Hollander, S. (1990), 'Ricardian Growth Theory: A Resolution of some Problems in Textual Interpretation', *Oxford Economic Papers*, vol. XLII, pp. 730–50.

Hutchison, T. W. (1952), 'Some Questions about Ricardo', *Economica*, vol. 19, Nov., reprint in Wood, J. C. (ed.). *Ricardo: Critical Assessments*, op. cit.

Kaldor, N. (1955–56), 'Alternative Theories of Distribution', *Review of Economic Studies*, vol. XXIII, pp. 83–100.

Kirman, A. (1989)), 'The Intrinsic Limits of Modern Economic Theory: The Emperor has No Clothes', *The Economic Journal*, vol. IC, pp. 126–39.

Knight, F. H. (1956), *On the History and Method of Economics*, University Press, Chicago, 1963.

Lancry, P. J. (1982), 'La Conception du Salaire chêz Turgot', in Bordes, C. and Morange, J., (eds), *Turgot, Economiste et Administrateur*, op. cit.

Levy, D. (1976), 'Ricardo and the Iron Law. A Correction of the Record', *History of Political Economy*, vol. VIII, no. 2, pp. 235–52.

Lowe, A. (1975), 'Adam Smith's System of Equilibrium Growth' in Skinner, A. S. and Wilson, T. (eds), *Essays on Adam Smith*, Clarendon, Oxford.

Macfie, A. L. (1967), *The Individual in Society. Papers on Adam Smith*, Allen & Unwin, London.

Macfie, A. L. and D. D. Raphael (1976), 'Introduction' to Smith, A. *Theory of Moral Sentiments*, op. cit.

McNulty, P. J. (1980), *The Origin and Development of Labor Economics. A Chapter in the History of Social Thought*, MIT Press, Cambridge Mass. and London.

Maffeo, V. (1987), *La teoria del fondo-salari da McCulloch a Taussig*, unpublished Doctoral Dissertation, University of Rome.

Marshall, A. (1920), *Principles of Economics*, (first edition 1890) Macmillan, London, 1982.

Marx, K. (1861–62), *Theories of Surplus Value*, Lawrence & Wishart, London, 1969.

Marx, K., (1887), *Capital*, edited by F. Engels, Lawrence & Wishart, London, 1974, vol. I.

Meek, R. L. (1953), *Marx and Engels on Malthus*, reprint as *Marx and Engels on the Population Bomb*, Berkeley, University of California Press, 1971.

Meek, R. L. (1954), 'Malthus: Yesterday and Today', *Science and Society*, vol. XVIII , pp. 21–5, reprint in Wood, J. C. (ed.), *Malthus: Critical Assessments*, op. cit.

Meek, R.L. (1967), 'The decline of Ricardian Economics in England' in *Economics and Ideology and Other Essays*, Chapman & Hall, London.

Mizuta, H. (1967), *Adam Smith's Library. A Supplement to Bonar's Catalogue*, Cambridge University Press for the Royal Economic Society, Cambridge.

Montani, G. (1985), 'The Theory of Compensation: a Case of Alternative Economic Paradigms', *Political Economy. Studies in the Surplus Approach*, vol. I, no. 1, pp. 109–37.

Morishima, M. (1989), *Ricardo's Economics. A General Equilibrium Theory of Distribution and Growth*, Cambridge University Press, Cambridge.

Morrow, G. R. (1969), *Ethical and Economic Theories of Adam Smith*, A. M. Kelley, New York.

O'Brien, D. P. (1970), *J. R. McCulloch. A Study in Classical Economics*, Allen & Unwin, London.

O'Brien, D. P. (1975), *The Classical Economists*, Clarendon, Oxford.

Panico, C. and Petri, F. (1987), 'Long run and short run', in Eatwell, J., Milgate, M., Newman, P. (eds), *The New Palgrave*, op. cit.

Pasinetti, L. (1959–60), 'A Mathematical Formulation of the Ricardian System', *Review of Economic Studies*, vol. XXVII, pp. 77–88

Pasinetti, L. (1981), *Lezioni di teoria della produzione*, Il Mulino, Bologna.

Pasinetti, L. (1982), 'A Comment on the "New View" of the Ricardian System' in Baranzini, M. (ed.), *Advances in Economic Theory*, Basil Blackwell, Oxford.

Peach, T. (1987), 'David Ricardo's Treatment of Wages' in Collison Black (ed.) *Ideas in Economics*, Macmillan, London.

Peach, T. (1988a), 'David Ricardo: A Review of some Interpretative Issues' in Thweatt, W. O. (ed.), *Classical Political Economy*, Kluwer, Boston.

Peach, T. (1988b), 'S. Hollander's Classical Economics: a Review Article', *The Manchester School*, vol. LVI , no. 2, pp. 167–76.

Peach, T. (1990), 'S. Hollander's 'Ricardian Growth Theory': A Critique', *Oxford Economic Papers*, vol. XLII , pp. 751–64.

Peach, T. (1993), *Interpreting Ricardo*, Cambridge University Press, Cambridge.

Picchio del Mercato, A. (1981), 'Il salario come prezzo naturale del lavoro nell'economia politica classica', *Ricerche Economiche*, no. 1, pp. 85–114.

Picchio, A. (1992), *Social Reproduction: the Political Economy of the Labour Market*, Cambridge University Press, Cambridge.

Pivetti, M. (1987), *Distribution Theories: Classical*, in Eatwell, J., Milgate, M., Newman, P. (eds), *The New Palgrave*, op. cit.

Robbins, L. (1970), *The Evolution of Modern Economic Theory*, Macmillan, London.

Roncaglia, A. (1974), 'Labour Power, Subsistence Wage and the Rate of Wages', *Australian Economic Papers*, XIII, no. 22, pp. 133–43.

Roncaglia, A. (1977), *Petty. La nascita dell'economia politica*, Etas, Milano.

Roncaglia, A. (1982a), 'Hollander's Ricardo', *Journal of Post Keynesian Economics*, vol. IV, Spring, pp. 339–59.

Roncaglia, A. (1982b), 'Rejoinder', *Journal of Post Keynesian Economics*, vol. IV, Spring, pp. 373–5.

Rosselli, A. (1985), 'The Theory of the Natural Wage' in Caravale, G. (ed.) *The Legacy of Ricardo*, Basil Blackwell, Oxford.

Rotwein, E. (1955), 'Introduction' to Hume, D. *Writings on Economics*, Edinburgh, Nelson.

Samuelson, P. A. (1978), 'The Canonical Classical Model of Political Economy', *Journal of Economic Literature*, vol. XVI, Dec., pp. 1415–1435.

Schumpeter, J. (1982), *History of Economic Analysis*, Allen & Unwin, London.

Seligman, E. R. A. (1899), *The Shifting and Incidence of Taxation*, (revised edition, 1927), Reprints of economic classics, A. M. Kelley, New York, 1969.

Sen, A. (1985), *The Standard of Living*, Cambridge University Press, Cambridge.

Sen, A. (1987), *On Ethics and Economics*, Basil Blackwell, Oxford.

Shoup, C. S. (1960), *Ricardo on Taxation*, Columbia University Press, New York.

Skinner, A. S. (1966), 'Introduction' to Steuart, J. *An Inquiry into The Principles of Political Oeconomy*, op. cit.

Skinner, A. S. (1976), 'General Introduction' to Smith, A. *Wealth of Nations*, op. cit.

Skinner, A. S. (1979a), 'A Conceptual System' in *A System of Social Science. Papers relating to Adam Smith*, Clarendon, Oxford.

Skinner, A. S. (1979b), 'Moral Philosophy and Civil Society', in *A System of Social Science. Papers relating to Adam Smith*, Clarendon, Oxford.

Skinner, A. S. (1982), 'A Scottish Contribution to Marxist Sociology?' in Bradley, I. and Howard, M. (ed.), *Classical and Marxian Political Economy*, Macmillan, London.

Skinner, A. S. and Wilson, T. (eds, 1975), *Essays on Adam Smith*, Clarendon, Oxford.

Smith K. (1951), *The Malthusian Controversy*, Octagon Books, New York, 1978.

Solow, R. (1980), 'On Theories of Unemployment', *American Economic Review*, vol. LXX , March, pp. 1–11.

Spengler, J. (1942), *French Predecessors of Malthus*, Duke University Press, Durham.

Spengler, J. (1945), 'Malthus Total Population Theory: a Restatement and Reappraisal', *Canadian Journal of Economics and Political Science*, vol. XI, Feb. and May, pp. 83–110 and 234–64.

Spengler, J. (1959), 'Adam Smith's Theory of Economic Growth', part 2, *Southern Economic Journal*, vol. XXVI , no. 1, pp. 1–12.

St Clair, O. (1965), *A Key to Ricardo*, A. M. Kelley, New York.

Sraffa, P. (1951–73, ed., with the collaboration of M. Dobb), *The Works and Correspondence of David Ricardo*, vols I–XI, Cambridge University Press for the Royal Economic Society, Cambridge.

Sraffa, P. (1951), 'Introduction' to Ricardo, D. *The Principles of Political Economy* in *Works and Correspondence*, vol. I, op. cit.

Sraffa, P. (1960), *Production of Commodities by Means of Commodities. Prelude to a Critique of Economic Theory*, Cambridge University Press, Cambridge.

Stigler, G. J. (1952), 'The Ricardian Theory of Value and Distribution', *Journal of Political Economy*, vol. LX , June, pp. 187–207.

Stigler, G. J. (1965), *Essays in the History of Economics,* University Press, Chicago.

Stigler, G. J. (1981), 'Review', *Journal of Economic Literature*, vol. XIX, pp. 100–102.

Stigler, G. J. (1990), 'Ricardo or Hollander?', *Oxford Economic Papers*, vol. XLII, pp. 765–8.

Taussig, F. W. (1896), *Wages and Capital – An Examination of the Wages Fund Doctrine,* Macmillan, London and New York.

Taylor, O. H. (1929), 'Economics and the Idea of Natural Laws', *Quarterly Journal of Economics*, vol. XLIV, Nov., pp. 1–39.

Tosato, D. (1985), 'Sraffa's Interpretation of Ricardo Reconsidered' in Caravale, G. (ed.) *The Legacy of Ricardo*, op. cit.

Vaggi, G. (1983), 'The Physiocratic Theory of Prices', *Contributions to Political Economy*, vol. II, March, pp. 1–22.

Vaggi, G. (1987), *The Economics of François Quesnay*, Macmillan, London.

Walsh, V. (1987), *Richard Cantillon*, in Eatwell, J., Milgate, M., Newman, P. (eds), *The New Palgrave*, op. cit.

Wermel, M. T. (1939), *The Evolution of Classical Wage Theory*, Columbia University Press, New York.

Weulersse, G. (1968), *Le Mouvement physiocratique en France*, Editions Mouton, Paris.

Wicksell K. (1934), *Lectures on Political Economy*, Routledge & Kegan Paul, London.

Wiles, R. C. (1968), 'The Theory of Wages in Later English Mercantilism', *Economic History Review*, vol. XXI, no. 1, pp. 113ff.

Wood J. C., (ed., 1983–84), *Adam Smith: Critical Assessments*, 4 vols, Croom Helm, Beckenham.

Wood J. C., (ed., 1985), *Ricardo: Critical Assessments*, 4 vols, Croom Helm, Beckenham.

Wood J. C., (ed., 1986), *Malthus: Critical Assessments*, 4 vols, Croom Helm, Beckenham.

Zamagni S. (1987), 'Economic laws', in Eatwell, J., Milgate, M., Newman, P. (eds), *The New Palgrave – The Invisible Hand*, Macmillan, London, 1989.

Index